Ageing, Dementia and
the Social Mind

Sociology of Health and Illness Monograph Series

Edited by Professor Ian Rees Jones
Cardiff School of Social Sciences
WISERD
46 Park Place
Cardiff
CF10 3BB
Wales, UK

Current titles

Ageing, Dementia and the Social Mind (2017)
edited by *Paul Higgs and Chris Gilleard*

The Sociology of Healthcare Safety and Quality (2016)
edited by *Davina Allen, Jeffrey Braithwaite, Jane Sandall and Justin Waring*

Children, Health and Well-being: Policy Debates and Lived Experience (2015)
edited by *Geraldine Brady, Pam Lowe and Sonja Olin Lauritzen*

From Health Behaviours to Health Practices: Critical Perspectives (2014)
edited by *Simon Cohn*

Pandemics and Emerging Infectious Diseases: The Sociological Agenda (2013)
edited by *Robert Dingwall, Lily M Hoffman and Karen Staniland*

The Sociology of Medical Screening: Critical Perspectives, New Directions (2012)
edited by *Natalie Armstrong and Helen Eborall*

Body Work in Health and Social Care: Critical Themes, New Agendas (2011)
edited by *Julia Twigg, Carol Wolkowitz, Rachel Lara Cohen and Sarah Nettleton*

Technogenarians: Studying Health and Illness Through an Ageing, Science, and Technology Lens (2010)
edited by *Kelly Joyce and Meika Loe*

Communication in Healthcare Settings: Policy, Participation and New Technologies (2009)
edited by *Alison Pilnick, Jon Hindmarsh and Virginia Teas Gill*

Pharmaceuticals and Society: Critical Discourses and Debates (2009)
edited by *Simon J. Williams, Jonathan Gabe and Peter Davis*

Ethnicity, Health and Health Care: Understanding Diversity, Tackling Disadvantage (2008)
edited by *Waqar I. U. Ahmad and Hannah Bradby*

The View From Here: Bioethics and the Social Sciences (2007)
edited by *Raymond de Vries, Leigh Turner, Kristina Orfali and Charles Bosk*

The Social Organisation of Healthcare Work (2006)
edited by *Davina Allen and Alison Pilnick*

Social Movements in Health (2005)
edited by *Phil Brown and Stephen Zavestoski*

Health and the Media (2004)
edited by *Clive Seale*

Partners in Health, Partners in Crime: Exploring the boundaries of criminology and sociology of health and illness (2003)
edited by *Stefan Timmermans and Jonathan Gabe*

Rationing: Constructed Realities and Professional Practices (2002)
edited by *David Hughes and Donald Light*

Rethinking the Sociology of Mental Health (2000)
edited by *Joan Busfield*

Sociological Perspectives on the New Genetics (1999)
edited by *Peter Conrad and Jonathan Gabe*

The Sociology of Health Inequalities (1998)
edited by *Mel Bartley, David Blane and George Davey Smith*

The Sociology of Medical Science (1997)
edited by *Mary Ann Elston*

Health and the Sociology of Emotion (1996)
edited by *Veronica James and Jonathan Gabe*

Medicine, Health and Risk (1995)
edited by *Jonathan Gabe*

Ageing, Dementia and the Social Mind

Edited by

Paul Higgs and Chris Gilleard

WILEY Blackwell

Contents

Notes on contributors

Emily Stella Andrews   Independent Scholar, London, UK

Simon Bailey   Alliance Manchester Business School, University of Manchester, Manchester, UK

Linda Birt   School of Health Sciences, University of East, Anglia, UK

Katherine Brittain   Department of Nursing, Midwifery and Health, Northumbria University, UK

Georgina Charlesworth   Research Department of Clinical, Educational and Health Psychology, University College, London, UK and Research and Development Department, North East London NHS Foundation, Trust, UK

Emese Csipke   Division of Psychiatry, University College, London, UK

Cathrine Degnen   School of Geography, Politics and Sociology, Newcastle University, UK

Claire Dickinson   Institute of Health and Society, Newcastle University, UK

Grant Gibson   School of Applied Social Science, Stirling University, UK

Chris Gilleard   Division of Psychiatry, UCL Faculty of Brain Sciences, London, UK

Marlene Goldman   Department of English, University of Toronto, Canada

Amanda Grenier   Department of Health, Aging and Society and Gilbrea Centre for Studies in Aging, McMaster University, Canada

Paul Higgs   Division of Psychiatry, UCL Faculty of Brain Sciences, London, UK

Anthea Innes   Faculty of Social Sciences, University of Stirling, Scotland

Ian Rees Jones   Wales Institute of Social and Economic Research, Data and Methods, Cardiff University, Cardiff, UK

Fiona Kelly   Centre for Person-centred Practice Research, Queen Margaret University, Edinburgh, UK

Paul Kingston   Centre for Ageing Studies, University of Chester, Chester, UK

Alexis P. Kontos   Human Rights Law Section, Department of Justice Canada, Canada

Pia Kontos   Toronto Rehabilitation Institute-University Health Network, Toronto, Canada and Dalla Lana School of Public Health, University of Toronto, Toronto, Canada

Liz Lloyd   School for Policy Studies, University of Bristol, UK

Joanne Middleton   School of Health Sciences, University of Manchester, Manchester, UK

Karen-Lee Miller   Toronto Rehabilitation Institute-University Health Network, Toronto, Canada

Patricia Mc Parland   School of Nursing and Human Sciences, Dublin City University, Dublin, Ireland

Chris Phillipson   School of Social Sciences, University of Manchester, UK

Fiona Poland   School of Health Sciences, University of East, Anglia, UK

Louise Robinson   Institute of Health and Society, Newcastle University, UK

Kezia Scales   Center for the Study of Aging and Human Development, Duke University, USA and School of Nursing, Duke University, USA

Justine Schneider   School of Sociology & Social Policy, University of Nottingham, Nottingham, UK

Edward Tolhurst   Faculty of Health Sciences, Staffordshire University, Stafford, UK

Bernhard Weicht   Department of Sociology, University of Innsbruck, Innsbruck, Austria

1

Ageing, dementia and the social mind: past, present and future perspectives

Paul Higgs and Chris Gilleard

The sociology of dementia has been a relatively neglected topic in studies of health and illness despite dementia becoming of increasing significance to most 'ageing societies'. For this reason alone an overview of developments and directions in the sociology of dementia seems both necessary and apposite. Worldwide, it has been estimated that there will be over 80 million people living with dementia by 2040 (Prince and Jackson 2013). The significance of this condition, we would argue, goes much further than its epidemiological significance. The effects of this 'major neurocognitive disorder' as it is described in the latest edition of the Diagnostic and Statistical Manual (DSM-5; Sachdev *et al.* 2014) are not confined simply to the numbers affected by the condition. It must also include the considerable impact that the condition has on the lives of patients and carers as well as the consequences for the health and social care professionals involved in providing support and care. Dementia is responsible for over half of all admissions to residential long-term care; it impacts more heavily upon families and carers than nearly all other medical conditions and it represents one of, if not the most feared aspects of growing older (Cantegreil-Kallen and Pin 2012, Luppa *et al.* 2010, Torti *et al.* 2004). Equally, the costs associated with providing care are constantly projected to grow with Alzheimer's Disease International (ADI) estimating that the worldwide combined cost of dementia care in 2015 was US$818 billion and that this figure is likely to rise to over US$ 1 Trillion by 2030 (Martin 2015). Alongside this has to be considered that the biomedical project to find a 'cure' for dementia which could potentially alleviate these costs has foundered (Lock 2013). While the latter decades of the twentieth century were marked by the concerted effort from the pharmaceutical industry to develop and market effective 'antidementia' drugs, since the beginning of the twenty-first century such efforts seem to have fallen by the wayside. Attention is turning toward 'pre-clinical' risk profiling and the public health implementation of 'dementia prevention' strategies (Imtiaz *et al.* 2014). All of this has complicated and extended the significance of dementia to researchers in the sociology of health and illness.

Dementia consequently has become identified as being at the heart of the 'problem' of ageing societies as many of the above features are rolled into the idea of 'apocalyptic demography' first advanced by Ann Robertson in 1990 and still going strong in many different contexts (Lundgren and Ljuslinder 2011, Martin *et al.* 2009). Furthermore, the increasing frequency of dementia as a topical news item in the media has meant that it has a growing influence on the social representations of old age as the messages about its effects spread more widely among the general population (Hunter and Doyle 2014). Such media exposure

Ageing, Dementia and the Social Mind, First Edition. Edited by Paul Higgs and Chris Gilleard.
Chapters © 2017 The Authors. Book Compilation © 2017 Foundation for the Sociology of
Health & Illness/Blackwell Publishing Ltd.

generates fears relating to the anticipated progressive loss of capacity of individuals who develop dementia. This fear of losing one's mind, and losing one's place in the adult world, has led to dementia being framed as a form of 'social death' (Sweeting and Gilhooly 1997). Despite the efforts of advocacy groups representing families facing the challenges of dementia and the articulation of the sufferer's voice in personal accounts of dementia, such fears have not diminished and may have prompted calls and means for voluntary euthanasia (Draper *et al*. 2010, Volicer 2016). This process appears to have occurred in parallel with what has been described as the 'Alzheimerisation of ageing' (Adelman 1995, Gilleard and Higgs 2000). Reinforced by media reports of 'institutional abuse' in nursing homes (Lloyd *et al*. 2014), the intensified search for 'a cure', and dire predictions of demographic apocalypse, the Alzheimerisation of ageing seems to contribute to the propagation of an associated and potentially negative 'neuro-culture' spread across the whole of society (Williams *et al*. 2012). In so doing the various contexts of dementia are re-setting the coordinates of what ageing and old age mean in contemporary societies. The increases in life expectancy and the improvement of health at later ages has shifted our understanding of what constitutes normal ageing (Jones and Higgs 2010) as well as creating a much more 'densified' and frail 'fourth age' (Gilleard and Higgs 2011). This transformation has been much discussed and debated within social gerontology but has not had as much attention within medical sociology (Higgs 2013).

This monograph then comes at an important time to take stock of the societal impact of dementia and its relation to health. The papers in it address several themes that exist at the intersection of dementia with a number of important concerns within the sociology of age, health and illness. The selection exemplifies our concern to further develop a critical but constructive sociology of dementia; one that is both critical in highlighting the social processes involved in dementia and dementia care as well as taking full account of the cultural and social representations of dementia that are present in everyday life. We do so to facilitate constructive engagement in the formulation of a range of potential responses to this condition. When first proposing this monograph, we drew heavily on our own understanding of the role of dementia in positioning a 'social imaginary' of the fourth age (Gilleard and Higgs 2010, Higgs and Gilleard 2015). We used the term social imaginary in order to project the idea that the fourth age has as much impact on those who are not enveloped by its corporeality as on those who by their dementia and frailty already are. We argued that using the term allows for a much greater recognition of the way in which social representations play a key role in understanding the dilemmas posed by dementia and how this may differ for those occupying the multiplicity of professional and social locations operating in this arena. This has led us to become interested in such key concepts as personhood, care work and the ethical and moral frameworks in which these practices are situated (Higgs and Gilleard 2016). These concerns are, we believe, brought out in this collection.

The volume covers four broad themes. While they are by no means exhaustive of the range of present and future possibilities for a sociology of dementia, they do serve as a sound basis from which to build one. The first theme concerns the importance of the construction of personhood in relation to dementia. This has been a key area for the development of social science thinking about what the condition of dementia means for those with the diagnosis as well as those dealing with it as both a family and a professional concern. A key point of departure has been the usefulness (or otherwise) of Kitwood's (1997) location of the 'problem' of dementia as the product of a 'malignant' social psychology. The tendency he observed for services to discount the concerns, feelings and interests of those with the condition led him to advocate a more 'person-centred' form of care as a way of recognising and supporting the 'personhood' of the individual concerned. For Kitwood, personhood was not 'dependent' on a Kantian assumption of individual rationality but on the relatedness of persons. This approach has been very influential and a number of the contributions to this volume explicitly discuss and defend that legacy. Kontos, Miller and Kontos in their paper 'Relational citizenship: Supporting embodied selfhood and relationality in dementia care' develop this line of thinking by explicitly arguing for a notion of 'embodied selfhood'. However the debate on personhood as developed, cannot help but overlap with discussions of citizenship given that many commentators have seen the issues of personhood better understood not as ones of 'personal capacity' or even 'personal relationships' but as ones that speak to the denial of citizenship rights (Bartlett and O'Connor 2007). Here an often implicit connection is made to the activism of the disability rights movement. This is brought out in Birt *et al.*'s paper 'Shifting dementia discourses from deficit to active citizenship' which seeks to consider the advantages to be gained from adopting a disability perspective to this area of practice and research, while recognising how profound cognitive disability may pose particular difficulties for this perspective.

The second theme concerns the issue of care. This topic interrelates with issues of personhood as shown in Tolhurst *et al.*'s paper 'Narrative collisions, sociocultural pressures and dementia: the relational basis of personhood reconsidered' and in Scales *et al.*'s paper 'Power, empowerment, and person-centred care: Using ethnography to examine the everyday practice of unregistered dementia care'. What these papers illustrate is the complexity of the care relationship within dementia and, as Andrews's paper 'Institutionalising senile dementia in 19th-century Britain' shows us, how these relations are historically contextualised within both medical discourses and institutional practices.

The third theme of the monograph addresses the social representations of dementia and in particular the way in which its presence has been inserted into contemporary culture. Work by Beard (2016), Beard and Neary (2013) and Lock (2013) has started to address this process. McParland *et al.*'s paper 'Dichotomising dementia: is there another way?' shows that as the title suggests, it would be a mistake to view living with dementia purely as a failure. They advocate accepting the condition as something more fluid and paradoxical in terms of the possibilities for continuing social inclusion. Brittan *et al.*'s paper 'When walking becomes wandering: representing the fear of the fourth age' describes aspects of the social imaginary of the fourth age that many working in the field are aware of and which represent symbolic processes as much as practical concerns. In a similar fashion, Goldman's paper 'Re-imagining dementia in the fourth age: the ironic actions of Alice Munro' examines the fictional representation of dementia. It reminds us also that the social imaginary of the fourth age operates at many different levels of cultural practice not just in bio-medical, nursing and social care discourses.

The fourth theme addresses what we would term the social contextualisation of dementia. Jones's paper 'Social class, dementia and the fourth age' offers an overview of the social determinants of dementia and dementia care, both in terms of their 'equalising' nature as well as those arenas where inequalities emerge. This is complemented by the paper by Grenier *et al.* entitled 'Precarity in late life: Rethinking dementia as a 'frailed' *old age*' which sees the many issues surrounding the fourth age as being better understood when viewed through the lens of contemporary work on 'precariousness' and the 'precariat' (Standing 2011). Such a conceptualisation places dementia and the fourth age within the broader context of statuses and positions that are less and less secured in present-day society. Among the many effects of this growing precariousness, they argue, is its role in deepening the social divisions of later life.

It is this wider contextualisation for which we are advocating; seeing the sociological problem of dementia within the broader context of family life, the social imaginary institutions of old age, the expansion of care work within the service sector of the economy, and the particular consequences of what Beck and Beck-Gernsheim (2002) have called the 'institutionalised individualism of second modernity' for those whose lives are made ever more difficult by the promulgation of an individualised reflexivity in contemporary culture. This focus continues into the care home where the issues of personhood and competence promote forms of 'third person agency' and 'proxy consumerism' (Vabø 2006).

What is perhaps one of the lacunae in this collection is the role that Alzheimer's plays within the domain of 'science, technology and society'. There has been research on the categories used in the development of the science and the development of categories within it (see, for example, Hedgecoe 2006, Moreira *et al.* 2009, Whitehouse and Moody 2006). The social representation of dementia extends beyond demographic fears, beyond considerations of the nature of autonomy in society and the related nature of care and the cultures of care. It is realised in and through media accounts and professional claims for dementia as a significant scientific and technological problem confronting society. If brain and consciousness represent one of the last 'frontiers' to be 'conquered' by science – the failure of researchers, of the pharmaceutical industry and of medicine to 'solve' the problem of dementia questions the limits of our scientific reach and of the modernist project itself.

Such concerns are raised whenever news of a breakthrough is followed by a period of media silence broken only when a new and often unrelated line of inquiry is opened. While, in the latter decades of the twentieth century, the work of the pharmaceutical industry was relatively successful in re-positioning 'dementia' from its status as part of the normative ageing process and expectations of decline from people as they reach ever greater ages, the re-branding of dementia as 'Alzheimer's and related disorders' has had minimal effect on society, beyond the evident increase in research funding associated with the condition. Cynically one might speculate that the most long lasting effect of the Alzheimerisation of old age has been to increase public anxiety and channel medical research toward a drive for a variety of cures and away from the previous concerns for improving care provision that dominated research before the era of the 'cholinergic' and the 'amyloidogenesis' hypotheses.

What then might constitute the most helpful directions of travel for research in dementia within the fields of medical sociology and the sociology of ageing? Does there need to be further research into 'the problems of care' or into the institutional practices of care? What scope is there for developing a social disability model of dementia? Or one based upon notions of 'justice' and 'citizens' rights'? Does the emergence of the social category of the 'precariat' offer a focus of resistance against the gradual erosion of services and reduction in public resources for those least able to navigate their way through what has been described by Post (2000) as a hyper-cognitive society? Are the issues surrounding dementia similar to the ones identified in the health inequalities literature and are the solutions broadly the same? What scope is there to support greater recognition – materially and socially – of the demanding and difficult work that is regularly performed by those in the care sector (Johnson 2015)? What of the challenges and points of resistance being created by an increasingly sophisticated range of technology designed to provide digital electronic support for this work?

What are the risks that can easily turn such systems of support into more oppressive forms of surveillance (Berridge 2016)? All of these are important questions that need to be developed and debated. The answers provided may reflect many different approaches but hopefully they will collectively take the field of social science dementia research forward so that it can fruitfully engage with policy and practice.

As we have pointed out earlier, as editors we have a definite approach to the questions posed by dementia and we have a clear idea of the concepts useful in answering them. Other than framing the call for papers we have not tried to endorse our views in this volume. The papers reflect a wide spectrum of opinion and we are grateful for that. We hope that this collection will help to draw wider attention to the debates and research occurring in an area that has not commanded the attention it deserves within the wider community of researchers working in the field of the sociology of health and illness. The debates and issues present inevitably reflect our own concerns but the multiplicity of the authors' approaches indicate that there are many ways of viewing the topic. While we believe that these papers focus on those areas and social relations where the social imaginary exerts its strongest influence, specifically on those caught up with the moral imperative of care and what is sometimes known as the 'reproductive labour' of care (Yeates 2012), it is also the case that all the papers share a desire to ensure that the social relations of dementia provide conceptual and empirical resources for establishing better ways of caring and of continuing to care.

Acknowledgements

Paul Higgs would like to acknowledge the support of two ESRC/NIHR funded research programmes: Managing Agitation and Raising QUality of lifE in dementia (MARQUE) ES/L001780/1 and Promoting Independence In Dementia (PRIDE) ES/L001802/1. The views expressed are solely in a personal capacity.

References

Adelman, R.C. (1995) The Alzheimerization of aging, *The Gerontologist*, 35, 4, 526–32.

Bartlett, R. and O'Connor, D. (2007) From personhood to citizenship: broadening the lens for dementia practice and research, *Journal of Aging Studies*, 21, 2, 107–18.

Beard, R.L. (2016) *Living with Alzheimer's: Managing Memory Loss, Identity, and Illness*. New York: NYU Press.

Beard, R.L. and Neary, T.M. (2013) Making sense of nonsense: experiences of mild cognitive impairment, *Sociology of Health & Illness*, 35, 1, 130–46.

Berridge, C. (2016) Active subjects of passive monitoring: responses to a passive monitoring system in low-income independent living, *Ageing and Society*, 1–24. doi:10.1017/S0144686X15001269.

Beck, U. and Beck-Gernsheim, E. (2002) *Individualization*. London: Sage.

Cantegreil-Kallen, I. and Pin, S. (2012) Fear of Alzheimer's disease in the French population: impact of age and proximity to the disease, *International Psychogeriatrics*, 24, 1, 108–16.

Draper, B., Peisah, C., Snowdon, J. and Brodaty, H. (2010) Early dementia diagnosis and the risk of suicide and euthanasia, *Alzheimer's & Dementia*, 6, 1, 75–82.

Gilleard, C. and Higgs, P. (2000) *Cultures of Ageing: Self, Citizen and the Body*. London: Pearson.

Gilleard, C. and Higgs, P. (2010) Ageing without agency: theorising the fourth age, *Aging & Mental Health*, 14, 121–8.

Gilleard, C. and Higgs, P. (2011) Frailty, disability and old age: a re-appraisal, *Health*, 15, 5, 475–90.

Harding, N. and Palfrey, C. (1997) *The Social Construction of Dementia: Confused Professionals?* London: Macmillan.

Hedgecoe, A. (2006) Pharmacogenetics as alien science: Alzheimer's disease, core sets and expectations, *Social Studies of Science*, 36, 5, 723–52.

Higgs, P. (2013) 'Disturbances in the field': the challenge of changes in ageing and later life for social theory and health, *Social Theory & Health*, 11, 271–84.

Higgs, P. and Gilleard, C. (2015) *Rethinking Old Age: Theorising the fourth age*. London: Palgrave Macmillan.

Higgs, P. and Gilleard, C. (2016) *Personhood, Care and Identity in Advanced Old Age*. Bristol: Policy Press.

Hunter, C. and Doyle, C. (2014) Dementia policy in Australia and the 'social construction' of infirm old age, *Health and History*, 16, 2, 44–62.

Imtiaz, B., Tolppanen, A.M., Kivipelto, M. and Soininen, H. (2014) Future directions in Alzheimer's disease from risk factors to prevention, *Biochemical Pharmacology*, 88, 4, 661–70.

Johnson, E.K. (2015) The business of care: the moral labour of care workers, *Sociology of Health & Illness*, 37, 1, 112–26.

Jones, I.R. and Higgs, P. (2010) The natural, the normal and the normative: contested terrains in ageing and old age, *Social Science and Medicine*, 71, 8, 1513–9.

Kitwood, T. (1997) *Dementia Reconsidered: The Person Comes First*. Buckingham: Open University Press.

Lock, M. (2013) *The Alzheimer Conundrum: Entanglements of Dementia and Aging*. Princeton: Princeton University Press.

Lloyd, L., Banerjee, A., Harrington, C., Jacobsen, F., *et al.* (2014) It is a scandal! Comparing the causes and consequences of nursing home media scandals in five countries. *International Journal of Sociology and Social Policy*, 34, 1/2, 2–18.

Lundgren, A.S. and Ljuslinder, K. (2011) Problematic demography: representations of population ageing in the Swedish daily press, *Journal of Population Ageing*, 4, 3, 165–83.

Luppa, M., Luck, T., Weyerer, S., König, H.H., *et al.* (2010) Prediction of institutionalization in the elderly: a systematic review, *Age and Ageing*, 39, 1, 31–8.

Martin, R., Williams, C. and O'Neill, D. (2009) Retrospective analysis of attitudes to ageing in *The Economist*: apocalyptic demography for opinion formers, *British Medical Journal*, 339, b4914.

Martin, P. (2015) *World Alzheimer Report 2015: The Global Impact of Dementia*. London: Alzheimer's Disease International (ADI).

Moreira, T., May, C. and Bond, J. (2009) Regulatory objectivity in action kild cognitive impairment and the collective production of uncertainty, *Social Studies of Science*, 39, 5, 665–90.

Post, S. (2000) The concept of Alzheimer disease in a hypercognitive society. In Whitehouse, P.J. and Maurer, K. (eds.) *Concepts of Alzheimer Disease: Biological, Clinical, and Cultural Perspectives*. Baltimore: Johns Hopkins Press.

Prince, M. and Jackson, J. (2013) *World Alzheimer's Report 2009 Executive Summary*. London: Alzheimer's Disease International (ADI).

Robertson, A. (1990) The politics of Alzheimer's disease: a case study in apocalyptic demography, *International Journal of Health Services*, 20, 3, 429–42.

Sachdev, P.S., Blacker, D., Blazer, D.G., Ganguli, M., *et al.* (2014) Classifying neurocognitive disorders: the DSM-5 approach, *Nature Reviews Neurology*, 10, 634–42.

Standing, G. (2011) *The Precariat: The New Dangerous Class*. London: A&C Black.

Sweeting, H. and Gilhooly, M. (1997) Dementia and the phenomenon of social death, *Sociology of Health & Illness*, 19, 1, 93–117.

Torti, F.M. Jr., Gwyther, L.P., Reed, S.D., Friedman, J.Y., *et al.* (2004) A multinational review of recent trends and reports in dementia caregiver burden, *Alzheimer Disease & Associated Disorders*, 18, 2, 99–109.

Vabø, M. (2006) Caring for people or caring for proxy consumers? *European Societies*, 8, 3, 403–22.

Volicer, L. (2016) Fear of dementia, *Journal of the American Medical Directors Association*, 17, 10, 875–8.

Whitehouse, P.J. and Moody, H.R. (2006) Mild cognitive impairment: a 'hardening of the categories'? *Dementia*, 5, 1, 11–25.

Williams, S., Higgs, P. and Katz, S. (2012) Neuroculture, active ageing and the 'older brain': problems, promises and prospects, *Sociology of Health & Illness*, 34, 1, 64–78.

Yeates, N. (2012) Global care chains: a state-of-the-art review and future directions in care transnationalization research, *Global Networks*, 12, 2, 135–54.

2

Relational citizenship: supporting embodied selfhood and relationality in dementia care

Pia Kontos, Karen-Lee Miller and Alexis P. Kontos

Introduction

In the dominant discourse of dementia there is a presumed existential erosion of selfhood 'until there is nothing left' (Davis 2004: 375). This discourse is a legacy of the 17th century rise of the 'modern self' in which the self and brain became consubstantial (Vidal 2009), implicitly relegating corporeality to a subordinate role. This introduces a belief in the body's fundamental passivity because it treats the brain as the organ responsible for the functions with which the self is identified (Whitehouse 2008). The perceived loss of self is, in turn, accompanied by assumptions of loss of agency, as well as citizenship status. An individual's status as citizen, which denotes an entitled connection to a community and country with rights and responsibilities as a community member and freedom from discrimination (Bartlett and O'Connor 2007), is seen as fundamentally and irrevocably eroded by dementia because communicative competence and intellectual capacities are inextricably linked to the practice and status of citizenship.

To redress the social and structural disadvantages of people with dementia, particularly those who are severely cognitively impaired, we advocate the need for a new model of citizenship – what we term 'relational citizenship' – that fully supports their contributions to social life and what they may expect as citizens in return. It is a model that is premised on the importance of interdependence, reciprocity, and the support of persons with dementia as active partners in their own care (Dupuis *et al.* 2009, Nolan *et al.* 2002). Another foundational tenet of the model is that the capacities, senses, and socio-cultural dispositions of the body are central to self-expression, interdependence, and the reciprocal nature of engagement (Kontos 2006, 2012a, 2012b). As such, relational citizenship is a model that stands to advance the discourse on citizenship by offering an important rethinking of notions of selfhood, entitlement, and reciprocity, which are central to a sociology of dementia.

We begin by tracing and critiquing the traditional paradigm of clinical and social care of individuals with dementia in order to contextualise key counter-paradigms, including citizenship and person-centred and relationship-centred approaches to care. We highlight important limitations of these paradigms, which we argue can be redressed with our relational model of citizenship (Miller and Kontos 2016, Kontos *et al.* 2016). To illustrate how relational citizenship can be supported, or undermined, at the micro level of direct care, we utilise empirical evidence from a study we conducted which explored the interactions between elder-clowns and persons with dementia residing in a long-term care facility.

Ageing, Dementia and the Social Mind, First Edition. Edited by Paul Higgs and Chris Gilleard.
Chapters © 2017 The Authors. Book Compilation © 2017 Foundation for the Sociology of
Health & Illness/Blackwell Publishing Ltd.

Paradigms of dementia care and treatment

The traditional paradigm of clinical and social care of individuals with dementia is characterised by the management of 'challenging behaviours' through control, containment, and pharmacology (Dupuis *et al.* 2012). Increasing disfavour towards this approach, due to concerns about inhumane consequences that include adverse medication effects (Katona 2001) and the harm caused by the pathologisation of distress as a dementia disease marker (Brannelly 2011), has led to alternative paradigms, including person-centred, relationship-centred, and arts-based approaches to care.

Person-centred dementia care (Kitwood 1997) recognises the intrinsic value and uniqueness of the individual with dementia. It shifts treatment emphasis from pathologising behaviour to understanding the meaningfulness of actions (Dupuis *et al.* 2012). Although it is the most important development in dementia care practice since the 1990s (Bartlett *et al.* 2010), it has nonetheless prompted newer paradigms intended to address its limitations, namely the decontextualising of the individual from relationships with others (Nolan *et al.* 2002) and the ways in which issues of agency and power differentials are profoundly ignored (Bartlett *et al.* 2010).

Relationship-centred care (Adams and Gardiner 2005) was developed to redress the focus on the person with dementia to the exclusion of those who informally or formally provide his or her care (Ryan *et al.* 2008). The impetus of relationship-centred care is to 'fully capture the interdependencies and reciprocities that underpin caring relationships' (Nolan *et al.* 2002: 203) and to make explicit the centrality of relationships to quality care. This paradigm makes two significant contributions to dementia care. The first is the conceptual shift from the autonomy and individuality that underpins person-centredness to interdependence and relationality (Dupuis *et al.* 2009). The second is the expectation that the person with dementia will retain status as an active partner in the dementia care experience (Bartlett *et al.* 2010). Nonetheless, even with relationship-centred care, the focus remains on care relationships, thus overlooking other relationships that individuals might have, such as those with the state and its institutions. Consequently, the person with dementia continues to be solely conceptualised within the in-need- of-care context (Bartlett *et al.* 2010).

A citizenship perspective redresses some of the gaps inherent in both person- and relationship- centred approaches to care (Bartlett and O'Connor 2007). In the context of dementia studies, social citizenship is defined as follows:

> A relationship, practice or status, in which a person with dementia is entitled to experience freedom from discrimination, and to have opportunities to grow and participate in life to the fullest extent possible. It involves justice, recognition of social positions and the upholding of personhood, rights and a fluid degree of responsibility for shaping events at a personal and societal level (Bartlett *et al.* 2010: 37).

A citizenship lens is fundamentally concerned with the misuse of power and thus is considered to be more apposite than a personhood perspective for improving the status and treatment of persons with dementia (Bartlett *et al.* 2010). Citizenship similarly extends relationship-centred care by incorporating an individual's relations with others into the sociopolitical landscape, thereby addressing influences on access to, and experience with, health and social care institutions (Bartlett *et al.* 2010). Unlike the empowered and politicised users of mental health services and cancer care, individuals with dementia had previously been excluded from the broader service user movement because they were seen as antithetical to the notion of 'the pro-active, rational consumer of services' (Smith *et al.* 2011: 1466).

This changed with campaigning activities that repositioned individuals with mild dementia as citizen-workers, and which yielded social and psychological benefits associated with activism, self-advocacy, and the companionship of others with similar impairments (Bartlett 2014). Nonetheless, this model of citizenship is premised on the ideological construct of 'self-cognisance' (Bartlett and O'Connor 2007), which deepens the social devaluation of those with more severe cognitive impairment who may not be able to make recognisable public contributions (Minkler and Holstein 2008).

One proposed corrective is the passive model of social citizenship. It is concerned with 'people getting what they are entitled to or have a right to expect as an equal citizen' (Bartlett *et al.* 2010: 108) without having to make a public contribution. With this corrective to the ethical principal of 'no rights without responsibilities' (Sevenhuijsen 2000: 8), citizenship is defined not by degree of participation but rather by the degree to which an individual's rights are recognised and upheld through care practices, policies, and institutions.

Both relationship-centred care and the passive model of citizenship offer important insights regarding the requirements of fair and equitable treatment of individuals with dementia. Yet, neither of these approaches has been significantly informed by the insights of critical gerontology's emerging theoretical subfield of embodiment and dementia, specifically, embodied selfhood (Kontos and Martin 2013). This is despite an explicit call to expand the notion of relationality to include embodied selfhood (Mitchell *et al.* 2013).

Embodied selfhood significantly advances examination of the lived body by foregrounding primordial as well as socio-cultural ways of being-in-the-world (Kontos and Martin 2013). It places body-self and body-world relations at the centre of a reconceptualisation of how dementia is represented and/or experienced. It advances a notion of selfhood that considers both the body's pre-reflective power of natural expression – manifest, for example, in basic bodily movements and the co-ordination of visual, tactile, and motor aspects of the body – and the style or content of bodily movements derived from socialisation and cultural upbringing over which the individual has no conscious mastery (Kontos 2012b).

Our proposed relational citizenship model extends the concept of social citizenship by presuming that support of the central tenets of relationship-centred care (i.e. interdependence, reciprocity, and the support of persons with dementia as active partners in their own care) and embodied selfhood theory (i.e. the primordial body and socio-cultural dispositions as the primary agential source of interactive and communicative practices for persons living with dementia) are necessary to more inclusively grant citizenship entitlements to persons living with dementia in long-term residential care (Miller and Kontos 2016, Kontos *et al.* 2016). Our intent here, by extension, is to examine the complex issue of how relational citizenship can be supported at the micro level of direct care. We do so through a focus on two forms of interactive and communicative expressions: creativity and sexuality. These are arguably among the most visible manifestations of relationality and embodied selfhood which are the central tenets of relational citizenship. Empirical evidence from our study on elder-clown practice (Kontos *et al.* 2015, 2016) is used as a heuristic to illustrate strategies and techniques that support and undermine relational citizenship. The intent is to prompt discussion on how relational citizenship can be supported by all members of a long-term care team.

Therapeutic and elder-clown practice

Participatory arts programmes are part of a 'major conceptual sea change' (Cohen 2006: 7) in long-term care. Some such programmes, particularly dance and drama, emphasise 'demonstrated potential for empowerment and pleasure for the moment' (Beard 2011: 11). The arts, with their creative-expressive focus, draw significantly on the body's potentiality for innovation and creative action and significantly support non-verbal communication and affect (Kontos and Martin 2013). The arts thereby offer an important means by which the citizenship of persons with dementia can be sustained. The most recent innovation in arts-based approaches in dementia care is elder-clowning (Hendriks 2012; Warren and Spitzer 2011).

The vast majority of clowns often begin as professional actors with theatrical training who then pursue post-graduate training at clown schools (Linge 2008). Since 2009, the University of Haifa has offered the only academic programme in medical clowning as a three year bachelor's track in the theatre department (Estrin 2012). The academicisation of the profession is designed to legitimise clowning as a paramedical profession (Estrin 2012).

Contemporary therapeutic clowning began in the 1970s in the United States (Roy 2009). Children are the primary target for most therapeutic clown programmes in acute care hospital settings (Warren 2007), although medicalised settings have seen clowns used for adult care in rehabilitation (Gervais *et al.* 2007) and assisted reproduction (Friedler *et al.* 2011). Since the late 1990s, clowning has been adapted for specific use with the dementia population (Killick 2003). The efficacy of elder-clowns has been demonstrated in qualitative (Thomson 2005, Warren 2008, 2009) and intervention studies (Kontos *et al.* 2015, Low *et al.* 2013).

Therapeutic clowns and elder-clowns share some similarities. Both don a red-nose and practise physical and verbal humour, reminiscence techniques, fantasy, surprise, inversion, dramatic movement, and storytelling (Warren and Spitzer 2011). They also both use body language ranging from subtle muscular movements of the face to more obvious gestural movements of the hands. Within the context of severe dementia, where verbal communication is often limited and may be non-existent, clowning utilises physically-oriented question-and-answer tactics such as eye contact, smiling, short actions, and slow movements. There is no expectation of active physical response by a resident; instead, even the observation of clown activities is perceived as a form of subtle communicative engagement (Thompson 1998).

Elder-clowns distinguish themselves from therapeutic clowns often seen in the paediatric context by avoiding the traditional heavily made-up white-faced clown with the exaggerated smile and oversized shoes (Warren and Spitzer 2011). Elder-clowns keep their faces natural with minimal make-up and wear clothing that evokes an earlier era such as 1950s swing dresses (Hendriks 2012, Kontos *et al.* 2015). To tailor their interactions to the adult context of long-term care residents, elder-clown activities rely upon a resident's biographical information (e.g. life history, preferences, and hobbies) which is typically provided by healthcare staff.

Methods

The study from which this data is drawn was a mixed-methods evaluation of a 12-week, embodied selfhood enhanced, elder-clown intervention in a nursing home in urban central Canada that embraces a holistic vision of health and well-being in its support of innovation and the arts. Relational citizenship discourse did not inform the original study.

The purpose of the study was to explore the impact of elder-clowning on residents of a longterm care home and to improve existing capacity to support embodied self-expression through training in embodied selfhood theory (for additional findings related to this study see Kontos *et al.* 2015, Miller and Kontos 2016, Kontos *et al.* 2016). Elder-clowns received study-specific training in embodied selfhood drawn from a curriculum developed for dementia care practitioners (Kontos *et al.* 2010). Educational modalities included didactic lecture, role-play, and a DVD presentation of *Expressions of personhood in Alzheimer's*, which is a research-based film that portrays dramatised resident-care practitioner interactions to highlight the significance of embodied selfhood for interactive and communicative practices for persons living with dementia (Kontos 2006, 2012a, 2012b), including how healthcare practitioners can support or suppress embodied selfhood in their approaches to care (Kontos *et al.* 2010, Kontos and Naglie 2006). Three of the elder-clowns had received professional training at recognised Canadian clown organisations, while the fourth was internationally trained.

Elder-clown-resident interactions
Elder-clowns visited residents twice weekly, approximately 10 minutes per visit, over a 12-week period. During each visit, the elder-clowns were free to utilise any modality (e.g. music or drawing) or prop (e.g. a miniature ukulele or a giant pen) they believed was appropriate to each resident's mood, interactional style, or clinical condition. Their decision-making was supported by the provision of information (e.g. family, work, and life biography) collected earlier by researchers via interviews with family care partners and health care practitioners.

Participants
Clowns are identified by pseudonyms (Cherry, Aksom, Zazzie, and Mitsy) during interactions when they are in clown character and by practitioner/clown pseudonyms (Holly/Cherry, Camilla/Aksom, Kate/Zazzie, and Ann/Mitsy) during videotaped reflections and interviews when they are reflecting on their clown characters' responses. All elder-clowns were women, but one elder-clown's character was a young male (Aksom). Twenty-three residents participated: the mean age was 87.8 years (SD = 8.0); 16 were female; and dementia diagnoses were predominantly Alzheimer's dementia (73.9%) followed by mixed Alzheimer's and vascular dementia (13.0%), Lewy body dementia (8.7%), and vascular dementia (4.4%).

Observations of videotaped clown-resident visits
Clown-resident visits predominantly took place in the residents' private rooms and were videotaped by a professional videographer. Four hundred and seventeen clown-resident visits (66 hours) were videotaped. One hundred and five visits occurred in public areas such as the hallway where videotaping was prohibited; these were reflected upon by the elder-clowns during videotaped reflections.

Independent and facilitated videotaped reflections
Elder-clowns are trained to reflect upon the work they do and consider factors that may help or hinder successful interactions (Stirling-Twist and Le Roux 2014). After each half-day of visits, the elder-clowns reflected on what transpired during visits (e.g. residents' active or passive verbal and non-verbal responses). For the purposes of this study, this reflective work was augmented by the researchers' questions related to embodied self-expression, as a component of the study's evaluation of the enhanced embodied selfhood training.

Interviews
Individual post-intervention interviews with all four elder-clowns were informed by our interim analysis of all video footage. This enabled us to further explore our interpretations of the interactions vis-à-vis resident responses and the techniques and strategies undertaken by the elder-clowns.

Analysis
Our interest here was to examine how the core tenets of relational citizenship (embodied self-hood and relationality) might be supported at the micro level of care practice. Towards this end, we restricted our interpretation to findings derived from clown data (in-person interviews and videotaped reflections) and clown-resident interactions (videotaped visits).

First, the entire corpus of video footage of clown-resident visits was viewed several times by authors PK and KLM, as is recommended when working with this type of data (Derry 2007). Videotaped interactions were then transcribed, as if they were occurring in real time, as non-participant observer field notes by authors PK and KLM, both of whom are trained in ethnographic observation. The verbatim transcriptions of the clowns' videotaped reflections and in-person interviews, as well as ethnographic descriptions of videotape footage, were analysed concurrently and recursively using a modified directed content analysis approach (Hsieh and Shannon 2005) in which code development is guided by sensitising concepts (Bowen 2008); in this case, relational citizenship. This involved analytic expansion of the data in order to investigate relational citizenship, which was not central to the original study. This approach is appropriate where secondary research questions can be traced back to the original data (Medjedović and Witzel 2008). Finally, analytical categories were examined to capture strategies and techniques that undermined the support of relational citizenship.

Findings

We focused on two experiential dimensions at the micro level (creativity and sexuality) because these are key visible manifestations of relationality and embodied selfhood, both of which are the central tenets of relational citizenship. Creativity and sexuality were then examined in situ vis-à-vis clown practices and techniques to determine how and in what ways relational citizenship was supported or undermined by the elder-clowns in their engagements with residents. Support was discerned from the elder-clowns' recognition and response to residents' reactions and contributions to the clown interactions versus undermining, such as when the clowns redirected or ignored such reactions or contributions.

The creative nature of elder-clown engagement
Research has explored how individuals with dementia express and interpret the non-verbal and verbal communication of others (Hubbard *et al.* 2002). Embodied selfhood importantly locates the body as a source of intentional interactive practices that not only support sociability and the maintenance of social norms but also distinctiveness and creativity (Kontos 2003, 2014). This underscores the ongoing relational and embodied nature of engagement undertaken by individuals with dementia and the importance of extending citizenship to include these dimensions of engagement. Here, we explore these dimensions of creativity through engagements involving the imagination, art, and music.

Engaging the imagination
Clowns often fully embraced the imaginary as a means to counteract residents' incoherent or nonsensical speech in the presence of reminiscence or delusion. This stands in stark contrast to the common response by health care professionals and family members who 'try to bring someone with dementia back to "normal" reality' (Symons 2012). Instead, elder-clowns 'surrender to the participant's reality' (Symons 2012) to co-construct imaginative scenarios. Here, the clowns coconstruct a narrative about authoring fiction in present time with a resident (Claire) whom they had learned through researcher-prepared biographies was an author in

her youth. The clowns (Cherry and Mitsy) built on her spoken and written use of the words 'America', 'Kate', and 'murder':

Claire awkwardly gestures writing with a semi-clenched left hand and asks Cherry, 'What do you want me to write down?' Cherry looks at Claire's moving left hand and queries whether she would like to write; Claire agrees. Mitsy places a multi-coloured mosaic glass pen near Claire's left hand, and Claire jerkily raises her right hand to take it. Once she has grasped it, she smoothly moves the pen from a grab hold to a writing position and asks, 'How do you want, how do you show it? How this in? Or, do you want just plain?' Both clowns exclaim in unison, 'Yeah!' ... Claire begins. She writes the word 'America' in shaky script and reads aloud as she is writing, 'I can't even America'. She draws small, disconnected lines, as if contemplating the rest of the sentence, and confidently reads, 'On the door'. Mitsy appears to also read the lines as if they are written words, and says affirmingly, 'Yeah'. Claire continues drawing small lines, and in a tone that suggests she is reading them aloud as text, says, 'Yeah, uh, here is that. It's half a line set. Simple. Example'. Mitsy says encouragingly, 'Uh huh. An example, yeah, that's good'. As Claire draws a few more small lines, Cherry looks on with increasingly excited anticipation, and Mitsy exclaims, 'Oh!', as if surprised at what is being written ... Claire connects a couple of lines as she says, 'Kate. So we bring her in, and ... '. Cherry asks with anticipation, as if waiting to hear what comes next, 'And? ... ' Claire pauses, then says as if announcing a climax, 'Murder!' Cherry exclaims, 'Murder?!!' Mitsy sounds shocked, as if she had not anticipated that, 'Oh!' Cherry says excitedly, 'Oh my goodness'. And then, as if realising something about the writing, she says, 'Oohh, it's a mystery! ... It takes a lot of focus, concentration ... '. Mitsy finishes her sentence, ' ... to write a murder mystery'.

Elder-clowns' recognition and support of the residents' embodied dimensions of storytelling is significant in that it models how individuals with dementia can make recognisably creative contributions despite the absence of sensical language.

Artful engagement
Given the expressive and emotive nature of art, it is another important example of how the relational citizenship of persons with dementia can be supported at the level of the body's potential for innovation and creative action. Consistent with embodied selfhood, one of the elder-clowns (Aksom) utilises his knowledge of a resident (Joseph) as an artist. The elder-clown then creatively uses his own body to visibly manifest an artist and canvas:

Joseph is lying in bed on his side facing the two elder-clowns. Mitsy is standing by the side of the bed gently stroking Joseph's arm as Aksom, who is beside her, reaches into his bag that he had placed on the night stand. He pulls out a black felt pen and moves to the base of the bed. Mitsy and Joseph watch as he extends his arm and begins to slowly sketch a landscape as if he were before a room-sized canvas. He squints one eye as if to sharpen his focus as he moves the pen up and down in grand gestures seemingly sketching a tall mountainous terrain; he is physically moving across the room given the expanse of the mountains. Joseph continues to watch Aksom's face but has not looked at his outstretched waving arm or the pen with which Aksom imaginarily draws. When Aksom turns his back to Joseph, assuming that Joseph is focused on the imaginary sketch, Joseph instead gazes downward at his bed sheets. Aksom's exaggerated sketching motions return him to Joseph's bed. Joseph looks up to Aksom's face, again ignoring Aksom's outstretched sketching hand.

Despite the elder-clown's nonverbal enactment of Joseph's vocation and training, a socio-cultural dimension of his embodied selfhood, the imaginary play was not at all effective in engaging Joseph's creative self. This is in striking contrast to a subsequent interaction with the same resident, described by Ann/Zazzie:

> When we [Zazzie and Mitsy] rounded the corner, Joseph was seated at a table with a [food] tray in front of him doing a movement with his orange juice [cup]. He took one cup, and he moved it to the edge [of the food tray], moved it down, back here, back up like this, and was moving this orange juice around the perimeter [of the food tray], and even into the middle. When I saw that movement, immediately I thought, 'He's drawing right now!' … I [opened] my little notebook to a blank page, got my big red oversized pen, and put them on the table in front of him … He took the pen and [drew] two eyes with eyebrows and [a] nose. He put the pen down. Mitsy took it and drew the mouth and the hair. Then it was my turn. Essentially, what was happening was a game of taking turns … He would draw, and then we would draw, and then he would add things, and then he would take [the pen] and hand it back to me, like there was a whole interactive thing going on. He was totally in the game … So there you go, embodied self, like, right there.

The elder-clown's astute interpretation of Joseph's bodily movements as artistic expression prompted her to support his efforts, which evolved into a reciprocal creative game. In the earlier example, the elder-clown attempted to engage Joseph not as an artist but rather as an audience member. This misses a fundamental premise of embodied selfhood in the context of creativity: that creative action is not an intellectual operation but rather it arises from practical involvement (Kontos 2014: 114). Artistic engagement required that Joseph himself be tactually involved; the act of creativity registered no meaning for Joseph detached from his own effort.

Musical engagement

The elder-clowns' success in recognising and supporting artistic self-expression is further demonstrated in the example below. Here, the elder-clowns and the resident co-create a highly improvised song:

> Betty is sitting in her wheelchair, which is tilted slightly back so that she reclines with her head against the head rest. Her eyes are closed, and her hands are clasped together across her lap. Zazzie strums a cord on her ukulele and sings, 'Da, da, da, da, da'. Cherry begins snapping her fingers to the beat of the tune. Both elder-clowns are gently swaying to the music; Cherry begins using her clutch purse filled with loose change as a tambourine. Without opening her eyes, Betty responds by tapping her left foot against the wheelchair footrest, pivoting her wrists downward so her clasped hands move to alternating beats of the music. As Zazzie continues to sing, Betty interjects melodically, 'Be boop', now moving her clasped hands to every beat of the music. Zazzie responds, 'Da, da, da, da'. Betty moves from interjecting words in the existing rhythm to embellishing and shaping the harmony. She sings, 'Ham and eggs, and ham and eggs', now intensifying the movements of her clasped hands by moving her forearms. Zazzie and Cherry repeat the lyric, 'And ham and eggs'. Cherry leans in close to Betty, as if

anticipating she will respond on the next beat. Betty does, warbling, 'Everywhere, there is a place for youuuuu'. The clowns sing in simultaneous reply, 'A place for you'. Betty responds, 'For you!' Zazzie and Cherry sing the lyric back to her. Betty slows the tempo by singing 'Here … Here … HERE!' She sharply punctuates each 'here' with a movement of her clasped hands. Zazzie matches each 'here' with a strum of her ukulele. Zazzie and Cherry mirror the same volume and sing-shout, 'HERE!' Betty softens her tone and lowers her pitch while resuming the up and down movements of her clasped hands, 'Ohhh, it's a big one'. Zazzie and Cherry repeat, 'It's a big one'. Betty warbles, 'And why? And why? And whyyy?' Zazzie and Cherry sing, 'Why, why, why?' Betty in the same tone, 'Take a gun through'. Zazzie and Cherry respond with surprise, and raise their pitch, 'Take a gun through!' Betty softly sings, 'Somebody loves me – but not anybody I know'. Betty's singing turns to incoherent phrasing and goes silent. She appears to have fallen asleep.

The techniques of communicative relating such as affect attunement (sharing an inner emotional state) and synchronisation (mutual conformability regarding speed and frequency of movement), which are integral to traditional elder-clown practice (Linge 2008), are beautifully illustrated in the previous example. In this study, the embodied selfhood training provided to the clowns also appears to have helped them understand the sociocultural aspects of the embodied nature of Betty's musical self and hence advanced their understanding of the importance of their relational support of her own music-making:

Kate/Zazzie: [In that interaction] I'm trying to kind of shape the [ukulele] music to what I'm seeing, the patterns of *her* musicality … So she's observing structures of musicality as well as embodiment of it, and she's in tune, so obviously she has music coming out her, you know, her entire being.

Holly/Cherry: Yeah. And we're going in with something then we let her take it over, and we start to follow her and let her build it, and we're supporting her.

Kate/Zazzie: There are a couple words that she said that are really interesting.

Holly/Cherry: Like 'getting a gun' … It could have been from 'Annie Get Your Gun', 'cause she was in that musical [when she was young].

Sexual dynamics in clown-resident engagement

Other studies have identified that caregivers find expressions of sexuality, and of sexual interest, by individuals living with dementia to be deeply troubling (Archibald 2003; Mahieu *et al.* 2015). This is largely due to issues related to the tendency to associate cognitive incapacity with a lack of moral permissibility to engage in intimate relations, and with ageism more broadly which associates sexuality with youth (Mahieu and Gastmans 2012). Caregivers have been found to ignore residents' sexuality and sexual interests, or to interpret sexual expressions as behaviour problems (Mahieu and Gastmans 2012) rather than as a primordial and relational human need for love and intimacy.

In our study, problematic sexual dynamics emerged between elder-clowns and several male participants. The problems were associated with sexualised clown play and the use of passive rather than direct techniques to dissuade sexual overtures. These problematic dynamics, and the ways in which expressed sexual desires were handled by the elder-clowns, undermined the support of relational citizenship. Elder-clowns sometimes engaged with male residents in a flirtatious manner, with clown plays characterised by verbal or physical teasing and storylines that focused on the elder-clowns' needs for male companionship. These interactions relied upon the demonstrative display of their own female bodies to respond to and invite the heterosexual male gaze. The following example is illustrative:

> The elder-clowns enter Edward's room where he is seated with his middle-aged son. The son says to his father, 'They're looking for you. You asked for younger women'. Both elder-clowns say at once, 'Ooh!' in a surprised but coquettish tone. The son says, 'Nice ladies. Beautiful' … Zazzie announces, 'And may I introduce to you my delightfully beautiful [then changes her tone to mimic a jealous older sister] tall, leggy, BLONDE sister?' Zazzie gestures in a presentational fashion to Cherry's body, and Cherry giggles and preens. Zazzie asks Edward if the man standing in the corner is his son, and Edward replies, 'He's a nice boy'. Zazzie asks, 'Is he single?' Edward responds, 'Yes, and he's looking for a nice girl, too'. Zazzie gasps and reaches into her purse for a jewelry box that she opens to reveal a faux plastic diamond solitaire ring. Zazzie asks Edward, 'Do you think, if I am really nice, that I might get proposed to? It's my engagement ring for when I find the man of my dreams' … Edward seems bewildered by the conversation, 'What are you saying?' Zazzie clarifies, 'I'm looking for a husband is what I am saying' … As the clowns prepare to exit, the son continues the romantic banter/storyline and says of his father, 'He's looking for a younger lady'. Zazzie stops mid-exit, and posing with an upheld arm and softened wrist which draws attention to her elongated torso, she says, 'Well look at that, a young lady *has* come to visit'.

At times, the legitimacy of the residents' sexual desires was not acknowledged by the elder-clowns. They instead made repeated jokes of the residents' requests for sexual engagement, including a resident's disappointment over the supposed virginity of the elder-clowns:

> Jacques asks Zazzie, 'Tu veux fourrer avec moi?' [Do you want to fuck me?] With a 'non' [no], Zazzie quickly turns away from him and attempts to divert his attention by introducing Aksom who hadn't yet met him … Jacques, returning to his initial question asks, 'Je n'ai pas compris. Pourquoi tu ne fourres pas avec moi?' [I didn't understand. Why won't you fuck me?]. Zazzie explains, 'Parce ce que c'est pas le jour pour ca' [Because it's not the day for that]. Jacques is asked by the elder-clowns if he wants some tea, and he responds, 'Pas de tea. Je veux des tits' [No tea. I want tits]. Jacques makes nipple grabbing or twisting motions with his fingers. Zazzie laughs loudly and says, 'Oh, Oh, Oh, like a cow'. Aksom pretends to milk a cow with sound effects, and Zazzie joins in mimicking milking with sounds akin to milk hitting a metal bucket … Jacques [switching to English] then asks Zazzie, 'Have you fucked before?' Zazzie responds, 'Me? Never', and makes an exaggerated face. Jacques says with surprise, 'Never?' and Zazzie confirms, 'No'. Jacques then asks the same of Aksom [whom he appears to understand is a woman despite her male clown character]. Aksom replies, 'I'm a virgin' … Jacques looks directly at the male videographer for the first time and makes a firm 'no' gesture with his hands. Jacques says forcibly, 'Good bye!' and indicates they should leave immediately. Zazzie laughingly says to Aksom, 'We are banished'. Turning to Jacques, she laughs and says gently, teasingly, 'Are we banished from your sight?' Jacques ignores her and again turns to the videographer and says, 'Elles sont vierges!' [They are virgins]. He closes his eyes and sighs deeply, appearing genuinely disappointed.

In other cases, the dismissal of residents' sexuality as significant and meaningful self-expression was evidenced by the amusement of the elder-clowns regarding residents' attempts to touch their breasts, and their own responses. On reflection, Kate/Zazzie noted that one of the male residents behaved 'like a kid with his hands in a cookie jar'. Ann/Mitsy found it funny when Aksom said to the same resident, 'Nothing there, nothing there', presumably referring to her small breasts, which he had tried to touch, apparently intuiting that she was biologically female, despite her male clown character.

The elder-clowns also resorted to passive approaches to responding to sexual overtures. These included blocking access to their bodies, redirection, and making appeals to propriety, including indicating current engagement in a primary romantic relationship with another man:

Kate/Zazzie: ... Oh, he's bringing up the tits again, like I had [the] redirection button [sounding], 'Redirection! Redirection! Redirection!' [mimics a robotic-sounding alarm]

Jacques says insistently, 'I want to feel you up', and reaches for Cherry's genital area. Zazzie holds her ukulele in front of Cherry's vagina and says in a goofy tone, 'There are rules around here, Sir! What about decorum?' Jacques replies, clearly joking, 'I'll feel him up too'. The elder-clowns burst into a loud laugh ... Jacques repeats his request to 'feel up' Zazzie. Zazzie responds in a very clearly faux and exaggerated tone of mannered exasperation, 'Sir, we are very dignified and very proper young ladies'. Jacques does not appear to understand the comment. Zazzie's voice changes, and she sounds more immature or youth-like, and more appeasing, 'And for one thing, Cherry's already got a guy friend'. Jacques asks Zazzie, 'And you?' Zazzie lowers her head and says with exaggerated disappointment, 'Not yet'. Jacques quickly responds, 'Let me feel you up ... I'll tell him if it's worthwhile'. The elder-clowns again burst into laughter.

Discussion

Our focus on creativity and sexuality facilitated the exploration of visible manifestations of relationality and embodied selfhood, both of which are the central tenets of relational citizenship. While our examination focused on the strategies and techniques of elder-clowns, our analysis importantly roadmaps how relational citizenship may be supported by the broader interdisciplinary health care team and not simply by elder-clowns.

Our analysis highlights the embodied nature of creativity as expressed through art, music, and imagination. Creative impulse is understood as emanating from deep within (Kontos 2003) and from 'ritualised patterns of action render[ing] cultural possibilities embodied inevitabilities' (Kontos 2014: 114). Elder-clowns' techniques, acquired through their standard clown training, were consistent with this understanding of embodied creativity as evidenced by their embodied communicative relating (e.g. affect attunement), synchronisation of creative offerings (emphasising residents' tactual involvement), and drawing on the sociocultural sources of residents' embodied creativity. These techniques were further enhanced in some interactions by the provision of embodied selfhood training, which emphasised moving from imaginative single-sided play (Aksom drawing) to creative practical co-involvement (Joseph drawing with the clowns).

There is research to suggest that racial and ethnic differences exist in social engagement in long-term care (Li and Cai 2014). However, in this study, we were unable to explore these differences in detail, given that that the racial backgrounds of the elder-clowns and residents were predominantly homogenous. Where ethnic and language differences existed, several clowns were bi- or tri-lingual, and enculturation appeared to have occurred for residents born outside Canada who had settled here decades earlier in their lives. We were therefore unable to explore how racial and ethnic differences might mediate clown-resident interactions or impact relational citizenship support. This is clearly an important area for future research.

Elder-clowning supports residents' creativity, whether generated spontaneously (e.g. recognising Joseph's drawing with the orange juice cup) or through reciprocal engagement (e.g. coconstructing the song with Betty). Other arts-based approaches to dementia care such as active story-telling (Fritsch *et al.* 2009) and song-writing (Basting 2009) provide important programme-based solutions to the 'aesthetic deprivation' (Moss and O'Neill 2014) that plagues long-term care settings. However, in our study, an important difference is that the residents' expressions of creativity were recognised and supported synchronously with the clown-resident interactions and thereby emerged from organic, spontaneous coconstructions. Such spontaneity removes the normative and artificial strictures of structured therapeutic programming (Genoe and Dupuis 2014) which may inadvertently thwart creative expression. The elder-clowns' strategies more fully support and nurture residents' embodied capacities and, in turn, their participation as relational citizens. Because these capacities exist *a priori*, and are central to selfhood, it is critical that they be supported and nurtured in all aspects of institutional life and not simply through elder-clowning specifically or even arts-based programming more generally. To this end, support of embodied selfhood through aesthetic enrichment not only promotes an ethic of mutuality (Mitchell *et al.* 2013) but also the more robust model of relational citizenship that we advocate.

Elder-clown strategies and techniques were not always exemplary of how relational citizenship can be inclusively and unconditionally supported in the context of long-term care. This was evidenced in relation to the problematic dynamics that emerged in the elder-clowns' responses to residents' expressed sexual desires including obfuscation ('I am a virgin'), humour, upping the play (e.g. joking about milking cows), redirection, and even provocation (using the female body as a source of humour) and mixed messaging ('because it's not the day for [fucking]'). This does not minimise the challenges faced by elder-clowns who were confronted by residents repetitively requesting sex or trying to touch their breasts or buttocks. Nor does this suggest that it was the elder-clowns' intentions to undermine relational citizenship. On the contrary, elder-clowns' responses appear akin to the broader social denigration of older adults and sexuality that is deeply entrenched in the culture of long-term care (Mahieu *et al.* 2014a). In long-term care, sexual desires and expressions are typically pathologised, stigmatised, and suppressed by care staff (Mahieu *et al.* 2014a), and organisational structures often fail to accommodate intimacy within institutional settings (Hajjar and Kamel 2004).

A relational citizenship model underscores the importance of critically examining these macro level barriers to cultivating residents' sexual expression. For example, modifications to the social environment (e.g. insisting staff knock before entering) would provide opportunities to engage in acts of intimacy free from the gaze of others and in a socially acceptable and responsible manner (Mahieu *et al.* 2014b). Some nursing homes in Germany and England have gone even further by introducing sex workers in nursing homes (Gardner 2013). Redressing heterosexist assumptions prevalent in institutionalised health care by supporting lesbian, gay, bisexual, transgender, and intersex sexuality (Archibald 2001, Kontos *et al.* 2016, Mahieu *et al.* 2014b) is also vital to the support of sexual expression in dementia care. Such support also necessitates training opportunities for staff to enable better understanding of residents' experiences and needs related to intimacy and sexuality along with a balance between such sensitivity and respect for the psychological and physical safety of staff (Kontos *et al.* 2016).

As elder-clowns are becoming increasingly more prominent in long-term care, it is critical that sexual ethics also be fundamental to their training. Traditionally, education on sexuality and later life, including dementia, has not been a component of training for most care providers in long-term care, and elder-clown training is no exception (Bauer *et al.* 2013, Couchman and Thomas 2014, Mahieu *et al.* 2015). This left the elder-clowns vulnerable to the reliance on clown techniques such as deflection and humour, which while understandable responses in the absence of any formal exposure to sexual ethics, were not supportive of relational citizenship. For our own part, sexuality has yet to be incorporated into pedagogical strategies premised on embodied selfhood to improve person-centred and relational care (Kontos *et al.* 2010), which we intend to redress. Given the importance of sexuality for embodied self-expression identified in this study, and for bodily integrity within a framework of an ethic of long-term care (Pirhonen 2015), it will be critical to redress this in future research and culture change efforts. It is precisely because of how sexuality has been marginalised that a model of citizenship is best positioned to redress the discriminatory practices of long-term care in relation to sexual expression. Yet an ethic of embodied relational sexuality under a relational citizenship model must achieve fuller definition. This will require future research that places sexuality at the intersection of primordial and relational expression within the socio-cultural landscape of long-term care.

Conclusion

The need to promote citizenship is gaining recognition within the dementia care literature (Bartlett and O'Connor 2007) but remains undertheorised within dementia practice and research. Much more needs to be done both in theory and practice to fully support individuals with dementia as relational citizens. The importance of reciprocity and embodied selfhood for citizenship troubles distinctions in the citizenship discourse between 'how to care for' and 'how to think about, relate to and increase the capacity' of individuals living with dementia (Bartlett *et al.* 2010). Our exploration of elder-clown strategies and techniques obviates this distinction and uniquely affords insight into how relational citizenship can be inclusively and fully supported in the context of long-term care.

Attention to citizenship importantly reflects the broader 'cultural turn' within sociology towards more relationally based explorations of social life (Bartlett and O'Connor 2007). Still, insights of the sociological discourses on embodiment, including those of embodied selfhood, remain absent from the ways in which citizenship is defined and conceptualised. By foregrounding the body's pre-reflective capacity to inform and express distinctiveness and relationality, relational citizenship more inclusively and unconditionally provides for the recognition and support of membership in, and contributions to, social collectivity despite even severe dementia.

Acknowledgements

Sincere thanks are owed to all participants of the study, and to the residents' families and private sitters for facilitating resident involvement. We also warmly thank Romeo Colobong for his smooth study coordination and Gilles Gagnon for sensitive and professional videography services. Clown scholars and teachers such as Lee-Fay Low, Peter Spitzer, and Bernie Warren were sage sources for both grant development and the clown intervention; we are deeply appreciative. This work was supported by the Canadian Institutes of Health Research Operating Grant (2012-14, MOP–114953).

Note

The views expressed in this article by the co-author Alexis Kontos are in his personal capacity and are not necessarily shared by the Department of Justice Canada.

References

Adams, T. and Gardiner, P. (2005) Communication and interaction within dementia care triads: Developing a theory for relationship-centred care, *Dementia*, 4, 2, 185–205.

Archibald, C. (2001) Sexuality, dementia and residential care: managers report and response, *Health and Social Care in the Community*, 6, 2, 95–101.

Archibald, C. (2003) Sexuality and dementia: the role dementia plays when sexual expression becomes a component of residential care work, *Alzheimer's Care Today*, 4, 2, 137–48.

Bartlett, R. (2014) Citizenship in action: The lived experiences of citizens with dementia who campaign for social change, *Disability and Society*, 29, 8, 1291–304.

Bartlett, R. and O'Connor, D. (2007) From personhood to citizenship: Broadening the lens for dementia practice and research, *Journal of Aging Studies*, 21, 2, 107–18.

Bartlett, R., O'Connor, D. and Mann, J. (2010) *Broadening the Dementia Debate: Towards Social Citizenship*: The Policy Press.

Basting, A.D. (2009) *Forget Memory*. Baltimore: Johns Hopkins University Press.

Bauer, M., McAuliffe, L., Nay, R. and Chenco, C. (2013) Sexuality in older adults: Effect of an education intervention on attitudes and beliefs of residential aged care staff, *Educational Gerontology*, 39, 2, 82–91.

Beard, R.L. (2011) Art therapies and dementia care: A systematic review, *Dementia*, 11, 5, 633–56.

Bowen, G. (2008) Grounded theory and sensitizing concepts, *International Journal of Qualitative Methods*, 5, 3, 12–23.

Brannelly, T. (2011) That others matter: The moral achievement – care ethics and citizenship in practice with people with dementia, *Ethics and Social Welfare*, 5, 2, 210–6.

Cohen, G.D. (2006) Research on creativity and aging: The positive impact of the arts on health and illness, *Generations*, 30, 1, 7–15.

Couchman, S. and Thomas, R. (2014) Reflective practice. Symposium on clowning in therapeutic environments, Toronto, Ontario.

Davis, D. (2004) Dementia: Sociological and philosophical constructions, *Social Science and Medicine*, 58, 2, 369–78.

Derry, S.J. (2007) Guidelines for video research in education: Recommendations from an expert panel, Available at http://drdc.uchicago.edu/what/video-research-guidelines.pdf (Last accessed 29 May 2015).

Dupuis, S.L., Gillies, J., Carson, J., Whyte, C., *et al.* (2009) Moving beyond patient and client approaches: Mobilizing 'authentic partnerships' in dementia care, support and services, *Dementia*, 11, 4, 427–52.

Dupuis, S., Wiersma, E. and Loiselle, L. (2012) Pathologizing behavior: Meanings of behaviors in dementia care, *Journal of Aging Studies*, 26, 2, 162–73.

Estrin, D. (2012) The healing clowns of Haifa, Available at http://pri.org/stories/2012-07-30/healingclowns-haifa (Last accessed 7 December 2013).

Friedler, S., Glasser, S., Azani, L., Freedman, L.S., *et al.* (2011) The effect of medical clowning on pregnancy rates after in vitro fertilization and embryo transfer, *Fertility and Sterility*, 95, 6, 2127–30.

Fritsch, T., Kwak, J., Grant, S., Lang, J., *et al.* (2009) Impact of TimeSlips, a creative expression intervention program, on nursing home residents with dementia and their caregivers, *The Gerontologist*, 49, 1, 117–27.

Gardner, B. (2013) Care home call girls: Staff invite prostitutes for residents, *The Argus*, 28 January. Available at http://www.theargus.co.uk/news/10189344.Care_homes_help_disabled_to_access_sex_surrogates/. (Last accessed 8 April 2016).

Genoe, M.R. and Dupuis, S.L. (2014) The role of leisure within the dementia context, *Dementia*, 13, 1, 33–58.

Gervais, N., Warren, B. and Twohig, P. (2007) 'Nothing seems funny anymore': Studying burnout in clown-doctors. In Warren, B. (ed) *Suffering the Slings and Arrows of Outrageous Fortune: International Perspectives on Stress*. Rodopi: Laughter and Depression, New York.

Hajjar, R.R. and Kamel, H.K. (2004) Sexuality in the nursing home, part 1: Attitudes and barriers to sexual expression, *Journal of the American Medical Directors Association*, 5, 2, S43–7.

Hendriks, R. (2012) Tackling indifference – clowning, dementia, and the articulation of a sensitive body, *Medical Anthropology Quarterly*, 31, 6, 459–76.

Hsieh, H.-F. and Shannon, S.E. (2005) Three approaches to qualitative content analysis, *Qualitative Health Research*, 15, 9, 1277–88.

Hubbard, G., Cook, A., Tester, S. and Downs, M. (2002) Beyond words: Older people with dementia using and interpreting non verbal behaviour, *Journal of Aging Studies*, 16, 155–67.

Katona, C.L. (2001) Psychotropics and drug interactions in the elderly patient, *International Journal of Geriatric Psychiatry*, 16, Suppl 1, S86–90.

Killick, J. (2003) 'Funny and sad and friendly': A drama project in Scotland, *Journal of Dementia Care*, 11, 1, 24–6.

Kitwood, T. (1997) *Dementia Reconsidered: The Person Comes First*. Buckingham: Open University Press.

Kontos, P. (2003) 'The painterly hand': embodied consciousness and alzheimer's disease, *Journal of Aging Studies*, 17, 151–70.

Kontos, P. (2006) Embodied selfhood: an ethnographic exploration of alzheimer's disease. In Cohen, L. and Leibing, A. (eds.), *Thinking about Dementia: Culture, Loss, and the Anthropology of Senility*. New Brunswick, N.J: Rutgers University Press.

Kontos, P. (2012a). Alzheimer expressions or expressions despite Alzheimer's?: Philosophical reflections on selfhood and embodiment. *Occasion: Interdisciplinary Studies in the Humanities*, 4, May 31, 1-12. Available at http://arcade.stanford.edu/sites/default/files/article_pdfs/OCCASION_v04_Kontos_053112_0.pdf. (Last accessed 8 April 2016).

Kontos, P. (2012b). Rethinking sociability in long-term care: an embodied dimension of selfhood, *Dementia: The International Journal of Social Research and Practice*, 11, 3, 329–46.

Kontos, P. (2014) Musical embodiment, selfhood, and dementia. In Hydén, L.C., Brockmeier, J. and Lindemann, H. (eds), *Beyond Loss*. New York: Oxford University Press, 107–19.

Kontos, P., Grigorovich, A., Kontos, A. and Miller, K.L. (2016). Citizenship, human rights, and dementia: towards a new embodied relational ethic of sexuality, *Dementia: The International Journal of Social Research and Practice*, 15, 3, 315–29.

Kontos, P. and Martin, W. (2013). Embodiment and dementia: exploring critical narratives of selfhood, surveillance, and dementia care, *Dementia: The International Journal of Social Research and Practice*, 12, 3, 288–302.

Kontos, P., Miller, K.L., Colobong, R., Palma Lazgare, L., *et al.* (2016) Elder-clowning in long-term dementia care: results of a pilot study, *Journal of the American Geriatrics Society*, 64, 2, 347–53.

Kontos, P., Miller, K.L., Mitchell, G.J. and Stirling-Twist, J. (2015). Presence redefined: the reciprocal nature of engagement between elder-clowns and persons with dementia, *Dementia: The International Journal of Social Research and Practice*, DOI: 10.1177/1471301215580895

Kontos, P., Mitchell, G.J., Mistry, B. and Ballon, B. (2010) Using drama to improve person-centred dementia care, *International Journal of Older People Nursing*, 5, 2, 159–68.

Kontos, P. and Naglie, G. (2006) 'Expressions of personhood in alzheimer's': moving from ethnographic text to performing ethnography, *Qualitative Research*, 6, 3, 301–17.

Li, Y. and Cai, X. (2014) Racial and ethnic disparities in social engagement among US nursing home residents, *Medical Care*, 52, 4, 314–21.

Linge, L. (2008) Hospital clowns working in pairs – in synchronized communication with ailing children, *International Journal of Qualitative Studies on Health and Well-Being*, 3, 27–38.

Low, L.F., Brodaty, H., Goodenough, B., Spitzer, P., *et al.* (2013) The Sydney Multisite Intervention of LaughterBosses and ElderClowns (SMILE) study: Cluster randomised trial of humour therapy in nursing homes, *BMJ Open*, 3.

Mahieu, L., Anckaert, L. and Gastmans, C. (2014a) Eternal sunshine of the spotless mind? An anthropological-ethical framework for understanding and dealing with sexuality in dementia care, *Medicine, Health Care and Philosophy*, 17, 3, 377–87.

Mahieu, L., Anckaert, L. and Gastmans, C. (2014b) Intimacy and sexuality in institutionalized dementia care: Clinical-ethical considerations, *Health Care Analysis*, 1–20, DOI: 10.1007/s10728-014-0287-2.

Mahieu, L., deCasterlé, B.D., Acke, J., Vandermarliere, H., *et al.* (2015) Nurses' knowledge and attitudes toward aged sexuality in Flemish nursing homes, *Nursing Ethics*, DOI: 10.1177/0969733015580813.

Mahieu, L. and Gastmans, C. (2012) Sexuality in institutionalized elderly persons: A systematic review of argument-based ethics literature, *International Psychogeriatrics*, 24, 3, 346–57.

Medjedovic, I. and Witzel, A. (2008) Secondary analysis of interviews: using codes and theoretical concepts from the primary study, *Historical Social Research/Historische Sozialforschung*, 33, 3, 148–78.

Miller, K.L. and Kontos, P. (2016) The use of elder-clowning to foster relational citizenship in dementia care. In Andreassen, T.A., Gubrium, J.F. and Solvang, P.K. (eds) *Reimagining the human service relationship*. New York: Columbia University Press, pp 158–77.

Minkler, M. and Holstein, M.B. (2008) From civil rights to … civic engagement? Concerns of two older critical gerontologists about a 'new social movement' and what it portends, *Journal of Aging Studies*, 22, 2, 196–204.

Mitchell, G.J., Dupuis, S.L. and Kontos, P. (2013) Dementia discourse: From imposed suffering to knowing other-wise, *Journal of Applied Hermeneutics*:1–19. http://jah.journalhosting.ucalgary.ca/jah/index.php/jah/article/viewFile/41/pdf. (Last accessed 8 April 2016).

Moss, H. and O'Neill, D. (2014) Aesthetic deprivation in clinical settings, *The Lancet*, 383, 9922, 1032–3.

Nolan, M., Ryan, T., Enderby, P. and Reid, D. (2002) Towards a more inclusive vision of dementia care practice, *Dementia*, 1, 2, 193–211.

Pirhonen, J. (2015) Dignity and the capabilities approach in long-term care for older people, *Nursing Philosophy*, 16, 1, 29–39.

Roy, J. (2009) Clowning within drama therapy group sessions: A case study of a unique recovery journey in a psychiatric hospital. Department of Creative Art Therapies, Montreal, PQ: Concordia University.

Ryan, T., Nolan, M., Reid, D. and Enderby, P. (2008) Using the Senses Framework to achieve relationship-centred dementia care services: A case example, *Dementia*, 7, 1, 71–93.

Sevenhuijsen, S. (2000) Caring in the third way: the relation between obligation, responsibility and care in Third Way discourse, *Critical Social Policy*, 20, 1, 5–37.

Smith, M., Gallagher, M., Wosu, H., Stewart, J., *et al.* (2011) Engaging with involuntary service users in social work: Findings from a knowledge exchange project, *British Journal of Social Work*, 42, 8, 1460–77.

Stirling-Twist, J. and Le Roux, K. (2014) *Core Competencies of the Therapeutic Clown Practitioner*. Toronto: Dr. Clown.

Symons, D. (2012) A study of elder clown programs in Scotland, the Netherlands, USA and Canada, Available at http://www.churchilltrust.com.au/media/fellows/2012_Symons_David.pdf (Last accessed 30 December 2014).

Thompson, K. (1998) Therapeutic clowning with persons with dementia, *The Hospital Clown Newsletter*, 3, 2, 1–4.

Thomson, R. (2005) *Evaluation of the use of a clown therapy group with dementia sufferers. Doctoral Thesis*. Edinburgh: University of Edinburgh.

Vidal, F. (2009) Brainhood, anthropological figure of modernity, *History of the Human Sciences*, 22, 1, 5–36.

Warren, B. (2007) *Suffering the Slings and Arrows of Outrageous Fortune: International Perspectives on Stress, Laughter and Depression*. New York: Rodopi.

Warren, B. (2008) Healing laughter: The role and benefits of clown-doctors working in hospitals and healthcare. In Warren, B. (ed) *Using the Creative Arts in Therapy and Healthcare*. London: Routledge.

Warren, B. (2009) Spreading sunshine … down memory lane: How clowns working in healthcare help promote recovery and rekindle memories, In Baum, N. (ed) *Come to Your Senses: Creating Supportive Environments to Nurture the Sensory Capital Within*, Toronto: Mukibaum Treatment Centres.

Warren, B. and Spitzer, P. (2011) Laughing to longevity – the work of elder clowns, *The Lancet*, 378, 9791, 562–63.

Whitehouse, P.J. (2008) *The Myth of Alzheimer's: What You Aren't Being Told about Today's Most Dreaded Diagnosis*. New York: Macmillan.

3

Shifting dementia discourses from deficit to active citizenship

Linda Birt, Fiona Poland, Emese Csipke and Georgina Charlesworth

Introduction

Sociological understandings of the experience of living with dementia are often situated within socio-political discourses. While definitions of citizenship can be located within civil or political domains (Marshall 1950), it is the notion of 'social citizenship' that is increasingly relevant to understanding the dementia experience (O'Conner and Nedlund 2016). Citizenship can be considered a social construct, actively shaped over time: 'it is a set of social practices which define the nature of social membership' (Turner 1993: 4). Understanding citizenship within a wider context than merely civil or political rights provides opportunities to explore what social structures are needed to enable people with dementia to participate in and belong to a community, and the distinctive ways in which citizenship roles can be enacted following a diagnosis of dementia. This is key in countering discourses which support the covert, or overt, exclusion of individuals with dementia from equal participation in social practices; participating as decision-makers and with an equal position in social groups from workplaces to care facilities. Bartlett and O'Conner (2010: 39) propose that social citizenship 'recognizes the person with dementia as an active agent with rights, history, and competencies'. This gains force by closer attention to Turner's (1993: 3) argument that citizenship is a 'dynamic social construction' the practices of which are shaped by history and political events. Such dynamic construction can be seen in the global response to the dementia challenge which has shifted discourses of dementia from being centred on individual experiences, to recognising the ways in which socio-political practices and discourses shape the imaginary of dementia.

In dementia studies we see the constructs of social citizenship as helping understand the practice of citizenship in 'ordinary places' (Bartlett 2016: 456). Exploring the macro and micro-practices of social citizenship enables a more specific understanding of how social rights, obligations and social structures can condition an individual's access as an equal to communities. Applying this understanding to how people with dementia are currently positioned as citizens, often within discourses of deficit, creates means to counter this by, instead, foregrounding the form and types of work people with dementia undertake as individuals and groups, so as to re-position themselves as active citizens within their communities.

From a sociological perspective, journeying with dementia will not entail chronological, unidirectional passage along an illness trajectory marked by pathological changes and healthdriven structures; rather it is a journey through different life events. This presents risks

Ageing, Dementia and the Social Mind, First Edition. Edited by Paul Higgs and Chris Gilleard.
Chapters © 2017 The Authors. Book Compilation © 2017 Foundation for the Sociology of
Health & Illness/Blackwell Publishing Ltd.

to, and opportunities for, social interactions. The movement along the illness trajectory is marked by changing social status, some of which can be stigmatising. The sociological concept of liminality provides a lens to explore those social structures which may constrain, or support, opportunities for people with dementia to move from the liminal state of ambiguity and uncertainty often triggered by diagnosis to a post-liminal state which can enable interdependency and provide the mechanisms for their own agentic actions to support social citizenship.

Medical and social discourses around dementia are bringing the condition of dementia increasingly into public view, together with a growing emphasis on early diagnosis (Prince *et al.* 2011), giving momentum to a socio-political agenda to raise public awareness of the challenges being encountered by people with dementia and their families (Department of Health 2013). Dementia defines a syndrome where symptoms are grounded in decline of brain function; specific symptoms differ across different neurological disease. However, for most people there will be social consequences to a diagnosis of dementia, therefore it is timely to examine the social structures which may shape the journey.

Illustrations in this paper are drawn from a scoping review of literature on social participation in dementia. The review has been used to ground the Promoting Independence in Dementia study (PRIDE) which seeks to explore the social and personal constructs of dementia. For the review we searched health and social science databases for literature reporting the experiences of social participation in people with dementia, living within the community. While we did not restrict country of origin, the literature retrieved mainly reported western experiences. Full details of the review are available from the authors.

Disrupted trajectories

A universal event in the dementia journey is the disruption triggered by a change in cognitive function. Such disruption may stem from the terror of suddenly not knowing where you are, or the gradual realisation that memory and processing skills are receding. Personal attributions for such cognitive changes are varied and situated within lived experiences (Hurt *et al.* 2011). Nonetheless, changes in cognition mark a key sociological event as the previous certainties of the form and function of social roles, statuses and planned life trajectories are threatened; the equilibrium of life is disturbed.

Becoming a person with dementia rarely happens at a single time point but rather across time situated within a sequence of physical and social changes either realised by the individual or by others. People may be living with uncertainty about cognitive changes for some time as the fear of being stigmatised can delay seeking help (Bamford *et al.* 2014). Once help-seeking is triggered a series of medical examinations usually precede diagnosis.

Receiving the diagnosis of dementia can be a watershed moment for how the person and others around them perceive their future (Aminzadeh *et al.* 2007, Vernooij-Dassen *et al.* 2006). It moves people along to an uncertain state and a place which is often defined by narratives of deficit. The diagnosis of dementia may be intrinsically linked both by the individual and others as a stigmatised condition (Milne 2010). A dementia diagnosis can be socially discrediting and lead to the person being 'unjustifiably rendered shameful, excluded and discriminated against' (WHO 2002: 8). Nonetheless people are themselves seen to use their diagnosis as a disclaimer enabling them to situate dementia and the accompanying cognitive changes as a sickness over which they have no control (MacRae 2010). Such difference in reactions to diagnosis indicates that there may be different personal or wider social structures which enable people to follow different trajectories following diagnosis. For all though, a diagnosis of dementia, even if its symptoms have been apparent for some time, places people on a different trajectory to their previously-envisaged selves.

Liminality

Chronic illnesses, including dementia, are ongoing processes with landmarks, transitions and changing demands. Rolland (1987) described three major phases of chronic illness: crisis, chronic and terminal, each with implications for individual and family adaptation and role changes. The social experiences of living in the 'crisis' period (pre-and post-medical diagnosis), may be considered as an example of 'liminality' or 'movement between fixed points' which is 'essentially ambiguous, unsettled, and unsettling' (Turner 1974: 274). During the liminal state people are often structurally invisible, without status: 'no longer classified and not yet classified' (Turner 1967: 96). In the post-liminal state they may be positioned within new groups and achieve new status.

For those living with chronic illness and cancer a clearly structured post-liminal state may not be possible. Bruce *et al.* (2014) in their work with people living with cancer, HIV/AIDS and chronic kidney disease identified the concept of 'pervasive liminality' as the delicate balance of the 'in between' experience. Shields (2015) describes the challenge of focusing on living lives while at the same time having an acute awareness of death and one's own mortality. People living with cancer can experience both acute and sustained liminality (Little *et al.* 1998). Diagnosis leads to the acute liminal state of uncertainty and confusion then over time a sustained liminal state is entered as people adapt and endure their illness; sustained liminality may become a permanent state (Little *et al.* 1998). The concept of liminality in health has also been explored through the experiences of family caregivers. Gibbons *et al.* (2014) report that diagnosis is often a pivotal point which thrusts caregivers into a liminal state, however in dementia the transition is often characterised by a gradual change in roles and social changes.

The concept of liminality within dementia research is relatively under-considered. Sweeting and Gilhooly (1997: 99) in their work exploring 'social death', introduced the notion of a person with dementia being 'a liminal', a non-person who was still making the 'transition from life to death'. Kelly (2008, 2010) working with people with AIDS dementia explored liminality from the perspective of people with a HIV diagnosis and their families. She drew attention to both social and emotional liminal states experienced when people received a diagnosis of dementia, drawing out the sense of uncertainty inherent in liminality. While in her later work Kelly (2010: 7) reports people as 'learning to live with liminality', rather than seeing the liminal state as a transitory state on the route to new roles and status. This has resonance with Bruce *et al.*'s (2014) description of pervasive liminality.

The unsettling and continuing nature of transition in dementia is reported in the findings of Godwin and Poland (2015) where people with dementia living in care homes are described as being in a liminal state. Participants expressed uncertainty about why or how they came to be the home; for some, liminality reduced wellbeing, while others seemed less troubled by the uncertainty. A potential strength of considering liminality as a concept to explore the dementia journey lies in its attention to the social, those social (and therefore shared) rituals and actions which shape experiences. Detailing the social rituals which surround the dementia trajectory can help us see how wider social and political discourses on dementia has an impact on individual experience and the inclusion, or otherwise, of people with dementia as social citizens.

Rites of passage

With the social recognition of illness comes then-recognised rites of passage: movement to status of patient, known or unknown norms of behaviour in medical spaces, changes to roles and responsibilities within families and communities. Van Gennep's (1960) social anthropological concept of staged rites of passage placed the initial focus on social rituals. However, increasingly rites of passage have since been applied to culturally-identified and managed life transitions. The transition from adolescence to adulthood is marked by social events, both positive and negative which guide child's passage; rites of passage may include a religious coming of age ceremonies or gaining the citizenship right to vote (Scheer *et al.* 2007). Such passages may often be marked by three phases: the pre-liminal phase, the point marking the end of the 'old' status; the liminal phase, where one is 'betwixt and between' statuses; and the post-liminal phase, of re-incorporation or re-assimilation into a new 'normal'.

Rites of passage are vital in moving people through liminality to a post-liminal state. In the dementia trajectory, the pre-diagnosis liminal state is increasingly well-structured. Memory tests, brain scans and being given a diagnosis can all be considered social rituals (see Figure 1). If diagnosis is viewed as a rite of passage which enables movement along the dementia trajectory, a ritual hiatus can occur when the diagnosis is either not provided or is denied by the person with cognitive symptoms. Diagnosis is not always straightforward, especially for people with mild symptoms or complex histories, and diagnoses may not be definitive (Phillips *et al.* 2012). An absence of a definitive diagnosis can cause uncertainty and ambiguity (Beard and Neary 2013, Samsi *et al.* 2014).

A diagnosis socially situates what can be expected of the 'patient' and the behaviour which others will tolerate as part of the disease (Jutel 2009). Disclosing a dementia diagnosis to those outside the family can help people move out of the liminal state and along a journey towards living well with dementia. The decision to disclose a diagnosis may be actively managed by the person as a way of retaining previous status and so potentially protecting the former self. Telling others of their dementia diagnosis creates opportunities to take control of social situations and use strategies to reduce the risk of stigma or embarrassment. Some people take control of social interactions by being explicit about the challenges they face

Rituals of becoming a person with dementia	Liminal state (uncertainty and ambiguity)	Post-liminal state	Characteristics of post-liminal state
• Discussions acknowledging possible memory lapses • Standardised memory tests • Brain scans • Formal confirmation of diagnosis or non-diagnosis • Status as mental health patient		Living in the shadow of the fourth age	Acknowledging frailty Agentic interdependence Preparing for the future
		Living as an active citizen with dementia	Disclosure of diagnosis Continuing social status Developing new networks Being a social citizen
		Living in extended liminality	Ambiguity of diagnosis Not able to develop new networks Becoming isolated

Post-liminal state influenced by:
Cultural beliefs, Reaction/expectation of others, Acceptance of diagnosis
Co-morbidities, Social capital reserves.

Figure 1   *Liminal states in dementia [Colour figure can be viewed at wileyonlinelibrary.com]*

and explaining to others how they can be helped with communication (MacQuarrie 2005, MacRae 2010). Beard and Fox (2008: 1513) report that some found being direct about their capabilities was the 'best way to handle things like that'. People were also explicit about the types of interaction which were not empowering, as 'when people ask me questions with no context' suggesting their good insight into the process and work of the social interaction (Beard *et al.* 2009: 230).

Macro structures shape the experience of the dementia journey. For example, the western socio-political emphasis on early diagnosis means that the 'taken for granted' forgetfulness of older age is challenged; memory is repeatedly tested through standardised tests which one passes or fails, with implications for social status. Yet taxonomies of 'acceptable' memory are arbitrary, being historically and culturally defined (Harding and Palfrey 1997, Katz 2013). A diagnosis of dementia does not change an individual's legal status, yet it is a pre-cursor to significant change. For example, in the UK a person with dementia must declare their diagnosis to the Driver and Vehicle Licensing Agency (DVLA); their ability to make decisions may be subjected to 'mental capacity' assessments and they are encouraged to put in place legal procedures to identify those who will act on their behalf once their mental capacity is found wanting. There are financial benefits to accepting a label of 'severe mental impairment', for example people with dementia can be 'completely disregarded' for the purposes of council tax (a local authority charge payable by residents of properties in England and Wales). In contrast to the UK's 'capacity' approach is that of self-determination, as applied in Sweden (see Österholm 2015).

Post-liminal destinations

Our scoping review generated evidence for a range of post-liminal states: 'living in the shadow of the fourth age', 'living as an active citizen with dementia' and 'living in extended liminality'. Identifying these distinct trajectories helps construct a sociologically-relevant debate around the dementia journey, bringing into view novel ways to shift discourses of deficit so as to also allow for discourses of active citizenship.

Living in the shadow of the fourth age
The non-citizen Ageing and dementia are currently intertwined in most cultures and the social imaginary of dementia is often embedded within the end-stage of the disease where an individual may be seen as frail and dependant, almost wholly unable to participate within their social world: socially dead (Cipriani and Borin 2014, Gilleard and Higgs 2014, McManus and Devine 2011, Zeilig 2013). Here people may be non-citizens, existing without rights, without agency, relining on others for physical care. Such an imaginary resonates with the conceptualisation of the oldest old living in the fourth age in a period of 'decrepitude and dependency' (Kertzer and Laslett 1995).

Western cultures attribute value to the 'productive autonomous self', and how living with dementia is framed may ultimately, if stigmatising, rob the person of their autonomy (Gilmour and Brannelly 2010). Unchallenged or unsupported, this can create tensions and challenges for the attempts of the person with dementia to assimilate changed status and roles framed in this way. Too often, stigmatising attitudes can lead to their exclusion from decisions, care options and social spaces (Batsch and Mittelman 2012). As dementia is more prevalent in older people, these individuals face the double jeopardy of the stigma of ageing and dementia. Dementia is here imagined as stripping the person of their very essence, to become a subaltern a nonperson (Gilmour and Brannelly 2010). In the extreme imaginaries of dementia, people are dependent on others to bestow care and compassion on them by virtue of their right to care, through their personhood (Kitwood 1997). Such concepts have resonance with those used by Gilleard and Higgs (2010) to characterise the cultural imaginary of the fourth age where people no longer have status, rather they live in a state of being. The concept of the fourth age and its imaginary around loss of agency for older people who are 'stripped of social and cultural capital' (Gilleard and Higgs 2010: 123), may be imposed on the older person by institutions, healthcare professionals and family rather than reflecting any aspects of the internal sense of self held by the older person (Lloyd *et al.* 2014). Others position people with dementia as living as non-citizens, socially dead, within a narrative of complete deficit. By too-readily positioning the oldest old and those with dementia in this place of deficit we risk ignoring the distinction between being and feeling frail (Gernier 2006) and too quickly close the discourse on whether people with advanced dementia can have a citizen status.

When considering the potential for active citizenship within the fourth age, the challenge is not only in supporting access to resources for the individual with dementia but also in addressing the stigmatising attitudes and behaviours of others. While those living with dementia may wish to continue to be agentic citizens, the opportunity for this is challenged if others do not recognise this ability or provide opportunities for agency. Kitwood (1997) describes how the actions of carers, although well-meaning, could lead to a pervasive erosion of the personhood of the person with dementia, their individual and human characteristics, designating this a 'malignant social psychology' (Kitwood 1997). Knowing people predominately by their diagnosis and not through their personal and socially-situated attributes increases the likelihood that the person with dementia will be given the social persona of 'dysfunctional patient' (Sabat 2002), reinforcing negative discourses.

The passive citizen Some people living with dementia will be frail and dependent as they live with decreasing cognitive ability and comorbidities; they will need the support of others to manage every day activities, yet being able to make decisions, choosing how and when to exercise rights and responsibilities, demonstrates agency and enacts citizenship status. Social citizenship acknowledges that some people will not be able to be active citizens in the sense of contributing to communities, rather they will be passive citizens. A rights, rather than needs, based discourse enables structural-stigma due to age or dementia diagnosis to be challenged (Bartlett and O'Conner 2010). People can live well in the fourth age as passive citizens if the actions of others recognise and acknowledge the nuanced ways in which people with severe dementia may display agency. People with severe dementia may continue to display embodied agency and with the appropriate social rituals can continue to live as recognised people, passive citizens, with the social rights to good quality care (Godwin and Poland 2015).

For some people, in some life stages moving to live 'in the shadow of the fourth age' can be a (destination) which is both realistic in accepting age-inherent physical challenges, while still offering opportunities for agentic actions. Moving into the fourth age may be an acceptable post-liminal state if people are able to review their lives and look back over a positive life (Wolverson *et al.* 2015). To ease the path along the journey to the fourth age there needs to be a realisation and imaginary of the fourth age as being not only a time of frailty, but also a time when some embodied agentic actions remain, even if it requires care workers to support such agency.

Living as an active citizen with dementia
The active citizen The narratives of deficit presented above are countered by narratives from people with dementia articulating and defending positive accounts of living well, engaging

in loving relationships, preserving identity and self, and living as recognised citizens in their communities (Bartlett 2014, Beard *et al.* 2009).

A growing body of qualitative research suggests that people with dementia continue in social interactions, able to contribute to their communities as a social citizen. Beard *et al.* (2009: 234) report that people with dementia demonstrate 'agency by actively accommodating dementia into their lives rather than allowing it to be imposed on them by structural forces', suggesting an awareness, certainly in the mild stages of dementia, of how social structures may facilitate or inhibit agency and citizenship for people.

Dementia support groups provide social structures within which people can perform social citizen roles, through actions that acknowledge both their diagnosis and their right to live free from discrimination in inclusionary ways. Accessing online support groups can help reduce the feelings of fear and social isolation (Clare *et al.* 2008). Interacting whether on-line or in person can help normalise problems, thereby potentially creating new groups to which the person can move to and belong in (Preston *et al.* 2007).Several studies report that people use humour in their verbal interactions with others (Clarke *et al.* 2010, Langdon *et al.* 2007, MacRae 2010). Humour is often present in liminal life stages and serves various social functions. Humour can control, unite or enable adjustment (Martineau 1972, Ziv 2010) and may be a way of relieving tensions in managing new social identities. In dementia humour may be a way of approaching and dealing with the inevitable losses which accompany changing status and roles: 'Since it is difficult to maintain my old social networks, I have begun to reach out to others online' (Beard *et al.* 2009: 230).

Social contact with others with dementia provides more than friendship and support for some people as it now it enables them to actively campaign for the citizenship rights of people with dementia. Having the distinct identity of person with dementia can create opportunities to campaign for social change and provide access to service user evaluations. Some have been seen to use their group not only to raise awareness but also to enable them to contribute to debates, 'DASNI (Dementia Advocacy and Support Network International) gives me entrée in a variety of places where I want to participate' (Clare *et al.* 2008: 19). Bartlett's (2014) longitudinal study with people who campaign for social justice through political lobbying and raising awareness of living with dementia presented a balanced view of the advantages but also the challenges of being an active citizen. She concludes 'campaigning can be energising and reaffirming of citizen identity because it (re)located a person within the realm of work'; however, 'individuals may experience fatigue due to their dementia and oppression linked to normative expectations about what someone with dementia "should" be like' (Bartlett 2014: 1300). It should be noted that not all people with mild dementia have the resources or the desire to undertake the work of active campaigning, but equally do not wish to be negatively positioned (Preston *et al.* 2007) objectified (MacQuarrie 2005) nor patronised or over-protected (Beard *et al.* 2009). They do not want the social status of 'sufferer' conferred on them (Beard *et al.* 2009).

People with dementia may participate as socially active citizens, giving to others, in ways not directly linked to their dementia and at a micro-level. Beard *et al.* (2009) recount the case of a man who had always been a basketball coach and who continued this activity after his diagnosis. Phinney *et al.* (2007) present a similar example of a man who had worked as a musician who continued to make music and to share this at his dementia group. However such active citizenship may need to be supported by others. Opportunities to remain a productive part of family life were sometimes created by the actions of family members: 'I leave her grandchildren with her because one it alleviates the fact she feels useless. You know, she's now, she's great with the kids' (Clarke *et al.* 2010: 109), yet the person with dementia must also be agentic in taking up the opportunity for active citizenship.

Many people with dementia give positive accounts of living with the condition emphasising the continued abilities and contentment with life while downplaying cognitive difficulties. Steeman *et al.* (2007) in critically exploring the positive narratives of older people living with mild dementia, suggest that there may be a constant balancing of 'being valued' against 'being worthless'. While people with dementia strive to affirm their competencies other may devalue their abilities and roles (Steeman *et al.* 2007: 126). Being confronted by losses and lacking the support of others to be active citizens can lead to restricted opportunities for citizenship, even while the person is striving to live as an active citizen with dementia.

Restricted citizen The cognitive abilities of a person with dementia decline over time. Family members are expected to take increasing responsibility for making proxy decisions for their relative (Samsi and Manthorpe 2013). However some people with dementia report that this happens too-readily, leading them to feel 'put down' (Langdon *et al.* 2007: 995). In these situations opportunities to be an active citizen are restricted rather than supported by others. Not being listened to or consulted about decisions appeared to lead to frustration and anger, 'Oh I was furious ... not to have talked to me ... we think this is best for you' (MacQuarrie 2005: 433). Being central to decision-making, however minor that decision may be, and being offered subtle support to enable purposeful contribution to the decisions, were all acknowledged as important, especially as people recognised their changing cognitive abilities (Featherstonhaugh *et al.* 2013).

People with dementia may be striving to be active in their families and communities but the actions of others constantly constrain their opportunities for agency. This can generate feelings of being disempowered when others take over tasks, and restrict opportunities for access to meaningful or enjoyable activities due to others perceiving them too risky (Clarke *et al.* 2010, MacQuarrie 2005). Having others restrict opportunities for people with dementia to be agentic, reflects the many frustrations and constraints experienced by those living in the shadow of the fourth age. Such uncertainties and threats to self, alongside the desire to remain an active citizen, are succinctly captured in the Beard and Fox (2008) study exploring how people with Alzheimer's disease resist becoming socially disenfranchised. They report one participant as saying 'I still have enough intelligence, you know, to be a person and not just someone you pat on the head as you go by ... it's devastating and it takes away your sense of self' (Beard and Fox 2008: 1516).

Attempts to participate as citizens by the person with dementia may be refuted by family (Clarke *et al.* 2010, Clemerson *et al.* 2014, Preston *et al.* 2007), illustrating the need for effective, understanding support systems if people are to enact citizenship roles. Families are often left to 'muddle through' and may struggle to find a good balance between protection and enabling of their relative with dementia. Retaining trusting relationships and sustaining effective social networks is important at a time when many people can experience depression and withdrawal from previous social networks (Burgener *et al.* 2015).

Living in extended liminality
Uncertain citizen Literature exploring liminality in chronic illness frequently refers to the concept of on-going liminality: pervasive liminality (Bruce *et al.* 2014); sustained liminality (Little *et al.* 1998). These liminal states are presented as non-problematic, without need to be resolved. We suggest that being in an extended state of liminality for people with dementia may be problematic as it may constrain opportunities for fulfilling the roles and accepting the rights of being an active citizen with dementia.

If a diagnosis is not accepted or the social structures, such as family and healthcare services do not assist the movement to either being a passive or active citizen, people may potentially become 'stuck' in extended liminality; a place where roles are contested and rights may not be readily accessible because the person does not have the status of 'person with dementia'. This post-liminal state is characterised by continuing ambiguity and uncertainty particularly about the diagnosis. Either the 'truth' of the medical label of dementia will be contested, or opportunities are not taken to disclose the diagnosis (Aminzadeh *et al.* 2007); an act seemingly necessary for enabling an active citizen's participative work. Nonetheless the cognitive decline inherent in dementia means that changes in roles and status can eventually become inevitable.

Some people have a confirmed diagnosis but are unable to acknowledge or act on this, perhaps relating to the agency they had in obtaining the diagnosis. Living within a state of 'extended liminality' can have negative social consequences, as failing to receive or act on a diagnosis of dementia may mean masking the symptoms of cognitive decline. While people are able to mask their difficulties in social interactions and social roles they can continue to pass as an intact self. However, if their ability to mask difficulties declines and others notice their potentially-deviant behaviours, the risk of being stigmatised increases. To avoid such risks to self, people may 'isolate themselves from others' (Robinson *et al.* 2005: 341), thus reducing opportunities for exercising their social citizenship.

More fully exploring the 'extended liminality' state may help delineate the social structures which block successful transition to a post-liminal place, and so enable us to develop new ways to support those with dementia and their families in ensuring agentic movement along the dementia journey.

Critiques of the citizen roles

In this paper we have drawn predominantly on literature which contextualises the western experience of living with dementia. We do, however, acknowledge ethnic variations of experiences within western (Dilworth-Anderson and Gibson 2002, La Fontaine *et al.* 2007) and nonwestern illness experiences (Cipriani and Borin 2014).

We accept that our representation of the dementia journey is linear whereas there can be sudden or gradual changes in cognitive function, alongside changes in physical abilities due to co-morbidities and that individual experiences will certainly be shaped by micro-social events. Changes in emotional well-being with depression may occur in those living with dementia making it difficult to enact agentic decisions. Further changes in social networks may be due to death of older friends and re-location connected to frailty. Nonetheless theorising liminality here provides ways to understand the impact of these physical, emotional, social and cognitive changes. Conceptualising post-liminal states provides new ways to understand the experience of moving along the dementia journey and to acknowledge positive as well as negative narratives in dementia.

Conclusion

The concept of liminality, being in a place of uncertainty and ambiguity, provides novel ways to understand the structures which move people along the dementia journey to post-liminal states. Bringing to the fore the post-liminal state of living well with dementia makes it possible to illustrate the various citizen roles held by people with dementia (passive or active citizen) as well as factors which may inhibitor opportunities to fulfil such roles (restricted or uncertain citizen).

By accepting and disclosing a diagnosis, people are creating opportunities to use the diagnosis as a tool for explaining any adaptations they may need in order to remain active in their social networks. Recognising and providing opportunities for the development of remaining personal attributes and skills, enables positive narratives rather than focusing on the deficits inherent in dementia. Working within a framework of social citizenship enables a more specific understanding of how social rights, obligations and social structures can condition an individual's access as an equal, to communities. Applying this understanding to how people with dementia are currently positioned as citizens, often within discourses of deficit, creates means to counter this by, instead, foregrounding the form and types of work people with dementia are undertaking as individuals and groups so as to re-position themselves as active citizens within their communities.

The social standing of the person with dementia may be more fully recognised by creating ways for giving citizenship more prominence in the social imaginary enabling their potential for continuing citizenship to be realised conceptually and in everyday practices, despite their changing expectations of cognitive capacity. By further exploring the ways in people may sustain such agentic roles in the face of change it may become possible to identify successful ways of managing the status transitions linked to receiving a diagnosis of dementia, enabling movement through the liminal phase. This opens up the possibility of moving interventions beyond behaviour modification to those which empower people with dementia to be active citizens who, therefore, can retain participatory roles in their social worlds.

Acknowledgments

We thank our reviewers whose insightful comments on an earlier version enabled us to develop our conceptual ideas thereby improving this paper. This work was supported by the Economic and Social Research Council/National Institute of Health [grant number ES/L001802/2]. This article presents independent research funded by the National Institute for Health Research (NIHR). The views expressed are those of the authors and not necessarily those of the NHS, the NIHR or the Department of Health.

References

Aminzadeh, F., Byszewski, A., Molnar, F.L. and Eisner, M. (2007) Emotional impact of dementia diagnosis: exploring persons with dementia and caregivers' perspectives, *Aging and Mental Health*, 11, 3, 281–90.

Bamford, S., Holley-Moore, G. and Watson, J. (2014) *New perspectives and approaches to understanding dementia and stigma*. London: ILC-UK.

Bartlett, R. (2014) Citizenship in action: the lived experiences of citizens with dementia who campaign for social change, *Disability and Society*, 29, 8, 1291–304.

Bartlett, R. (2016) Scanning the conceptual horizons of citizenship, *Dementia*, 15, 3, 453–61.

Bartlett, R. and O'Conner, D. (2010) *Broadening the dementia debate: towards social citizenship.* Bristol: Policy Press.

Batsch, N.L. and Mittelman, M.S. (2012) *World Alzheimer report: overcoming the stigma of dementia*. London: Alzheimer Disease International.

Beard, R.L. and Fox, P.J. (2008) Resisting social disenfranchisement: negotiating collective identities and everyday life with memory loss, *Social Science and Medicine*, 66, 7, 1509–20.

Beard, R.L., Knauss, J. and Moyer, D. (2009) Managing disability and enjoying life: how we reframe dementia through personal narratives, *Journal of Aging Studies*, 23, 227–35.

Beard, R.L. and Neary, T.M. (2013) Making sense of nonsense: experiences of mild cognitive impairment, *Sociology of Health & Illness*, 15, 1, 130–46.

Bruce, A., Sheilds, L., Molzahn, A., Beuthin, R., *et al.* (2014) Stories of liminality: living with life-threatening illness, *Qualitative Research*, 32, 1, 35–43.

Burgener, S.C., Buckwalter, K., Perkhounkova, Y. and Liu, M.F. (2015) The effects of stigma on quality of life outcomes in persons with early-stage dementia: longitudinal findings: Part 2, *Dementia*, 14, 5, 609–32.

Cipriani, G. and Borin, G. (2014) Understanding dementia in the sociocultural context: A review, *International Journal of Social Psychiatry*, 61, 2, 198–204.

Clare, L., Rowlands, J.M. and Quin, R. (2008) Collective strength: the impact of developing a shared social identity in early-stage dementia, *Dementia*, 7, 1, 9–30.

Clarke, C.L., Keady, J., Wilkinson, H., Gibb, C.E., *et al.* (2010) Dementia risk: contested territories of everyday life, *Journal of Nursing and Healthcare of Chronic Illness*, 2, 2, 102–12.

Clemerson, G., Walsh, S. and Isaac, C. (2014) Towards living well with young onset dementia: an exploration of coping from the perspective of those diagnosed, *Dementia*, 13, 4, 451–66.

Department of Health (2013) *Dementia: a state of the nation report on dementia care and support in England.* Available at https://www.gov.uk/government/uploads/system/uploads/attachment_data/file/262139/Dementia.pdf. (Last accessed 1 July 2016)

Dilworth-Anderson, P. and Gibson, B.E. (2002) The cultural influences of values, norms, meanings and perceptions in understanding dementia in ethnic minorities, *Alzheimer Disease and Associated Disorders*, 16, s52, s56–63.

Featherstonhaugh, D., Tarzia, L. and Nay, R. (2013) 'Being central to decision-making means I am still here!': the essence of decision-making for people with dementia, *Journal of Aging Studies*, 27, 2, 143–50.

Gernier, A. (2006) The distinction between being and feeling frail: exploring emotional experiences in health and social care, *Journal of Social Work Practice*, 20, 3, 299–313.

Gibbons, S.W., Ross, A. and Bevans, M. (2014) Liminality as a conceptual frame for understanding the family caregiving rite of passage: an integrative review, *Research in Nursing and Health*, 37, 5, 423–36.

Gilleard, C. and Higgs, P. (2010) Aging without agency: theorizing the fourth age, *Aging and Mental Health*, 14, 2, 121–8.

Gilleard, C. and Higgs, P. (2014) Studying dementia: the relevance of the fourth age, *Quality in Ageing and Older Adults*, 15, 4, 241–43.

Gilmour, J.A. and Brannelly, T. (2010) Representations of people with dementia – subaltern, person, citizen, *Nursing Inquiry*, 17, 3, 240–7.

Godwin, B. and Poland, F. (2015) Bedlam or bliss? Recognising the emotional self-experience of people with moderate to advanced dementia in residential and nursing care, *Quality in Ageing and Older Adults*, 16, 4, 235–48.

Harding, N. and Palfry, C. (1997) *The social construction of dementia: confused professionals?.* London: Jessica Kingsley.

Hurt, C.S., Burns, A., Brown, R.G. and Barrowclough, C. (2011) Why don't older adults with subjective memory complaints seek help? *International Journal of Geriatric Psychiatry*, 27, 4, 394–400.

Jutel, A. (2009) Sociology of diagnosis a preliminary review, *Sociology of Health & Illness*, 31, 2, 278–99.

Katz, S. (2013) Dementia, personhood and embodiment: what can we learn from medieval history of memory? *Dementia*, 12, 3, 303–14.

Kelly, A. (2008) Living loss: an exploration of the internal space of liminality, *Mortality: Promoting the Interdisciplinary Study of Death and Dying*, 13, 4, 335–50.

Kelly, A. (2010) Lost the feel for the game: meanings of onset and diagnosis of AIDS dementia for significant others, *Qualitative Health Research*, 20, 4, 531–40.

Kertzer, D.I. and Laslett, P. (eds) (1995) *Aging in the past: demography, society, and old age.* Berkeley: University of California Press.

Kitwood, T. (1997) *Dementia reconsidered: the person comes first.* Buckingham: Open University Press.

La Fontaine, J., Ahuja, J., Bradbury, N.M., Phillips, S., *et al.* (2007) Understanding dementia amongst people in minority ethnic and cultural groups, *Journal of Advanced Nursing*, 60, 6, 605–14.

Langdon, S.A., Eagle, A. and Warner, J. (2007) Making sense of dementia in the social world, a qualitative study, *Social Science and Medicine*, 64, 4, 989–1000.

Little, M., Jordens, C.F.C., Paul, K., Montgomery, K. and Philipson, B. (1998) Liminality: a major category of the experience of cancer illness, *Social Science and Medicine*, 47, 10, 1485–94.

Lloyd, L., Calnan, M., Camerson, A., Seymour, J. and Smith, R. (2014) Identity in the fourth age: perseverance, adaptation and maintaining dignity, *Ageing and Society*, 34, 1, 1–19.

MacQuarrie, C.R. (2005) Experiences in early stage Alzheimer's disease: understanding the paradox of acceptance and denial, *Aging and Mental Health*, 9, 5, 430–41.

MacRae, H. (2010) Managing identity while living with Alzheimer's disease, *Qualitative Health Research*, 20, 3, 293–305.

Marshall, T.H. (1950) *Citizenship and social class.* Cambridge: Cambridge University Press.

Martineau, W.H. (1972) A model of the social functions of humor. In Goldstein, J.H. and McGhee, P.E., (eds) *The psychology of humor: theoretical perspectives and empirical issues.* New York: Academic Press.

McManus, M. and Devine, P. (2011) *Dementia: public knowledge and attitudes*, Research update, 77, Access Research Knowledge. Available at http://www.ark.ac.uk/publications/updates/update77.pdf. (Last accessed 28 June 2016)

Milne, A. (2010) The D word: reflections on the relationship between stigma and dementia, *Journal of Mental Health*, 19, 3, 227–33.

O'Conner, D. and Nedlund, A. (2016) Editorial introduction: special edition on citizenship and dementia, *Dementia*, 15, 3, 285–88.

Österholm, J.H., Larsson, A.T. and Olaison, A. (2015) Handling the dilemma of self-determination and dementia: a study of case managers' discursive strategies in assessment meetings, *Journal of Gerontological Social Work*, 58, 6, 613–36.

Phillips, J., Pond, C.D., Paterson, N.E., Howell, C., *et al.* (2012) Difficulties in disclosing the diagnosis of dementia: a qualitative study in general practice, *British Journal of General Practice*, 62, 601, e546–53.

Phinney, A., Chaudhury, H. and O'Conner, D.L. (2007) 'Doing as much as I can do': the meaning of activity for people, *Aging and Mental Health*, 11, 4, 384–93.

Preston, L., Marshall, A. and Bucks, R.S. (2007) Investigating the ways that older people cope with dementia: a qualitative study, *Aging and Mental Health*, 11, 2, 131–43.

Prince, M., Bryce, R. and Ferri, C. (2011) *World Alzheimer's report 2011: the benefit of early diagnosis and intervention.* London: Alzheimer's Disease International.

Robinson, L., Clare, L. and Evans, K. (2005) Making sense of dementia and adjusting to loss: psychological reactions to a diagnosis of dementia in couples, *Aging and Mental Health*, 9, 4, 337–47.

Rolland, J.S. (1987) Chronic illness and the life cycle: a conceptual framework, *Family Process*, 26, 2, 203–21.

Sabat, S.R. (2002) Surviving manifestations of selfhood in Alzheimer's disease: a case study, *Dementia*, 14, 1, 11–9.

Samsi, K. and Manthorpe, J. (2013) Everyday decision-making in dementia: findings from a longitudinal interview study of people with dementia and family carers, *International Psychogeriatrics*, 25, 5, 949–61.

Samsi, K., Abley, C., Campbell, S., Keady, J., *et al.* (2014) Negotiating a labyrinth: experiences of assessment and diagnostic journey in cognitive impairment and dementia, *International Journal of Geriatric Psychiatry*, 29, 1, 58–67.

Scheer, S.D., Gavazzi, S.M. and Blumenkrantz, D.G. (2007) Rites of passage during adolescence, *The Forum for Family and Consumer Issues*, 12, 2. Avalailble at http://ncsu.edu/ffci/publications/2007/v12n2-2007-fall/index-v12n2-nov-2007.php. (Last accessed 28 June 2016)

Shields, L., Molzahn, A., Bruce, A., Schick Makaroff, K., *et al.* (2015) Contrasting stories of life threatening illness: a narrative inquiry, *International Journal of Nursing Studies*, 52, 1, 207–15.

Steeman, E., Godderis, J., Grypdonck, M., De Bal, N. and Dierckx de Casterle, B. (2007) Living with dementia from the perspective of older people: is it a positive story? *Aging and Mental Health*, 11, 2, 119–30.

Sweeting, H. and Gilhooly, M. (1997) Dementia and the phenomenon of social death, *Sociology of Health & Illness*, 19, 1, 93–117.

Turner, B.S. (1993) Contemporary problems in the theory of citizenship. In Turner, B.S. (ed) *Citizenship and social theory*. London: Sage Publications.

Turner, V. (1967) *The forest of symbols aspects of Ndembu ritual*. London: Cornell University Press.

Turner, V. (1974) *Dramas, fields and metaphors: symbolic action in human societies*. New York: Cornell University Press.

Van Gennep, A. (1960) *The rites of passage*. Chicago: University of Chicago Press.

Vernooij-Dassen, M., Derksen, E., Scheltens, P. and Moniz-Cook, E. (2006) Receiving a diagnosis of dementia: the experience over time, *Dementia*, 5, 3, 397–410.

Wolverson, E.L., Clarke, C. and Moniz-Cook, E.D. (2015) Living positively with dementia: a systematic review and synthesis of the qualitative literature, *Aging and Mental Health*, 20, 7, 679–99.

World Health Organization (WHO) (2002) *Reducing stigma and discrimination against older people with mental disorders*. Geneva: WHO.

Zeilig, H. (2013) Dementia as a cultural metaphor, *The Gerontologist*, 54, 2, 258–67.

Ziv, A. (2010) The social function of humor in interpersonal relationships, *Society*, 47, 1, 11–8.

4

Narrative collisions, sociocultural pressures and dementia: the relational basis of personhood reconsidered
Edward Tolhurst, Bernhard Weicht and Paul Kingston

Introduction: the conceptualisation of personhood

Personal relationships are recognised as a key contextual influence upon the experience of dementia. An exclusive focus on dementia as a state of disease and the substantial strain it places upon people's lives can result in the challenges of the condition being exacerbated and, at worst, lead to cruelty due to lack of care. As a consequence, person-centred approaches (in contrast to illness-centred) offer counterbalance by emphasising that people live their lives within interdependent relationships, which can enable people with dementia to sustain a positive personal identity.

The relational basis of experience pertains to the concept of personhood, which was pioneered by Tom Kitwood who is recognised as one of the most influential authors on the experience of dementia (Baldwin and Capstick 2007). Kitwood (1997: 8) defined personhood as 'a standing or status that is bestowed upon one human being, by others, in the context of relationship and social being. It implies recognition, respect and trust'. Dementia, accordingly, cannot be understood solely with reference to the neurodegenerative impacts of the condition, as human life is based on the interconnectedness and interdependencies of relationships. An individualised perspective of neurological or biological being does not, therefore, represent the essence of lived experience. The relational basis of experience endures for a person with dementia, and this means that those with the condition should not be 'downgraded into the carriers of an organic brain disease' (Kitwood 1997: 7).

The maintenance of personhood therefore depends upon positive relational conditions, for example, the endorsement and support of other people. Kitwood (1990) however also warned that negative relational conditions can impact upon people with dementia, contributing to a 'malignant social psychology'. This refers to attitudes and behaviours adopted by (well-meaning) carers that undermine the experiential conditions of people with dementia. The nature of relationships and the care environment require an appropriate degree of scrutiny, so that such 'malignant' social factors can be identified and resisted.

While the importance of immediate relationships, prompted by Kitwood's approach to personhood, offers a significant advancement of the understanding of dementia, several authors have highlighted that there is a tendency to overlook how these relationships are framed by sociocultural factors (e.g. Bartlett and O'Connor 2010; Innes 2009). The grounding of Kitwood's psychological approach has been offered as one of the reasons why the

Ageing, Dementia and the Social Mind, First Edition. Edited by Paul Higgs and Chris Gilleard.
Chapters © 2017 The Authors. Book Compilation © 2017 Foundation for the Sociology of
Health & Illness/Blackwell Publishing Ltd.

experience of dementia remains scrutinised in limited terms within social science. For example, while Kitwood sought to address defective contexts of care, he drew little on concepts from sociology and consequently more extensive social influences were given little consideration (Baldwin and Capstick 2007). Furthermore, his 'unwavering commitment to the *person* with dementia' (Davis 2004: 376 original emphasis) offers an individualistic rather than a genuinely relational conceptual starting point. Hence, Kitwood's approach advances understandings of dementia beyond a limited view of its biological basis, but then offers a narrow view of experience which itself requires broader contextualisation.

Higgs and Gilleard (2015) also warn that under Kitwood's approach, personhood is a status attributed to the person by others. Personhood is thus not asserted by people with dementia themselves, which means that their own agency in the process is lacking: it is a status bestowed, rather than something actively shaped by the person with the condition (Baldwin and Capstick 2007). Taking personhood seriously therefore requires a comprehensive, sociological analysis of the constructions and attributions impacting upon all those involved in the maintenance of interpersonal relationships.

A sociologically-informed perspective drawing on the broad feminist literature on care and the ethics of care (Bowlby *et al.* 2010; Tronto 1993; Twigg 1997; Weicht 2015) offers resources that can help to expand this narrow orientation, by embedding experience and interactions between partners in relationships within sociocultural structures and understandings. It has been claimed that academic endeavours have devised an effective relationship-focused approach, illuminating impacts upon wellbeing at an interpersonal level, and that this can be supplemented by attention to sociocultural elements of the social fabric (Keady and Burrow 2015). It is something of a category mistake, however, to view the interactional order and broader social conditions as neatly separable domains of enquiry. These conditions do not comprise a discrete element of analysis to be addressed in *post hoc* fashion, but are constitutive of the interactional situation: the 'conditions *of* the situation are *in* the situation' (Clarke and Friese 2007: 364 original emphasis).

In addition to this theoretical scrutiny and societal embedding, personhood also requires particular methodological reinforcement. It is not just the case that personhood is conceptually devised in narrow social terms, but that the interactional basis of relationships also requires greater research attention (Molyneaux *et al.* 2012). Social contexts cannot simply be appended to interaction in a top-down theoretical manner. Instead, a socially-framed understanding of dementia requires a cogent empirical platform at the level of experience and immediate relationships.

Even when dyadic research approaches are employed, interaction has received insufficient direct attention. Joint interviews valuably enable access to the subjective viewpoints of two respondents, but also enable insights into conversational exchanges. Nevertheless, one notable tendency is for data to be presented in an individualised format with interactions not directly conveyed. Such a pattern is evident in Robinson *et al.* (2005), who focus exclusively on individual responses and do not present what can be termed 'interactional data'; that is, data which shows conversational interactions between participants. The interview is treated as a site where subjective viewpoints are obtained (and disaggregated from their relational context), rather than as a setting whereby interaction comprises a phenomenon for investigation in itself.

Based on the model of personhood inspired by Kitwood, this article focuses on the societal conceptualisations that shape the experience of dementia within concrete relationships. By drawing upon qualitative research that explored relationships between men with dementia and their spousal carers,[1] this article illuminates how a sociological perspective can help to construct and utilise an empirical platform which can fortify the understanding of personhood. A joint interview approach allows the exploration of both subjective perspectives and interactional exchanges within spousal dyads where one member of the couple has been diagnosed with dementia. Within this exploration the term 'narrative collisions' is advanced, which sets out to illuminate the breadth of influences and pressures that shape interpersonal negotiations.

Literature context: spousal dyads and interaction

While it is noted above that interaction has received limited empirical attention, a small number of qualitative dementia studies do set out to convey the conversational exchanges within spousal couples. A joint interview study that addresses interactional data extensively is Molyneaux *et al.* (2012), and this is the exclusive format of data that they present. Their article builds upon the notion of 'couplehood' (Hellström *et al.* 2007), which asserts how couples strive positively to maintain the balance of their relationship. The identified interactional themes in Molyneaux *et al.* therefore focus on reciprocity and the mutual basis of experience, including how couples maintain their relationship and adopt a shared approach to the challenges posed by the condition. The orientation is thereby to the positive co-construction of a shared identity (see also Davies 2011). It can be queried, however, whether this focus on couplehood could potentially lead to the distinctive subjective perspectives of the members of the dyad being under-represented.

Clare and Shakespeare (2004) also present an exclusive focus on interactional data in their study of how the impact of forgetting is negotiated. Short conversations between people with dementia and their spousal carers were recorded (without an interviewer present). This process demonstrated how the conversational strategies of each partner might conflict. For example, the person with dementia sometimes adopted a 'psychological' resistance to the condition, offering a normalising account in the endeavour to resist being positioned negatively and as a burden. In response, carers would not always 'collude' with these accounts, presenting instead a 'political' resistance to their circumstances: this relates to the requirement to 'retain a voice, and to be able to express and discuss fears and feelings openly and honestly' (Clare and Shakespeare 2004: 226).

Studies that focus on interactional data therefore draw out different factors which shape relationships that are affected by dementia: this relates to the need to reconcile individual identities with the shared identity of the spousal relationship. The concept of couplehood, endorsed by Molyneaux *et al.* (2012), indicates that a shared identity is readily pursued and achieved by people with dementia and their carers. Clare and Shakespeare (2004), on the other hand, suggest that this goal is rendered challenging by the competing subjective positions of the person with dementia and the carer.

These alternative perspectives demonstrate that there is an enduring requirement to engage in exploration of how personhood is sustained within relationships. It is crucial, however, from both a theoretical and a methodological perspective, to situate the subjective accounts and the conversational exchanges within an analysis of the socially constructed meanings of what matters to the couple. In order to identify how these meanings intersect with palpable relational negotiations this article draws upon a joint interview study, focusing on one case specifically. This approach allows the different elements that shape and configure the meaning and experience of dementia within the context of a particular relationship to be traced.

Method

This article utilises data from a dyadic case study drawn from a qualitative research project. A joint interview approach was undertaken with 14 dyads: men with dementia and their spousal carers were interviewed together in their family home.[2] The gender-based orientation of this research was adopted to obtain in-depth insights into spousal relationship dynamics when the man has been diagnosed with dementia. The research set out to obtain an understanding of the experience of living with dementia, via elaborate respondent accounts on their spousal relationship, relationships with other family members, and the professional support they were accessing. Dyads were interviewed twice in the endeavour to obtain extensive experiential insights, with a six-month interval between these interviews.

The couple from which this article draws its data was selected as their interviews were among the most balanced in this research in terms of input from both respondents. The man with dementia, David,[3] was 64 at the time of the first interview, while the carer, Florence, was 52. David is defined as having 'early onset dementia', which refers to the onset of the condition prior to the age of 65 (Alzheimer's Society 2015). The focus on a person with early onset dementia is also useful, as research has tended to focus on older people with the condition (Clemerson *et al.* 2014).

Both David and Florence are still in employment: David works in a distribution business, while Florence works in a clinical role within health/social care. They have been married for 10 years. David was diagnosed with Alzheimer's disease six months prior to their first interview in this research. Each of the joint interviews (with David and Florence interviewed together) lasted for approximately 90 minutes. The couple was recruited via a National Health Service (NHS) trust's dementia service.[4]

In keeping with the endeavour to obtain extensive accounts from respondents, narrative analysis was undertaken of transcripts (Riessman 2008). The aim of the analytical process was to establish the key subjective themes expressed by the man with dementia and the carer respectively, but also how these narrative themes intersect within conversation. In practical terms, the transcript was parsed on multiple occasions with respective focus on these analytical stages, to establish key narrative themes and their relational construction. The first stage required the interrogation of the subjective account presented by the man with dementia; the second stage focused on the carer's account; while the final stage evaluated interaction, i.e. how subjective perspectives were negotiated within conversational exchanges. Building upon this analytical approach, a distinctive incremental approach to the presentation of findings is conveyed: the (socially-framed) subjective perspective of each participant is addressed, and this offers a springboard to the evaluation of how these viewpoints are interwoven within interactional exchanges. This approach shows how narrative relates to the presentation of personal identity; however, it also demonstrates how stories are co-constructed by talk-in-interaction with others (Squire *et al.* 2008).

It has to be recognised that relationships are diverse and shaped by a breadth of factors: the specific experiences noted in the findings and the format of their expression are, of course, particular to the selected dyad. *Inter alia*, this couple was among the youngest in the sample, and age is a factor that will shape experience. It should also be recognised that David had only recently been diagnosed with dementia, and was able to communicate his views clearly and extensively. When a person is in a more advanced stage of dementia this is likely to impact upon their scope to negotiate conversational exchanges (Clare and Shakespeare 2004). Nevertheless, the selected case does represent the principal subjective themes and conversational strategies that were identified across the 14 dyads that participated in this research. Focusing on one couple to articulate these factors offers a coherent representation of the construction and co-construction of narratives, and the challenges of reconciling a personal account with a shared account of the relationship.

Subjective perspectives[5]

The man with dementia

It appeared that a key aim for David in the interviews was to present a positive depiction of his experience since being diagnosed with dementia. In the following excerpt David acknowledges that he had encountered threats to his self-esteem at the onset of the condition, but he also states that the impacts of the medication following the diagnosis have ameliorated these difficulties. For example, his scores within cognitive function tests have improved, thus re-establishing his sense of competence:

> I suppose once they actually, definitely diagnosed that I'd got early stages of Alzheimer's, at that point they began to input with drugs. Things like that which gave me a lot more security and made me feel a lot happier and I just felt that I wasn't as dim as I thought I was [laughs]. Because I really had a bad time before all this happened. I was really struggling and I felt embarrassed about struggling. But the girls that have come out to me, they've come out and they've put me on different tests and as I work my way through the tests I've got better and better at working out the tests. In fact the last test I had I think I got 34 out of 35.

David also refers to his interactions within his workplace. His reference to other people regarding him as normal indicates the social pressures engendered by the anticipated impacts of the dementia. David, however, expresses his ability to function well in interpersonal situations, which offers a sense of continuity with his previous levels of performance:

> I just feel most folks regard me at the moment as perfectly normal. The drivers will all wander in and make coffee, there's chatter and a natter. Nobody looks at me and says you are completely off your rocker or whatever.

In the following excerpt, David discusses his working role, and also his ability to engage in a manual task with skill and precision. The centrality of ongoing competence to David's sense of self is apparent in his discussion of his retained abilities. The emphasis on both the still functioning body and the positive recognition by others not only reinforce the normativity of 'vitalism' (Greco 2009) but also the discursively created 'polarity between dependent, vulnerable, innocent, asexual children and competent, powerful, sexual, adult citizens' (Shakespeare 2000: 15). The importance for men with dementia to retain a sense of purposeful activity is also captured by Phinney et al. (2013). The assertion of sustained levels of skilful endeavour seems to relate to a sense of personal value and contribution:

> I've had a busy day today. We ship an awful lot of barbeques all over the country. I spent most of my day building. You have to wrap them, put timbers under these big concrete barbeques and nail them together [...] I can hit the hammer on a nail dead-on every time.

The importance of social contribution is also underscored below. David mentions that he has been offered the opportunity to attend a dementia support group; however, he does not yet wish to attend and if he does in the future it would be to help others rather than to seek help for himself. In fact both the opportunity to help others (being able to provide help to those needing it) and to reject help himself (the horror of needing help) appear to enhance David's sense of self and status (see also Dean and Rogers 2004). Again, the focus of his account is on his personal improvement. The use of the word 'we' is also notable, and this indicates a shared experiential orientation within the couple:

> I must admit we haven't taken it up. Because I feel very happy with how things are going. I'm not saying that in the future we wouldn't. If things get a bit – it could possibly be a good place to go to, and talk to other people in the same position. Or give advice to people in there who are perhaps newly diagnosed. I could be some help to them. To say that I've been there and I've done it and there are ways of improving yourself.

The carer

While David acknowledged the trials of the diagnostic process he converted this into a positive account of his situation. Florence, however, focused more closely on the emotional strains she encountered during this process. Below she discusses the impact of the clinician delivering the diagnosis of Alzheimer's and refers to their particular disquiet with the clinician's reference to life expectancy:

> I just wanted to gag her. I wanted to say, 'I don' t want this now. Come back and tell us that on another day, I don't want David to hear this.' […] when she had gone it was the first thing David said. We then just sat and sobbed.

Florence considers the changes to their circumstances and also contemplates the impacts that this will have in the future. She states her need to reconcile her caring role with her work commitments, which indicates the tension between balancing her own needs with providing care (Quinn *et al.* 2015). David is currently able to drive, but Florence anticipates the implications of the time when his driving licence might be revoked and he is subsequently no longer able to go to work:

> I really hope the licence can continue. That's a big thing, because I'll be sitting at work thinking I need to go now because David will have been on his own from ten-to-seven in the morning. But I'm planning, I might have to ask if I can work at home more and stuff, but again that changes your dynamics and work with your staff.

The anticipation of care responsibilities and how they will impact on her life is not the only difficulty faced by Florence. She discusses the frustrations she encounters with David's behaviour but also expresses guilt at feeling these emotions. It has been noted that recognition of the impact of the condition upon behaviour can remove the 'legitimacy' of carers' frustrations, with such feelings replaced by guilt (Walters *et al.* 2010). This indicates that there is something of a recursive challenge associated with caring: negative emotions such as frustration beget other negative emotions:

> I try and not feel selfish, because at times sometimes I want to kill you don't I? If you lose things and so on. And that's quite difficult because then you feel mean. Because there's a reason, there's a condition that's causing it.

A further moral trial is presented when Florence contemplates the idea of attending a support group for carers. She would not feel able to attend for personal reasons related to her work role, as she believes she would be unable to relinquish her clinical mindset within the support group setting. This perspective generates feelings of guilt: Florence appears to perceive that she is placing her own preferences ahead of the shared needs of the couple, and accordingly she feels selfish:

> I think what I would tend to do is become the clinician in that. And I would be doing the 'have you thought of doing this, and have you thought of doing that?' Now maybe that is very selfish of me, but I kind of don't want to do that because I do it every day. No, maybe we'll get to that stage where we'll feel it will be helpful, but I almost feel – so maybe that's very selfish, that is very selfish. But I don't want to do it at the moment.

Social influences upon subjective accounts

The analysis of the data above shows the different perspectives of David and Florence. David offers a positive account oriented to ongoing activity, independence and enduring capabilities. Alternatively, Florence's account is more negative and oriented to her changing circumstances and associated feelings of frustration and guilt. She finds herself in the position of having to juggle competing societal expectations of remaining independent/active with being a good carer (Pickard 2010). While the immediate interactional setting of the interview (comprising the man with dementia, the carer and the interviewer) will influence the expression of these views, the impact of wider social influences must also be acknowledged. This relates to the dialogic basis of the narrative analytical approach: this recognises how subjective 'voices' within conversation are not just directed to co-present individuals, but are also pervaded by sociocultural representations and ideals. Narrative is thereby never a singular phenomenon but is 'polyphonic', with the influence of social discourses detectable within the person's account (Sullivan 2012).

As indicated, for the person with dementia there are a range of discourses likely to compound personal challenges. A condition such as dementia intersects with the aim to sustain a preferred identity (Charmaz 1994), as it presents the threat that the person will be labelled as defective with reference to key sociocultural values. A duty and necessity to cope self-sufficiently defines the increasingly individualised basis of contemporary social conditions (Bauman 2011). As a corollary, a strong value is placed upon the importance of personal independence and autonomy, alongside related moral imperatives of rationalism and economic contribution (Post 2000). Dementia is accordingly positioned as the antithesis of agentic mental competence (Williams et al. 2012).

David repeatedly asserted his ability to continue his life as an independent and competent person despite his diagnosis of dementia. This could be to counter the threat that he will be judged negatively if he cannot measure up to the core societal values of independence, autonomy and individual contribution. Such cultural norms of independence/dependence relate closely to conceptualisations of personhood: 'Dependency is a sign of not being healthy, of being passive, of not being self-reliant and not being a 'proper' person in society' (Weicht 2011: 214). David's perceived role at the dementia support group, helping others but not needing help himself, underscores the potency of these social norms. This could represent the goal to resist societal constructions of dementia that could position him in a 'helpless victim role' (MacRae 2008). Maintaining a sense of personal contribution could also reinforce David's position within the spousal relationship, thus maintaining a relationship of equals and resisting a carer/cared-for relational configuration.

The carer's personal context is also strongly shaped by cultural discourses, and these relate to the aforementioned constructions of illness. As illness is associated with an undesirable state of dependency, it requires the person who undertakes caring duties to be defined as a committed and selfless person who places the interests of the 'sick' before their own. While this discourse might ostensibly offer an endorsement of the value of 'caring', it risks imposing pressure upon carers to fulfil their roles with unremitting commitment. This accordingly prompts feelings of guilt if the carer feels emotions not consistent with such values, as represented by Florence's feelings when she acknowledges her frustrations with David's behaviour.

The feminist literature on care has continuously shown that care relationships cannot be understood without a focus on the societal meaning of gender constructions (Bowlby *et al.* 2010). Labels associated with illness related to passivity, dependence and a subordinated status (Charmaz 1994) clash with societal notions of masculinity that are predicated on autonomy and control. 'Being a patient contradicts the very definitions of manhood, leaving a person vulnerable, weakened and dependent' (Coston and Kimmel 2013: 194). Again, this is consistent with the sense that David's positive assertions of purposeful activity, social contribution and competence are offered to resist such threatening cultural norms. The influence of other characteristics, such as age, should also not be discounted. As a younger person with dementia, David is confronted with the risk of being prematurely aligned with negative discourses on old age associated with infirmity and dependency (Higgs and Jones 2009).

Gendered meanings of care also affect the experience of carers. For example, caring is defined as a natural female role associated with nurturing, maternal values (Coston and Kimmel 2013; Ungerson 2000). This impinges upon female identity, defining feminine subjectivity as well as moral worthiness (Paoletti 2002). It is also argued that female self-identity is acutely defined by significant relationships: women are consequently placed under particular pressure with regard to what could be termed 'relational competence'; that is, their ability to maintain positive close relationships (O'Connor 1995). These pressures could relate to the intense moral concerns apparent in Florence's deliberations over attending a support group for carers. Cultural constructions of femininity mean that 'a concern with individual survival comes to be branded as "selfish" and to be counterpoised to the "responsibility" of a life lived in relationships' (Gilligan 1982: 127). An ethics of care that moves beyond a 'carer/ cared for' dichotomy, and which acknowledges that interdependency is the defining feature of social relationships, could help to overcome such gendered conceptualisations of caring (Weicht 2015).

Interactional data

The collision of socially-framed narratives
The exploration of data thus far demonstrates how the alternative narrative strategies of both interviewees are positioned with reference to broader sociocultural factors that shape roles, relationships and individual narratives. The way that these subjective perspectives are interwoven within interactional exchanges is now evaluated. The following conversational exchange shows David's preference for presenting a positive view of his situation, and also Florence's tendency to present a more negative account:

David: I just feel a lot more in charge of myself, with working and doing things. I just feel much happier. I've got a goal. I've got something to do. Being at work helps me dramatically [...]

Florence: But I think for me, it gave me all the responsibility. Having that diagnosis I then felt I've got to deal with this. It will be me managing this situation. And I think for me, it was a huge impact. Absolutely huge.

It is not just the case, however, that alternative views are held by each person, but that these perspectives interrelate and present potential problems that will require negotiation. Below, Florence again refers to the impact of being informed about life expectancy at the diagnosis. Her response collides with David's endeavour to offer a more positive account that seeks to distance him from this particular period. He concentrates on his improvement and reasserts that the medication regime offers him a sense of control over, and resistance to, the condition so that he has essentially recaptured his 'past self' (Charmaz 1994):

Florence: It was a difficult delivery compounded by information about longevity and then we were asked to feed back on the delivery and neither of us was in a fit state to do that. But my feedback would have been that neither of us wanted to hear about life expectancy at that point. I think it was difficult enough having to think about the diagnosis without having the extra burden of that.

Interviewer: Is that how you felt as well David?

David: Well to be honest with you, when [the psychiatrist] came in and she told me that, I was somewhat shocked but almost relieved that I knew there was something there. The way that she put it to me, 'I know, yes you've hit upon it.' I mean, she told me in a very nice way, didn't she?

Florence: But in terms of the life expectancy?

David: Oh yes, the life expectancy was – I mean I feel it's up to me to try and do what I can do. And listen to what they have to tell me. To take the drugs at exactly the right times [...] because the drugs, the Aricept, has just sort of really turned me around. It's had a great deal of effect on me and improved me completely.

The different approaches within the interview, by the two participants, mean that one person's expressed outlook can potentially impede the cogency of the other's account. In the excerpt below, David is concluding a lengthy section of narrative on his role at work; however, Florence then reports that David now encounters some difficulties with him feeling lonely. David, in turn, does not accept this account and reasserts a more affirmative view of his circumstances, highlighting his self-sufficiency:

David: I do all that, get all the bits of wood back together, in case we sometimes have to slice open the plastic things and wrap the wrapper all round to make it tidy.

Florence: Sometimes you are a bit lonely aren't you? You are sent to do jobs without much support, so your days can be a bit lonely so I think that's the difference.

David: Sometimes I am actually quite happy on my own.

Florence: Okay.

David: I've got a great friend of mine who I've known for years, he's a local farmer [...] just lately we've had to clear out the barns and get them ready for reuse, and it's always me that gets the job of clearing out the barn and doing everything else and sorting it all out. But I'm quite happy with that [...] I quite enjoy my own company at times, quite honestly.

The requirement for Florence to convey the source of some of her frustrations also collides with David's objective to present himself as competent and carrying on as normal. This is reminiscent of the findings of Clare and Shakespeare (2004), noted above, where it was found that spousal carers do not always 'collude' with face-saving and normalising accounts. Florence states the difficulty of David losing things which David tries to resist with humour. Florence's elaboration on this topic draws further resistance from David, which reflects his need to position any undesirable impacts of dementia in the past. The use of 'we' by Florence in this instance perhaps indicates an endeavour to claim a shared responsibility, limiting any sense she is blaming David. Alternatively, this approach could undermine David as it reduces a sense of his capacity to take personal responsibility. However, Florence also appears to seek to diminish the impact of her statements by commenting on her own fallibility:

Florence: It's the losing things.
David: I shouldn't have a coat with so many pockets in.
Florence: No, we all lose things. But we've lost a couple of mobile phones haven't we, and hearing aids somewhere. I think we just get on with it don't we.
David: You're going back a bit. We did used to lose quite a few things. We used to leave places and realise I'd not picked something up, whereas now I'm a little bit more …
Florence: Yes, because that's mainly on holiday isn't it. Because I actually go 'have you got it, where is it?' You know, things like that. You'll frequently go out in the evening without a wallet, which is a good ploy! But I can't comment because you'd got your wallet last night, and I'd left my purse at work.

With reference to the exchanges shown above, Florence to some extent seeks catharsis from the interview process and appears to feel the need to offer a credible account, from her vantage point, of the problems that they are encountering. Her feelings in relation to her caring role are gainsaid to a degree by the overtly positive account presented by David. If the situation does not contain a substantial degree of change and hardship then Florence's frustrations might not be justifiable to herself. This could, accordingly, prompt an additional personal concern that such frustrations are not morally acceptable. The incommensurability of their respective vantage points, however, also presents difficulties to David. His expressed stoicism and appeals to enduring skills and competence were challenged within the interactional exchanges: Florence's more pessimistic account risks hindering David's attempts to sustain his preferred narrative strategy.

The influence of the dementia generates particular personal and relational challenges for the couple to negotiate. This relates to the direct neurological impact of the condition, with David pursuing a psychological resistance to the condition. It also pertains to a carer/cared-for dynamic: Florence sets out to highlight the challenges of caring she is encountering and anticipating, but also appears mindful that this could subvert David's endeavour to convey a more positive impression of their circumstances. Gender-related norms are also likely to link with these relational pressures. These elements combine to generate a context where narrative collisions are a potential outcome of respective endeavours to express a coherent subjective identity.

The different relational positions of the man with dementia and the female carer (with reference to the condition, one another, and wider social discourses) therefore generate interactional issues for both parties. People are narrative beings, with their self-identities narratively constituted in association with others (Baldwin 2005). Narratives are therefore inherently relational and different subjective approaches can conflict with one another. David's requirement to offer a positive account based on normalcy and continuity collides with Florence's requirement to present a more negative account based on the changes she is encountering. Additionally, both construct their own narratives in response to societal demands for independence and self-sufficiency. What has accordingly been demonstrated is a dialectical collision of narrative strategies, rather than simply the carer bestowing a negative frame of reference upon the person with dementia.

These findings show two people contending with the intense biographical disruption (Bury 1982) prompted by dementia: both individuals struggle to maintain respective preferred identities within a disrupted interactional locale, which is shaped by multiple sociocultural pressures. If the analytical orientation were to remain on co-presence (divorced from its sociocultural embeddedness) then human agency is likely to be overstated with causal powers disproportionately imputed to individuals (Archer 1995). The source of the person with dementia's problems would then be identified solely at the interpersonal level.

Positive care dynamics are associated with the ability and willingness of carers to support the person with dementia (Keady and Nolan 2003), and their capacity to put the other person's needs before their own (Shim *et al.* 2012). The emphasis is accordingly on the individual efforts and dispositional qualities of the carer. These are, of course, factors that need to be considered when supporting people with dementia, and it is vital to address attitudes and behaviours that are expressed in the interpersonal environment (Tanner 2013). There are, however, implications with addressing care dynamics in a manner that understates how interactional settings are shaped by wider social influences. Ultimately, a narrow conceptualisation of relationships is compatible with a blame-oriented explanatory model (Baldwin and Capstick 2007; Bartlett and O'Connor 2010). While Kitwood (1997) set out to distance his critique of care environments from informal carers in his later work, it can be argued that the thrust of malignant social psychology risks compounding the pressures of caring: it suggests that carers are complicit in the process of generating conditions that undermine personhood (Davis 2004).

Conclusion: seeking a balanced relational approach

As noted in the introduction, Kitwood's influential approach to personhood has been critiqued for failing to embed personhood within a sufficiently rich and extensive social context. This article has demonstrated one means by which this limitation can be addressed by supplementing the concept of personhood with findings, informed by the sociology of care, that seek to reconcile the influences of subjective, interactional and wider social factors. Within this analysis, the development of the term 'narrative collisions' is of particular value. This highlights the challenges inherent to interpersonal negotiations while acknowledging the complex breadth of contextual factors that shape potentially competing narrative vantage points.

The empirical identification of interactional challenges in this article in no way suggests that an intrinsic negativity underpins relationships shaped by dementia. The overall dynamic and tone of the interviews with David and Florence indicated that this was a loving and mutually supportive relationship. This was consistent more widely across the sample of this research: relationships were supportive, but narrative collisions were still apparent. The narrative collisions that were identified within spousal dyads across this research, as represented in the case study above, reinforce the findings of Clare and Shakespeare (2004) who highlighted the different strategies people with dementia and their carers employ when resisting the impacts of the condition. This article expands upon the identification of such personal strategies, relating them to broader sociocultural influences.

David and Florence both offered a sense of unity through the use of language and often ascribed the word 'we' to their experiences, which indicates the aim to co-construct a congruent joint narrative (see also Hydén and Nilsson 2015). The different conversational strategies that they employ, however, shows how their distinctive subjective positions and responses to social pressures render the attainment of a unified couplehood challenging. A combined

48 Edward Tolhurst et al.

account of the relationship is difficult to sustain, as it is constructed from two different socially-framed individual perspectives. The interactions demonstrate how 'individual' narratives and negotiated 'shared' narratives are shaped by the interdependencies within a care relationship (Bowlby *et al.* 2010). Both persons relate to a number of societal demands and constructions of meanings in relation to the experience of dementia, the normativity of independence and the moral construction of the ideal care relationship.

The exploration of data in this article therefore underscores the truism that relationships are not amenable to binary categorisation (being either positive or negative): they are complex phenomena that must be understood with reference to a breadth of experiential, interactional and contextual factors. Nevertheless, there is a trend within academic discourse that could diminish the recognition of this relational complexity. For example, the academic promotion of personhood is aligned with resistance to excessively discouraging representations of dementia. This is reinforced by a policy discourse associated with 'living well' with dementia (Department of Health 2009). This approach sets out to provide a counterbalance to the prevailing view that neurodegenerative decline and carer burden are the defining aspects of lives affected by dementia. As highlighted by La Fontaine and Oyebode (2014), there is the scope for researchers within this academic context to suppress material that does not endorse a positive portrayal of experience.

While ostensibly seeking a more integrated view of relationships by reducing the distinction between people with dementia and 'healthy others' (Sabat *et al.* 2011), the promotion of a more positive outlook on dementia still fails to transcend a limited standpoint. The individualistic residue of the 'personhood' concept endures and this means that, even when the wider social context is addressed (via the aim to counter negative societal representations of dementia), this is confronted in a unitary manner that fails to account for the interdependencies of relationships. The accounts of David and Florence capture how different narrative strategies might be adopted by people living with dementia, with carers tending to express a more pessimistic worldview than their partners. The carer's more negative perspective does not align readily with the ideal being advanced under individualised academic discourses.

A manufactured stance of positivity thus generates a zero-sum situation: the aim to bolster the position of the person with dementia requires the vantage point of the carer to be diminished. The well-intentioned attempt to elevate the status of people with dementia has thereby introduced new imbalances into academic thought. The goal to counter negative societal perceptions of dementia, however, should not lead to the difficulties of carers being invalidated. Moreover, insights into the interpersonal challenges encountered by people with dementia could also be underplayed.

A conceptual basis that asserts the person with dementia 'comes first' (Kitwood 1997) generates a prioritisation of the individual which offers a less than optimal starting point for a genuinely balanced exploration of relationships (Davis 2004). Even when a 'couplehood' approach has been promoted this has tended to be imbalanced, focusing on the construction of a shared identity with the aim of endorsing what is perceived to be the best interests of the individual with dementia. The views of carers are accordingly at risk of being suppressed, or held accountable for generating malignant social conditions. A credible and balanced account of the experience of dementia will be more valuable to people with the condition than a perspective that undermines carers, potentially rendering relational conditions even more challenging. This article has shown how the application of incremental analytical focus to (socially-framed) subjective perspectives and interaction can inform an academic understanding that neither prioritises one person's account over the other, nor conflates individual viewpoints under a shared 'us' identity.

Acknowledgement

The authors would like to thank Mark Lovatt at Staffordshire University for his comments on earlier drafts of this article.

Notes

1 While the term 'carer' is used in this article, it is acknowledged that this term should be used with caution, as it implies the relationship is defined by a carer/cared-for dynamic (Bartlett and O'Connor 2010).
2 A further two carers were interviewed on a one-to-one basis, as their partners did not have the mental capacity to take part.
3 The names of the interviewees have been changed.
4 Ethical clearance for this research was granted by an NHS Research Ethics Committee.
5 An ellipsis in square brackets highlights that some text has been removed from an interview excerpt. This is to aid the presentation of the findings and does not alter the basis of expressed perspectives, or interactions.

References

Alzheimer's Society (2015) What is young-onset dementia? Available at http://www.alzheimers.org.uk/site/scripts/documents_info.php?documentID=164. (Last accessed 15 April 2016).
Archer, M. (1995) *Realist Social Theory: The Morphogenetic Approach*. Cambridge: Cambridge University Press.
Baldwin, C. (2005) Narrative, ethics and people with severe mental illness, *Australian and New Zealand Journal of Psychiatry*, 39, 11–12, 1022–9.
Baldwin, C. and Capstick, A. (eds) (2007) *Tom Kitwood on Dementia: A Reader and Critical Commentary*. Maidenhead: Open University Press.
Bartlett, R. and O'Connor, D. (2010) *Broadening the Dementia Debate: Towards Social Citizenship*. Bristol: The Policy Press.
Bauman, Z. (2011) *Collateral Damage: Social Inequalities in a Global Age*. Cambridge: Polity Press.
Bowlby, S., McKie, L., Gregory, S. and MacPherson, I. (2010) *Interdependency and Care over the Lifecourse*. London: Routledge.
Bury, M. (1982) Chronic illness as biographical disruption, *Sociology of Health & Illness*, 4, 2, 167–82.
Charmaz, K. (1994) Identity dilemmas of chronically ill men, *The Sociological Quarterly*, 35, 2, 269–88.
Clare, L. and Shakespeare, P. (2004) Negotiating the impact of forgetting: dimensions of resistance in task-oriented conversations between people with early-stage dementia and their partners, *Dementia*, 3, 2, 211–32.
Clarke, A. and Friese, C. (2007) Grounded theorizing using situational analysis. In Bryant, A. and Charmaz, K. (eds) *The Sage Handbook of Grounded Theory*. London: Sage.
Clemerson, G., Walsh, S. and Isaac, C. (2014) Towards Living Well with Young Onset Dementia: an Exploration of Coping from the Perspective of Those Diagnosed, *Dementia*, 13, 4, 451–66.
Coston, B. and Kimmel, M. (2013) Aging men, masculinity and Alzheimer's: caretaking and caregiving in the new millennium. In Kampf, A., Marshall, B. and Petersen, A. (eds) *Aging Men, Masculinities and Modern Medicine*. London: Routledge.
Davies, J.C. (2011) Preserving the 'us identity' through marriage commitment while living with earlystage dementia, *Dementia*, 10, 2, 217–234.
Davis, D.H. (2004) Dementia: sociological and philosophical constructions, *Social Science & Medicine*, 58, 2, 369–78.

Dean, H. and Rogers, R. (2004) Popular discourses of dependency, responsibility and rights. In Dean, H. (ed) *The Ethics of Welfare: Human Rights, Dependency and Responsibility*. Bristol: The Policy Press.

Department of Health (2009) *Living Well with Dementia: A National Dementia Strategy*. London: DH Publications.

Gilligan, C. (1982) *In a Different Voice: Psychological Theory and Women's Development*. Cambridge, MA: Harvard University Press.

Greco, M. (2009) On the art of life: a vitalist reading of medical humanities, *The Sociological Review*, 56, 2, 25–45.

Hellstrom, I., Nolan, M. and Lundh, U. (2007) Sustaining 'couplehood': spouses' strategies for living positively with dementia, *Dementia*, 6, 3, 383–409.

Higgs, P. and Gilleard, C. (2015) *Rethinking Old Age: Theorising the Fourth Age*. London: Palgrave.

Higgs, P. and Jones, I.R. (2009) *Medical Sociology and Old Age: Towards a Sociology of Health in Later Life*. London: Routledge.

Hydén, L.-C. and Nilsson, E. (2015) Couples with dementia: positioning the 'we', *Dementia*, 14, 6, 716–33.

Innes, A. (2009) *Dementia Studies: A Social Science Perspective*. London: Sage.

Keady, J. and Burrow, S. (2015) Quality of life for persons with dementia living in the community. In Kazer, M.W. and Murphy, K. (eds) *Nursing Case Studies on Improving Health-Related Quality of Life in Older Adults*. New York: Springer Publishing.

Keady, J. and Nolan, M. (2003) The dynamics of dementia: working together, working separately, or working alone? In Nolan, M., Lundh, U., Grant, G. and Keady, J. (eds) *Partnerships in Family Care: Understanding the Caregiving Career*. Maidenhead: Open University Press.

Kitwood, T. (1990) The dialectics of dementia: with particular reference to Alzheimer's disease, *Ageing & Society*, 10, 2, 177–96.

Kitwood, T. (1997) *Dementia Reconsidered: The Person Comes First*. Buckingham: Open University Press.

La Fontaine, J. and Oyebode, J. (2014) Family relationships and dementia: a synthesis of qualitative research including the person with dementia, *Ageing & Society*, 34, 7, 1243–72.

MacRae, H. (2008) Making the best you can of it: living with early-stage Alzheimer's disease, *Sociology of Health & Illness*, 30, 3, 396–412.

Molyneaux, V., Butchard, S., Simpson, J. and Murray, C. (2012) The co-construction of couplehood in dementia, *Dementia*, 11, 4, 483–502.

O'Connor, D. (1995) Caring for a memory-impaired spouse, *Journal of Women and Aging*, 7, 3, 25–42.

Paoletti, I. (2002) Caring for older people: a gendered practice, *Discourse & Society*, 13, 6, 805–17.

Phinney, A., Dahlke, S. and Purves, B. (2013) Shifting patterns of everyday activity in early dementia: experiences of men and their families, *Journal of Family Nursing*, 19, 3, 348–74.

Pickard, S. (2010) The 'good carer': moral practices in late modernity, *Sociology*, 44, 3, 471–87.

Post, S. (2000) *The Moral Challenge of Alzheimer Disease: Ethical Issues from Diagnosis to Dying*, 2nd edn. Baltimore, MD: Johns Hopkins University Press.

Quinn, C., Clare, L. and Woods, R. (2015) Balancing needs: the role of motivations, meanings and relationship dynamics in the experience of informal caregivers of people with dementia, *Dementia*, 14, 2, 220–37.

Riessman, C.K. (2008) *Narrative Methods for the Human Sciences*. London: Sage.

Robinson, L., Clare, L. and Evans, K. (2005) Making sense of dementia and adjusting to loss: psychological reactions to a diagnosis of dementia in couples, *Aging & Mental Health*, 9, 4, 337–47.

Sabat, S., Johnson, A., Swarbrick, C. and Keady, J. (2011) The 'demented other' or simply 'a person'? extending the philosophical discourse of Naue and Kroll through the situated self, *Nursing Philosophy*, 12, 4, 282–92.

Shakespeare, T. (2000) *Help*. Birmingham: Venture Press.

Shim, B., Barroso, J. and Davis, L. (2012) A comparative qualitative analysis of stories of spousal caregivers of people with dementia: negative, ambivalent and positive experiences, *International Journal of Nursing Studies*, 49, 2, 220–29.

Squire, C., Andrews, M. and Tamboukou, M. (2008) Introduction: what is narrative research? In Andrews, M., Squire, C. and Tamboukou, M. (eds) *Doing Narrative Research*, 2nd edn. London: Sage.

Sullivan, P. (2012) *Qualitative Data Analysis: Using a Dialogical Approach*. London: Sage.

Tanner, D. (2013) Identity, selfhood and dementia: messages for social work, *European Journal of Social Work*, 16, 2, 155–70.

Tronto, J. (1993) *Moral Boundaries: A Political Argument for an Ethic of Care*. London: Routledge.

Twigg, J. (1997) Deconstructing the 'social bath': help with bathing at home for older and disabled people, *Journal of Social Policy*, 26, 2, 211–32.

Ungerson, C. (2000) Thinking about the production and consumption of long-term care in Britain: does gender still matter? *Journal of Social Policy*, 29, 4, 623–43.

Walters, A.H., Oyebode, J. and Riley, G. (2010) The dynamics of continuity and discontinuity for women caring for a spouse with dementia, *Dementia*, 9, 2, 169–89.

Weicht, B. (2011) Embracing dependency: rethinking (in)dependence in the discourse of care, *The Sociological Review*, 58, 2, 205–24.

Weicht, B. (2015) *The Meaning of Care: The Social Construction of Care for Elderly People*. Basingstoke: Palgrave Macmillan.

Williams, S.J., Higgs, P. and Katz, S. (2012) Neuroculture, active ageing and the 'older brain': problems, promises and prospects, *Sociology of Health & Illness*, 34, 1, 64–78.

5

Power, empowerment, and person-centred care: using ethnography to examine the everyday practice of unregistered dementia care staff

Kezia Scales, Simon Bailey, Joanne Middleton and Justine Schneider

Introduction

An estimated 46 million people currently live with dementia worldwide, and this number is projected to rise to 131.5 million by 2050 (ADI 2015). This means that a significant proportion of older adults receiving care across medical and residential care settings have dementia; for example, one quarter of National Health Service (NHS) beds are used by patients with dementia (RCP 2013), and more than 60 per cent of care home residents have dementia (Knapp *et al.* 2007). Dementia is caused by a number of underlying pathologies and is associated with progressive impairment across the domains of learning and memory, attention, executive function, language and communication, perceptual-motor function, and social cognition. Historically, persons with dementia have been socially positioned in terms of their increasing impairments and treated primarily as dependent bodies requiring management and care (Innes 2002, Sabat 2001) or, worse, as 'empty shells' (Bryden 2005) enduring a 'living death' (Woods 1989).

'Person-centred care' challenges the stigmatised social positioning of persons with dementia and the associated, depersonalising care they receive (Kitwood 1997). Related to a wider movement to improve patients' and service users' care experiences and outcomes through increased engagement in assessment and treatment decisions (Harding *et al.* 2015), personcentred care emphasises the preservation of choice and dignity through specific care strategies. These strategies include privileging the individual's preferences over organisational demands, for instance with regard to meals, bedtimes, occupational activities, and decor. In the long-term care sector, and particularly in nursing homes in the United States, person-centred care has been adopted as a central component of 'culture change', which is aimed at transforming nursing homes from medicalised, routine-driven institutions to personalised, home-like settings where care is organised around each individual, regardless of their cognitive or functional capacity (Koren 2010).

Person-centred approaches place new responsibilities on health-care providers to proactively elicit and address individuals' preferences and goals for care (AGS 2016), rather than imposing their own. Person-centred care places particular responsibility on direct-care staff[1] to facilitate opportunities for choice and independence rather than prioritising tasks and routines (Fetherstonhaugh *et al.* 2016).[2] Most notably in long-term care settings in the United States, this responsibility has been framed as 'empowerment' of these otherwise marginalised workers (Bowers and Nolet 2011, Chalfont and Hafford-Letchfield 2010). It has been

Ageing, Dementia and the Social Mind, First Edition. Edited by Paul Higgs and Chris Gilleard.
Chapters © 2017 The Authors. Book Compilation © 2017 Foundation for the Sociology of
Health & Illness/Blackwell Publishing Ltd.

operationalised in a number of ways, including through enhanced autonomy for care staff in daily decisions, their increased participation in formal care-planning processes, and the introduction of consistent assignment to facilitate communication and relationship-building between staff and care recipients (Barry *et al.* 2005, Caspar *et al.* 2009, Castle 2011).

There is some evidence to suggest that attempts to empower frontline staff have had positive impacts on job satisfaction and job retention, as staff feel more valued, respected, and heard (Banaszak-Holl and Hines 1996, Kostiwa and Meeks 2009); on the provision of individualised care (Caspar and O'Rourke 2008); and on family members' perceptions of service quality (Hamann 2014). However, other studies have highlighted the limitations of empowerment in the broader context of care delivery; for example, one longitudinal study of an intervention to empower certified nursing assistants (CNAs) in five nursing homes in the United States found generally positive effects on absenteeism and turnover, but mixed effects on job performance and attitude due to the competing priorities involved (such as attending meetings versus providing direct care) and inconsistent recognition of their empowerment by nursing leadership (Yeatts and Cready 2007).

A key challenge is that empowerment has been conceptualised and implemented inconsistently and with limited analysis of the mechanisms by which it operates (Bowers and Nolet 2011, Harding *et al.* 2015). Notably missing is an understanding of how the empowerment of direct-care workers (as implied or explicitly required by different person-centred approaches) aligns with their broader disempowerment as a workforce which carries out the 'dirty work' delegated by professional nurses, with little training, remuneration, or opportunity for advancement (Kessler *et al.* 2015, Twigg 2000). Further, the majority of evidence on empowerment focuses on direct-care workers in nursing/care homes who care for residents with a range of complex clinical and social care needs. Less attention has been given to the empowerment of direct-care staff who work exclusively with people with dementia in acute settings – despite recognition of the potential benefits of person-centred dementia care beyond long-term care (Goldberg *et al.* 2013, Webster 2011).

This article will contribute to efforts to advance the provision of person-centred dementia care by examining the notion of empowerment within a Foucauldian understanding of power and knowledge (Foucault 1982), with reference to empirical data. Our specific aim is to determine whether a Foucauldian approach can help us better understand and conceptualise directcare workers' empowerment in the context of dementia care. Drawing on fieldnotes and interview data from ethnographic studies of three dementia wards in the National Health Service (NHS) and one dementia care unit in a private care home, we examine whether Foucault's notion of power as relational and productive helps explain how staff constitute, and are constituted by, the relations of power in these settings. We begin by describing power in Foucauldian terms before presenting the empirical findings in a three-section narrative which describes the relatively disempowered positioning of care staff, their negotiation of this positioning, and the implications for their practical accomplishment of daily care. We conclude with a discussion of how our reading of the data through a Foucauldian lens can help inform and expand efforts to empower staff in ways that improve quality of care for persons with dementia without undermining job satisfaction or other outcomes.

Power, knowledge, and legitimacy

To examine how direct-care staff experience and engage with their own empowerment/ disempowerment in the dementia care context, we start with Foucault's conceptualisation of power. Foucault (1984: 292) suggests that power is both 'relational' and 'productive':

relational because it is present in all human relationships, whether 'amorous, institutional, or economic', and productive because, rather than merely repressing, it also produces or enables particular ways of being (while disabling others). Underpinning this conceptualisation is the essential connection between power and knowledge: 'there is no power relation without the correlative constitution of a field of knowledge, nor any knowledge that does not presuppose and constitute at the same time power relations' (Foucault 1977: 27). According to Foucault, power/knowledge constitutes both what we are as subjects and what we know as objects of knowledge. The task of analysis, therefore, is to focus not on how one person or group wields power over another, but by what tools, techniques, and technologies power relations work 'through and upon individuals' (O'Malley 1996: 189).

Foucault (1977) identifies 'discipline' as a key mechanism by which power works through and upon individuals. Discipline has two closely linked meanings: first, discipline is a set of practices enacted upon the body or a group of bodies, including surveillance, distribution, and segregation. Second, a discipline is a body of knowledge that develops from the application of such techniques. At the heart of disciplinary power is 'normalisation', understood as the creation of norms against which 'individual uniqueness can be recognized, characterized and then standardized' (O'Malley, 1996: 189). Of particular relevance to this article is the mobilisation of these normalising forces within institutions, such as hospitals and 'asylums' as well as prisons, schools, and army barracks. Foucault (1981: 10) defined institutions as the 'crystallisations' over time of programmes of disciplinary power exercised to address specific problems. Dementia, as an example, can be understood as a category by which older persons who exhibit particular, 'problematic' signs and symptoms are defined and socially positioned through the disciplinary forces of power. Over time, as the disease progresses, they are likely to be moved into institutions (Alzheimer's Society 2007), in which their aberrant behaviour can be supervised and 'normalised' through caregiving routines and/or medication (Hyde *et al.* 2014, May 1992).

Foucault's account suggests that the social order which crystallises in institutions is both 'taken for granted' and, at the same time, highly fragile, contingent, and contestable. Institutional theorists following Foucault have developed the idea that there are micro-processes of both 'structuration' and 'destructuration', or deinstitutionalisation, thereby inherent in any process of institutionalisation (Clegg 2010). This strand of institutional theory suggests that the extent to which significant change may occur within institutions, however, is constrained by the formation of 'legitimate' ways of knowing and doing which preclude alternative possibilities for action. By bringing the concept of 'legitimacy' back to Foucault's dynamic notion of power/knowledge, we can consider the conditions under which particular 'legitimate' ways of knowing and doing become possible. We can then consider 'legitimacy' as the emergent property of ongoing conflict between different ways of ordering the world which are temporarily stabilised 'when it becomes the norm for authorities to structure institutions and actions relative to that order' (Clegg 2010: 5). From this perspective, change is not only possible but inevitable, as the struggle for legitimacy is never fully resolved; the degree and direction of change, however, is always contingent upon existing relations of power. To enact change, individuals or groups must act in 'entrepreneurial' (Clegg 2010) ways that not only diverge from the norm but question its very legitimacy. Following Foucault's (1980a: 141) view that an individual can never hold a position 'outside' power relations, the notion of institutional entrepreneurs does not suggest 'hypermuscular agency' (Clegg 2010: 5) on the part of individuals or groups, but it does help draw attention to the creative, opportunistic, and risky acts designed to temporarily 'escape' or 'disengage' power (Foucault 1980b: 138).

Through this lens, we can see that 'person-centred care', as a discourse inscribed in policy and practice, aims to disrupt the institutional order which positions persons with dementia as beyond cure or hope by promoting instead their personhood and capacity for self-expression. In this paper, we consider how Foucauldian notions of power/knowledge and institutional-isation help us understand the position and practices of the staff who are responsible for directly providing dementia care and who are, in principle, 'empowered' to enact person-centred care. Considering the idea that power works 'through and upon individuals', the analysis that follows is guided by two broad questions: first, in what ways are care staff and their work shaped by disciplinary techniques in these settings (Brijnath and Manderson 2008, St Pierre and Holmes 2008), and second, what are the implications of this understanding of power for analysing attempts to empower staff and transform institutionalised patterns of care?

Research design and methods

The analysis presented here draws primarily from a multi-sited ethnographic study of the challenges and rewards experienced by healthcare assistants (HCAs) working in hospital-based dementia assessment and treatment wards. Contrasting evidence is drawn from a sec-ond study of knowledge translation about person-centred care in long-term care homes. The first study was conducted in 2008–2009 by the authors across three wards within one mental health trust in the East Midlands of England, which we have called Wards A, B and C: Ward A (24 beds) was an assessment ward located within a large urban teaching hospital; Ward B (13 beds) was a specialist 'challenging behaviour' unit in a small suburban hospital; and Ward C (10 beds) was another assessment unit in a rural community hospital. From these wards, most patients were referred or returned to care homes, while a minority returned to the com-munity. The second study was conducted in 2011–2012 by KS in a specialist, 20-bed demen-tia unit ('Vintage Vale') within a 65-bed skilled nursing and residential care home ('Forest Lodge') located in the East Midlands, which was owned by a large corporate provider.[3] The main aim of the second study was to describe how ideas about person-centred care translated (or failed to translate) into frontline care practices in long-term care settings.

As 'active participants' (Spradley 1980) in both studies, the researchers undertook the required training for care assistants in each setting – namely, a four-day NHS induction and a two-day course on 'managing violence and aggression' for the HCA study and a half-day 'moving and handling' training at Forest Lodge – before providing hands-on assistance with the full range of direct care, including bathing, dressing, toilet/incontinence care, mobil-ity and meals. The researchers in the first study spent four months each on their assigned ward, completing an average of three eight-hour shifts per week of participant observa-tion as supernumerary care assistants. On Vintage Vale, KS completed approximately two months of participant observation, again adhering to a part-time shift pattern across the day, evening, and overnight shifts. In addition, in-depth interviews were conducted in both studies with care assistants, nurses, managers and administrators (35 across the three NHS wards, eight on Vintage Vale). Prior to the start of fieldwork in both studies, members of the research team introduced the research at staff meetings and placed posters within view of staff, residents, and visitors. In the first study, the research question was described in terms of the experiences, challenges, and rewards of the HCA role in dementia care; in the sec-ond study, KS described her interest in how staff acquire, apply, and share knowledge and expertise related to direct care in nursing homes. Direct-care staff were asked to give their consent to be included in the researchers' written observations, and those who participated in interviews were asked to provide separate informed consent. Although fully participat-ing as members of the care team, the researchers maintained transparency about the reason for their presence in the field through conversation and informal 'member checking' of their emerging findings with staff while on shift.

Observations were recorded as brief 'jottings' (Emerson *et al.* 1995) on shift and converted into full-length fieldnotes thereafter. Taking an inductive approach, the research team for the first study began by collaboratively analysing the fieldnotes and interview transcripts through line-by-line coding, then built these open codes into themes; examples included routines, challenging behaviour, humour, and the team. (See Scales *et al.* (2011) for a more detailed discussion of this study's methodology.) KS followed the same process to analyse the data-set from the second study. In developing this manuscript, KS and SB reanalysed both data-sets in order to draw out comparisons between them with regards to the issues of power, positioning, and individualised care.

Formal ethical approval was granted for the HCA study by the local Research Ethics Committee and for the care home study by the School of Sociology and Social Policy at the University of Nottingham and the research-governance committee of Forest Lodge.

Findings

Guided by Foucault's concept of disciplinary power, we examine in the following sections how care assistants experienced but also actively engaged with their subject positioning within these dementia care settings, thereby generating new, albeit limited, possibilities for action.

'Only a carer'

As discussed in the Introduction, person-centred approaches place considerable responsibility on direct-care staff to promote the personhood of individual patients/residents. Such increased responsibility implies an 'empowered' workforce who are able to act creatively and autonomously to facilitate opportunities for choice, self-expression, and social engagement. The evidence from the two studies described in this article suggests that the experience of empowerment for our participants was not clear-cut, but rather characterised by conflict and negotiation. In contrast to feeling empowered, participants from both settings more often expressed a sense of being undervalued and disregarded. 'I have actually been told "you're a shit shoveller", well, I'm not', reported an HCA from Ward A.[4] She went on to say that HCAs 'deserve respect as well [as nurses], and sometimes we don't get that'. HCAs often expressed this lack of respect as a reflection of the marginalisation of their patients. One HCA from Ward C asserted that dementia care was the 'poor relation of the health service ... because they're elderly and they're mentally ill, nothing gets done'.

Care staff referred in particular to their lack of input into decisions about the organisation and delivery of care. This sense of exclusion related also to communication of information about patient/resident needs and generated considerable frustration among care staff. According to an HCA from Ward C: 'sometimes we don't get that respect, we don't get seen, we can pass things on and it's "what would you know?" ... You can pass it on again, and again, and you never know all the time if it's been picked up on'. This and similar comments about feeling ignored or invisible indicate carers' limited capacity to act, due to their perceived lack of voice or impact. As one HCA said about attempts to raise concerns: 'you relay your views, it filters through ... but, you just think, "you're not really listening to what I'm trying to say"... we're all feeling the same and yet we're in the same situation, no change has been made'. The picture that emerged here was not consistent with empowerment in relation to communication and decision-making within these care settings.

To some extent, Forest Lodge presented a contrast to the NHS wards in terms of engagement and empowerment. All care assistants on Vintage Vale participated in person-centred dementia care training which emphasised their influential role in promoting residents' personhood. Day-to-day, they participated actively in handover with qualified nurses or gave their own shift reports and they were encouraged to contribute directly to residents' care notes and to collaborate in the organisation of daily care and activities.

However, the scope of their input remained limited. The practice of writing notes had quickly stalled because it was not considered an essential element of the carers' role; that is, staff were not required to write notes nor evaluated for doing so. We observed that some carers who started working after the practice of note-taking had been discontinued were uncertain about whether they were authorised to even read the notes. Even when they had been writing notes, the carers felt constrained about what they were allowed to write. In the following fieldnote, KS paraphrases a conversation that she had with one care assistant about writing notes:

> [The care assistant said] mind you, you're not allowed to put negative things in, though, so it's a matter of choosing your words. I [KS] asked for an example, and she said 'for our residents who wander', you're not allowed to say they wander, say instead that they're 'exploring their environment'.

Paradoxically, the emphasis on using person-centred language may have limited the carers' capacity to express, in their own words, what they had witnessed, experienced, or addressed, which may have had negative consequences for their feelings of empowerment.

Like the HCAs, care assistants on Vintage Vale also expressed a general sense of exclusion from decisions about care, including formal assessment and care-planning processes. One care assistant talked about being a 'lowly employee' on the 'lower rung of it all', linking this status to low reimbursement and job insecurity. Another said that progress towards achieving personcentred practices on the unit had been undermined by recent leadership changes, which she expressed as 'rumblings with management' which had compromised care quality. She qualified her comments with disclaimers, however, such as 'it's just my opinion' and 'what do I know? I'm only a carer!' Another carer made a similar point: '[W]e worked our arses off to get it to the unit that it was then, now we feel like our work's just completely gone out the window'.

The fieldnote below, in which KS summarises a conversation that took place on Ward A, illustrates how HCAs characterised their 'lowly' status in us/them terms:

> [The HCAs were talking about how] 'nobody gets it': nobody from outside Ward A understands what it's like to work here … they don't really even talk about their work to their partners, and if they have a bruise or mark from one of the patients, they'll dismiss it as an accident – because 'they don't understand what it's like here'.

The notion that 'nobody gets it' sometimes included managers and other health-care professionals as well as outsiders. As an HCA from Ward B explained: '[managers] don't understand, how can they understand when they're sat in an office? Not just managers here, even these people that come up with these surveys … how can they know?' Similarly, on Ward C, an HCA referred to the modern matron (a registered nurse who holds supervisory responsibility over an area of care) as someone who 'waltzes in', lives in a 'fairy world', and 'has no idea of what the ward actually needs … just wants it all to be pretty and lovely'. This discourse suggests that carers perceived that their work was largely unseen and unappreciated.

In summary, across both settings the dementia care staff referred to feeling unseen, unheard, overlooked, or dismissed. However, their acknowledgement of this subject positioning did not constitute unreflective acceptance; rather, they actively attempted to negotiate it through a number of strategies, as discussed in the next section.

'We're the ones that see it'
The carers challenged their marginalisation through careful maintenance of a strong collective identity. This can be read as an effort to reposition themselves in the power relations characterising each care setting, thereby opening up new opportunities for action. Central to this repositioning was the carers' claim to superior – but largely unrecognised – experience and expertise. In other words, the care staff based their collective identity on the claim that, notwithstanding their lack of formal authority or recognition, they exercised informal authority over patient care and the ward environment. 'I think that the running of the ward is down to the HCAs mainly', said an HCA from Ward B in an interview. 'I'm not just saying that because I'm an HCA – it's because we understand the patients a lot better than management do because we're hands-on. We know exactly what's going on'. A carer from Vintage Vale made a similar point:

> We're the ones that see [residents] on a day-to-day basis, we're the ones that … know what hurts us, what hurts them, what's best for them, what's not best for them. Although the nurses have the authority, they don't always see it, you know, we're the ones.

In this and many other examples, carers explicitly challenged the dominant biomedical discourse which positioned them as less knowledgeable or expert relative to nurses and other health-care professionals.

These strategies for repositioning themselves appeared, to some extent, protective and productive for the care staff. They were protective in the face of alternate, stigmatising objectifications (as described in the previous section), and they were productive because care staff drew on this alternate discourse of authority to act in 'empowered' ways, more or less overtly challenging the formal limits of their role. One HCA from Ward A, for example, talked about working beyond her job description, saying 'why as care assistants we can't take what we're capable of doing off [nurses], you know, it's not their fault that we're not paid to do that'. The implications of this productive repositioning will be discussed further in the next section.

Paradoxically, the strategies by which carers challenged their position in the social order also served to reinforce the occupational boundaries which delineated their exclusion from broader relations of multidisciplinary teamwork. That is, maintaining a favourable us/them distinction required carers to devalue the expertise or contribution of others, to a certain extent. This was indicated by their criticism of nurses who 'shut themselves in the office' rather than providing bedside care (Ward C); overt scepticism of medical expertise, expressed as 'the white coat fallacy' (Ward B); and censure of co-workers who crossed the boundary line, as with the HCA who was labelled a 'brown-noser' for waving to a consultant in the corridor (Ward A). The implication is that carers' own efforts to maintain their occupational boundaries may have contributed to their exclusion from the interdisciplinary communication of information which is required for effective care. (For a further discussion of the HCAs' in-group identity and interprofessional working, see Lloyd *et al.* (2011)).

Maintaining their occupational boundaries further limited the HCAs' opportunity for participation in collective, multidisciplinary reflection. This helps explain practices that were observed to be individualised but not necessarily person-centred. For example, on Ward A, there was a patient who was known for her loud and repetitive vocalisations. The type of individualised attention that she received as a result was noticeably non-person-centred, as suggested by this fieldnote:

> As we were talking, the patient came up to the table and began speaking to the HCAs in a loud voice. One HCA dismissed her quite sharply, then turned to say to me [KS] that 'you just have to ignore this one – because otherwise she just gets worse'.

Although the carers were 'empowered' to see and interpret this patient's behaviour in individualised ways, their interpretation (without the benefit of collective, interdisciplinary reflection) led to the reproduction of disciplinary power rather than promotion of the patient's personhood. Other examples included open discussions of individuals' anatomy, disposition, habits or proclivities, or sensitive details of their personal history – making them visible as persons (not just patients/residents) but without promoting the dignity that underpins personhood.

We also found evidence that maintaining an exclusive claim to the experience of providing dementia care risked obscuring problematic aspects of the work. One aspect was the prevalence of physical injury, which carers largely interpreted as an element of their occupational experience and identity rather than a problem. When KS was scratched during one of her first shifts on Ward A, one HCA remarked to another 'she's a real HCA now!' – indicating that learning to tolerate violence was a rite of passage from novice to expert. An HCA from Ward C reflected: 'it just becomes normal for them to boot, kick you, punch you and I think "oh you've done it again"'. Whether that's a good thing or a bad thing, I don't know'. This comment suggests the dual implications of the caregivers' claims to superior insight and expertise: being the only 'ones who see it' promoted their occupational identity and value, but may have also undermined the opportunity to identify and addresses the risks and challenges of their role.

In the first section, we suggested that the dementia care staff were constituted by the prevailing relations of power as low-skill, low-wage workers with minimal influence. Here, we have demonstrated how they re-engaged power to claim a different position characterised by informal authority over direct care and the treatment environment. We described the protective and productive implications and highlighted some potentially divisive consequences. In the next section, we examine the possibilities for action that became available through this repositioning, focusing on the provision of individualised care (as central to person-centred care) within the institutional setting.

'Knowing, watching and understanding'

The carers' claim to authority and expertise, as described above, hinged largely on their extensive knowledge of each patient/resident as an individual, articulated in comparison to nurses who spent more time on 'paperwork' and other health-care professionals who visited infrequently. While such individualised knowledge can be misused, as noted above, it is nonetheless fundamental to person-centred dementia care, as expressed by this HCA from Ward B:

> [T]here is a big difference in people with dementia; it's knowing, watching and understanding the parts of the illness and the different behaviours ... it's just treating people with respect, with individuality.

Other respondents made similar comments such as 'it's getting to know them, isn't it, every patient's an individual' (Ward C) and 'they are still people at the end of the day, aren't they, even if they are severely impaired ... it's all about their individual choice ... you have got to give them as much choice or option as possible' (Ward A). They also highlighted individual needs and preferences when modelling the provision of personal care, as described in the following fieldnote from Ward A:

> [The HCA] moved slowly and deliberately but with confidence as she removed the bloodsoaked dressing, washed the wound, and applied fresh bandages. She was also careful to tell me exactly what to do, and to point out the patient's preferences; e.g. she prefers not to wear the net knickers because they are too tight, she prefers to leave her upper body and feet uncovered by the sheet, etc.

The following interview excerpt from Ward B illustrates how staff operationalised an individualised approach to care:

> One patient was so used to going to work, he still believes that he should be working, he doesn't realise that he's retired … so he still gets up in the morning thinking he's going to work and we'd say 'no, you're not going to work' so … well, it was my idea actually, [we started] a rota where we give him a specific task to do and he did it and it did work … So we try each day and see which mood he's in, if he moans about his work we give him little jobs to do and if he don't, then we leave it.

In this example, the carers attempted to redirect the confusion and frustration of the patient into an activity that would be productive and satisfying for him, although still within institutional parameters related to routines and responsibilities.

On Vintage Vale, carers also pursued strategies to personalise residents' care within institutional parameters; one carer referred to this as being 'interchangeable', depending on the day, each resident's mood, and so on, and another expressed it as following a 'non-routine routine', balancing individual preferences against clinical standards of care. Echoing the example from Ward B (above), in this interview excerpt a care assistant discusses how she organised daily care around individual preferences and medical needs, taking personal history into account:

> I've tried to think of … a balance between things, for example, I try to get Leo up early because Leo's diabetic, and I feel that … to sleep in is not very good for his diabetes, and I think that that affects his moods as well … he is an early riser, because that's always been his routine, when he was working.

The carer went on to describe other residents' morning routines in similar detail, concluding that 'all these things are running through my mind while I'm also on the floor working'.

Furthermore, there was also evidence of strategic efforts to break rules that were perceived as antithetical to individualised or person-centred care. The 'Dining Experience' programme at Forest Lodge provides a good example. Although promoted by the corporate provider as an alternative to conventional, depersonalising institutional mealtimes, the Dining Experience was perceived by care staff as a top-down mandate that sometimes restricted, rather than facilitated, their ability to personalise care. For example, as shown in the following fieldnote, the rules mandated that meals were served one course at a time, but carers made an exception for a resident who chose to eat in his bedroom:

> [The care assistant] took the resident's lunch tray to him, then came back saying, 'I took both courses together but made sure to say loudly as I went in, 'here's your soup and main course together, [Resident], just the way you like it!' – because the nurse was in the office nearby.

Although it may have also saved time, this strategic transgression was framed in terms of promoting the preferences of the individual. As another example, a care assistant from Vintage Vale talked about resisting messages about 'efficiency' that he felt contradicted person-centred care:

> I've refused to, in any sense, try to become more efficient, in inverted commas – I still take the time I think it takes. And if [the care home management] don't like that, I think morally I'm on the high ground, and they're not.

This same carer also openly admitted to small transgressions, such as applying skin cream without using gloves, to preserve the resident's dignity, as described in the following fieldnote:

> [The care assistant] explained that 'you're probably supposed to use gloves' but spreading it on with latex 'just doesn't seem very nice'; adding that some rules were so risk-averse that he preferred to just bypass them and do what made sense to him, 'as long as you're careful'.

However, these efforts to individualise care were limited by the parameters of the existing institutional order. One HCA from Ward C described the limits of her ability to adapt morning care:

> I don't agree that they should be up for half past 8. If that patient wants to stay in bed, that patient should be able to stay in bed. Where's the patient individuality? ... I tried to talk this out with the deputy manager, and got bawled out ... I mean, she's saying 'it's patient care' and 'you're not doing your job', but you are doing your job.

This example represents the HCA's struggle for autonomy and ownership over direct care, which as discussed is a key source of empowerment for this workforce – but from a disempowered position.

In summary, this empirical analysis has explored how the possible actions of direct-care staff were shaped by their subject positioning within the relations of power characterising different dementia care settings in the UK. The first section ('only a carer') explored carers' general experience of 'powerlessness' rather than 'empowerment'. The second section ('we're the ones that see it') suggested, however, that care staff attempted to negotiate this marginalised subject positioning by collectively claiming a privileged, if largely unrecognised, perspective on the experiences and challenges of dementia care. This renegotiation had mixed implications: although opening up new possibilities for 'empowered' action, it also risked perpetuating the carers' marginalised role. The third section ('knowing, watching, and understanding') looked further at these possibilities for action, exploring in particular how carers undertook the challenge of individualising care, in more or less subversive ways. In the next section, we discuss these findings in terms of Foucault's conception of power and the person-centred discourse of empowerment, drawing out implications for policy and practice change.

Discussion

As described in the Introduction, person-centred dementia care challenges the stigmatised social positioning of persons with dementia by emphasising their enduring capacity for selfexpression and social engagement and their right to dignity, respect, and choice. This denotes a shift away from routinised and task-oriented care practices in formal organisational settings. In Foucauldian terms, the person-centred discourse thus challenges the dominant power/knowledge regime that positions those with dementia according to a master narrative of inevitable decline, which has previously led to practices of containment and management (Sabat 2008). Person-centred care thereby also challenges the marginal status of those who provide dementia care: no longer unskilled labourers providing custodial care for persons with diminished personhood, care staff are credited with the capacity to directly facilitate (or undermine) personcentred outcomes. For example, in Kitwood's (1997) influential work on personhood in dementia, care staff carry the weight of responsibility for creating positive or malignant social psychology through their 'enabling' versus 'detracting' actions and behaviours; this implies much more than 'basic' care. This aspect of person-centred care is cast, more or less explicitly, in terms of the 'empowering' of the direct-care workforce to improve outcomes through more flexible, personalised caregiving techniques. The Foucauldian perspective suggests that becoming empowered in this sense entails more than individual-level practice change; rather, it entails a challenge to the immediate and extended relations of power that inform current, taken-for-granted ways of working in this context of care.

In the first section of empirical findings, we saw limited evidence that the 'destructuration' (Clegg 2010) implied by staff empowerment had actually been achieved; rather, participants clearly expressed a sense of enduring disempowerment. Taking a broader view, we can see that their disempowerment is produced and maintained through various 'technologies' of the formal organisation that are distinct from the discourse of person-centred care; for example, their contractual status defines their low occupational status, low pay, and limited opportunities for training, and links to their lack of involvement in formal assessment and care-planning processes.

Nonetheless, the second empirical section suggested that care assistants engaged in collective attempts to resist their marginalised position by promoting their skilled contribution to care. These attempts at resistance could be described as 'institutional entrepreneurship', which Clegg (2010: 10) defines as 'a strategic face of power reliant on skilled analysis, deployments, and coordination grounded in local knowledge with which to outflank dominant actors with superior resources'. In Foucauldian terms, this collective entrepreneurship is an important response to disciplinary power, which operates through processes of separation, division, and segregation. The care assistants' deployment of their ownership of 'basic care' is a prominent example. Although this ownership was linked to their structural disempowerment (as the 'dirty workers' who take on tasks relinquished by professional nurses), within the caring environment it also represented an important resource from which to develop a stronger and more autonomous (or 'empowered') occupational identity. Konrad (2011: 53) describes the development of 'group consciousness' among direct-care workers in the United States in a similar way: 'the members of this occupational group mutually recognise each other, positively affirm their own and each other's worth, and widely empathize with their fellows as participants in certain common tasks, among which are the securing of public recognition as members of an invigorated group that possesses and demonstrates collective agency'. For the HCAs on the dementia care wards, part of this collective effort involved identifying their marginalised status with that of their patients/residents, as expressed by comments like '[dementia care] is the poor relation of the health service'. In contrast with reports of 'dirty workers' distancing themselves from care recipients (Ashforth and Kreiner 1999, Isaksen 2002), our evidence indicates that care staff actively highlighted the parallels in their structural and social status.

From these collective attempts at empowerment, care assistants in our study found new local possibilities for person-centred actions, as described above. This involved different degrees of negotiation with the existing order: sometimes attempting to negotiate a 'non-routine routine' as one carer put it, and sometimes deliberately transgressing institutionalised norms such as 'efficiency' in order to provide more personalised care. However, these possibilities were limited by two interrelated factors: first, by their own disempowered subject positioning as described above, and second, by other 'legitimate' organisational demands. By this we mean that person-centred practices were not necessarily recognised as 'legitimate' when put alongside, for example, the predictable completion and documentation of tasks. We also found that an organisation-wide approach to 'person-centred care', such as the Dining Experience, sometimes proved counterproductive to the provision of personalised care. In response, carers' own assertion of personcentred practices could appear illegitimate rather than empowered. This finding aligns with Kontos *et al.*'s (2010: 11–12) observation that direct-care workers in a study in Canadian nursing homes broke certain organisational rules 'as a strategy to individualize care because full compliance with rules [constrains] their ability to do so'. The problem is that such situated rule-breaking or disruptive action, undertaken covertly to avoid disciplinary action, may have failed to disrupt the relations of power that have produced and legitimated non-person-centred norms.

These findings point to the need for better recognition of the care workers' collective claim to knowledge, skills and expertise as an important step towards meaningful empowerment. An affirmative response from those who are more 'empowered' within the current institutional order, that is, would help legitimise the carers' claims to authority. This legitimation would necessitate a shifting of the power relations that currently, as we have shown, have adverse implications, such as carers' marginalisation within the multidisciplinary team and their associated defensiveness about their occupational boundaries and reluctance to reflect on their own practices. Legitimation represents a different mechanism of empowerment than 'giving' or 'allowing' more autonomy, since a gift – whether given or withheld – leaves existing relations of power intact.

The importance of external recognition is reflected to a certain extent in 'culture change' attempts to promote and formalise direct-care staff's involvement in organisational practices such as shift handovers and care-planning meetings. In the United States, the Green House model of long-term care (Loe and Moore 2012) provides a prominent example. Here, care staff have been promoted to 'universal workers' (known as *Shahbazim*) who take responsibility for running each small household, including creating work schedules and planning meals and activities as well as providing direct care. Even in this model, however, evidence suggests that 'empowerment' is interpreted and implemented in quite different ways, with more or less favourable outcomes in terms of interdisciplinary collaboration and resident outcomes (Bowers *et al.* 2015). In challenging the view of power as a property which can be given or taken away, Foucault helps us consider how action and consequences are shaped by innumerable forces and relations, some of which may be beyond the individual or collective actors' immediate field of vision. Thus, we can see that 'culture change' approaches to empowerment may not succeed if they do not adequately account for the complex power relations – including those related to quality, safety, accountability, profit, and so on – which inform the possibilities for action in any particular care setting while rendering other actions 'unthinkable' (Deetz 1992: 143). We must consider what actions are available to or 'thinkable' for staff, and with what outcomes; for example, how thinkable is the action of applying skin cream without gloves for someone whose responsibility is to enforce accepted standards of safety and hygiene? And if the transgressive act is ignored to 'save' the worker from disciplinary action, then power has been disengaged, to some extent, but without potential for the act to prompt further change. More radical change would require transgression to be treated as an invitation to collectively question disciplinary norms; however, this presupposes the existence of conditions of openness and mutual trust, which the evidence presented here does not support.

Another important step towards public recognition of the 'invigorated' direct-care role is the establishment of training and performance standards. The Care Certificate, which came into force in the UK in April 2015, is a notable example which establishes a minimum level of training for non-regulated care workers across health and social care settings. However, training standards alone, especially when minimally enforced, are not sufficient to offset the marginalisation of the workforce; this has been shown in the United States, where nursing assistants are required to complete a federal minimum of 75 hours of training and certification but who nonetheless remain an underpaid, undervalued workforce (PHI 2009). Further, it is important to remember that with recognition and formalisation comes an intensification of disciplinary power in the form of increased scrutiny; to empower is not to set free, following Foucault, but to set in motion a new set of power-knowledge relations which shape a new field of possible action. By recognising care staff as an occupational group, and beginning to regulate their practice through training and performance standards, there is a risk of further individualising what might otherwise be understood as the collective phenomena of practice – if recognition serves primarily to distinguish and discipline individuals who fall short of those standards, rather than legitimising the 'generative and creative nature of care practices' (Mol *et al.* 2011: 77) implemented by this workforce as a whole.

Person-centred care has substantial normative legitimacy (Scott 2001), as part of broader movements toward individualisation, anti-stigmatisation, and user involvement across health and social care. It is supported by national action plans and policy and practice guidelines (e.g., in the UK: Department of Health 2009, 2010, 2013, Department of Health, Cabinet Office and Prime Minister's Office 2015, NICE 2006) and spelled out for nursing staff in particular in the NHS Commissioning Board's (2012) Compassion in Practice report. Therefore, person-centred discourse provides an external force which could set in motion the wider 'abandonment of widespread taken-for-granted practices' (Maguire and Hardy 2009: 148) in dementia care, as in other settings, which is the necessary adjunct to deinstitutionalisation. However, we have argued that there is a limit to the reform or 'abandonment' that is likely to result from the locally empowered moves of caregivers, without simultaneous attention to their persistent structural disempowerment and the deeply rooted legitimacy of non or pre-person-centred practices, such as economic rationalisation. In other words, if the responsibility to transform institutional norms through person-centred practice is placed solely on the shoulders of caregivers through their ostensible 'empowerment', limited change will result. Transformation of care requires changes in both the organisational settings where practices occur and the broader relations of power which produce them. Nevertheless, focussing on those everyday practices, as we have done here, draws attention to the creative capacity of this workforce and their potential role in collectively producing change. Realising this potential requires a sense of 'balanced responsiveness' (Deetz 1992: 338) in institutional dementia care, in order to recognise the tensions created by multiple interests and to encourage disciplinary power to be enacted in more collective and participatory ways.

Conclusion

This article has examined the role of unregistered care staff in dementia care settings, with particular attention to the relations of power which define their experiences and possibilities for action. The starting point for the analysis was person-centred care, a concept with considerable traction in health and social care discourse which places the responsibility for promoting personhood largely on direct caregivers. The analysis was framed within Foucault's work on knowledge and power, which emphasises the productive nature of these twin forces in shaping everyday realities and offers the means to analyse the possibilities, as well as the constraints, that actors face.

The empirical findings illustrated the various ways that direct-care staff enacted their own 'empowerment' from a position of persistent 'disempowerment'. Through this examination, we considered the extent to which they could impact the legitimate order of the institution through their collective resistance and action, rather than 'just' the individual experience at the point of care. We concluded by suggesting that more needs to be done to recognise, support and develop the creative work of direct-care staff in order to generate greater correspondence between the everyday action we observed and broader normative shifts towards more empowering models of dementia care.

Acknowledgements

The HCA study was funded by the Service, Delivery and Organisation programme of the National Institute of Health Research (NIHR), now the Health Services and Delivery Research programme (SDO #08/1819/222). The care home study was supported by a doctoral studentship from the NIHR-funded Collaboration for Leadership in Applied Health Research and Care for Nottinghamshire, Derbyshire and Lincolnshire (CLAHRC-NDL). All views and opinions expressed here are the authors' own and do not reflect those of the NIHR. We give our thanks to the staff, patients, and residents from Wards A, B, and C and Forest Lodge; to all those who supported and advised both studies; to Paula Hyde, Ruth McDonald, and Damian Hodgson for their thoughtful input; and to the journal editors and reviewers for their careful review and comments.

Notes

1   Direct-care staff comprise the largest practitioner group and provide the majority of hands-on care across health and social care settings (Moran *et al.* 2011). This workforce has many labels; here, we use 'care assistant', 'direct-care worker', and 'carer' interchangeably, but 'healthcare assistant' (HCA) when referring specifically to the NHS setting. 'Caregiver' is used when referring to informal care or to caregiving in general. Finally, the term 'patient' is used for the NHS setting and 'resident' for long-term care.

2   It should be noted that informal caregivers, including family, friends, and neighbours, provide the majority of care for the two-thirds of people with dementia who live in the community. Although discussions about power, personhood, and person-centred care are relevant to their experiences and actions as well, the focus here is paid staff in formal organisational settings.

3   The second study comprised two comparative cases: Forest Lodge and a family-owned, 80-bed skilled nursing facility located in the north-eastern United States. Although the majority of residents at both facilities had some degree of cognitive impairment, those in the US nursing home and on the skilled nursing unit at Forest Lodge also tended to have more acute physical health needs, which impacted the organisation and delivery of care; therefore, the data discussed here are drawn exclusively from 'Vintage Vale', the secure dementia unit at Forest Lodge, where residents' acuity was similar to that of the patient population of the NHS wards in the first study.

4   Quotation marks in fieldnote excerpts indicate verbatim wording of research participants; otherwise, the conversations described in fieldnotes have been paraphrased by the author of the fieldnote. False starts and repetitions have been removed from verbatim quotes to enhance readability. Ellipses signify omitted text from fieldnotes or interview excerpts, and square brackets are used for clarifying text.

References

Alzheimer's Disease International (ADI). (2015) *World Alzheimer Report 2015: The Global Impact of Dementia*. London: ADI.

Alzheimer's Society. (2007) *Home From Home: A Report Highlighting Opportunities for Improving Standards of Dementia Care in Care Homes*. London: Alzheimer's Society.

American Geriatrics Society Expert Panel on Person-Centered Care (AGS). (2016) Person-centered care: A definition and essential elements, *Journal of the American Geriatrics Society*, 64, 1, 15–8.

Ashforth, B.E. and Kreiner, G.E. (1999) "How can you do it?": dirty work and the challenge of constructing a positive identity, *Academy of Management Review*, 24, 3, 413–34.

Banaszak-Holl, J. and Hines, M.A. (1996) Factors associated with nursing home staff turnover, *The Gerontologist*, 36, 512–7.

Barry, T., Brannon, D. and Mor, V. (2005) Nurse aide empowerment strategies and staff stability: effects on nursing home resident outcomes, *The Gerontologist*, 45, 3, 309–17.

Bowers, B. and Nolet, K. (2011) Empowering direct care workers: lessons learned from the Green House model, *Seniors Housing & Care Journal*, 19, 1, 109–20.

Bowers, B., Roberts, T., Nolet, K. and Ryther, B. (2015) Inside the green house 'black box': opportunities for high-quality clinical decision making, *Health Services Research*, 51, Suppl 1, S378–97.

Brijnath, B. and Manderson, L. (2008) Discipline in chaos: Foucault, dementia and aging in India, *Culture, Medicine and Psychiatry*, 32, 4, 607–26.

Bryden, C. (2005) *Dancing with Dementia: My Story of Living Positively with Dementia*. London: Jessica Kingsley Publishers.

Caspar, S. and O'Rourke, N. (2008) The influence of care provider access to structural empowerment on individualized care in long-term-care facilities, *The Journals of Gerontology Series B: Psychological Sciences and Social Sciences*, 63, 4, S255–65.

Caspar, S., O'Rourke, N. and Gutman, G.M. (2009) The differential influence of culture change models on long-term care staff empowerment and provision of individualized care, *Canadian Journal on Aging*, 28, 2, 165–75.

Castle, N.G. (2011) The influence of consistent assignment on nursing home deficiency citations, *The Gerontologist*, 51, 6, 750–60.

Chalfont, G. and Hafford-Letchfield, T. (2010) Leadership from the bottom up: reinventing dementia care in residential and nursing home settings, *Social Work and Social Sciences Review*, 14, 2, 37–54.

Clegg, S. (2010) The state, power, and agency: missing in action in institutional theory? *Journal of Management Inquiry*, 19, 1, 4–13.

Commissioning Board Chief Nursing Officer and DH Chief Nursing Adviser (2012) *Compassion in Practice*. London: Department of Health and NHS Commissioning Board.

Deetz, S. (1992) *Democracy in an age of Corporate Colonization: Developments in Communication and the Politics of Everyday Life*. Albany, NY: State University of New York Press.

Department of Health (2009) *Living Well with Dementia: A National Dementia Strategy*. London: Department of Health.

Department of Health (2010) *Essence of Care: Benchmarks for the Fundamental Aspects of Care*. London: The Stationery Office.

Department of Health (2013) *The NHS Constitution*. London: Department of Health.

Department of Health, Cabinet Office and Prime Minister's Office. (2015) *Prime Minister's Challenge on Dementia 2020*. London: Department of Health.

Emerson, R.M., Fretz, R.I. and Shaw, L.L. (1995) *Writing Ethnographic Fieldnotes*. Chicago: University of Chicago Press.

Fetherstonhaugh, D., Tarzia, L., Bauer, M., Nay, R., *et al.* (2016) 'The red dress or the blue?': how do staff perceive that they support decision making for people with dementia living in residential aged care facilities? *Journal of Applied Gerontology*, 35, 2, 209–26.

Foucault, M. (1977) *Discipline and Punish: The Birth of the Prison*. New York: Random House.

Foucault, M. (1980a) *Knowledge/Power: Selected Interviews and Other Writings*. New York, NY: Pantheon Books.

Foucault, M. (1980b) Power and strategies. In Gordon, C. (ed.) *Power-Knowledge: Selected Interviews and Other Writings, 1972–1977*. Brighton: Harvester.

Foucault, M. (1981) Questions on method: an interview, *Ideology & Consciousness*, 8, 1, 3–14.

Foucault, M. (1982) The subject and power. In Dreyfus, H. and Rabinow, P. (eds) *Michel Foucault: Beyond Structuralism and Hermeneutics*. Brighton: Harvester Press.

Foucault, M. (1984) The ethics of the concern for self as a practice of freedom. In: Rabinow, P. (ed) *The Essential Works of Michel Foucault, Volume 1: Ethics: Subjectivity and Truth*. New York: New Press.

Goldberg, S.E., Bradshaw, L.E., Kearney, F.C., Russell, C., *et al.* (2013) Care in specialist medical and mental health unit compared with standard care for older people with cognitive impairment admitted to general hospital: randomised controlled trial, *BMJ*, 347, f4132.

Hamann, D.J. (2014) Does empowering resident families or nursing home employees in decision making improve service quality?, *Journal of Applied Gerontology*, 33, 5, 603–23.

Harding, E., Wait, S. and Scrutton, J. (2015) *The State Of Play In Person-Centred Care: A Pragmatic Review Of How Person-Centred Care Is Defined, Applied And Measured, Featuring Selected Key Contributors And Case Studies Across The Field*. London: Health Policy Partnership.

Hyde, P., Burns, D., Hassard, J. and Killett, A. (2014) Colonizing the aged body and the organization of later life, *Organization Studies*, 35, 11, 1699–717.

Innes, A. (2002) The social and political context of formal dementia care provision, *Ageing and Society*, 22, 4, 483–99.

Isaksen, L.W. (2002) Toward a sociology of (gendered) disgust, *Journal of Family Issues*, 23, 7, 791–811.

Kessler, I., Heron, P. and Dopson, S. (2015) Professionalization and expertise in care work: the hoarding and discarding of tasks in nursing, *Human Resource Management*, 54, 5, 737–52.

Kitwood, T. (1997) *Dementia Reconsidered: The Person Comes First*. Buckingham: Open University Press.

Knapp, M., Comas-Herrera, A., Somani, A. and Banerjee, S. (2007) Dementia: international comparisons – Summary report for the National Audit Office. London: Personal Social Services Research Unit, London School of Economics and Political Science, and Section of Mental Health and Ageing, The Institute of Psychiatry, King's College London.

Konrad, T.R. (2011) The direct care worker: overcoming definitions by negation. In Kronenfeld, J.J. (ed.) *Access to Care and Factors that Impact Access, Patients as Partners in Care and Changing Roles of Health Providers*. Bingley: Emerald Group Publishing Limited.

Kontos, P.C., Miller, K.L., Mitchell, G.J. and Cott, C.A. (2010) Dementia care at the intersection of regulation and reflexivity: a critical realist perspective, *The Journals of Gerontology: Series B*, 66B, 1, 119–28.

Koren, M.J. (2010) Person-centered care for nursing home residents: the culture-change movement, *Health Affairs*, 29, 2, 312–7.

Kostiwa, I.M. and Meeks, S. (2009) The relation between psychological empowerment, service quality, and job satisfaction among certified nursing assistants, *Clinical Gerontologist*, 32, 3, 276–92.

Loe, M. and Moore, C.D. (2012) From nursing home to green house: changing contexts of elder care in the United States, *Journal of Applied Gerontology*, 31, 6, 755–63.

Lloyd, J.V., Schneider, J., Scales, K., Bailey, S., *et al.* (2011) Ingroup identity as an obstacle to effective multiprofessional and interprofessional teamwork: findings from an ethnographic study of healthcare assistants in dementia care, *Journal of Interprofessional Care*, 25, 2, 354–1.

Maguire, S. and Hardy, C. (2009) Discourse and deinstitutionalization: The decline of DDT, *Academy of Management Journal*, 52, 1, 148–78.

May, C. (1992) Nursing work, nurses' knowledge, and the subjectification of the patient, *Sociology of Health & Illness*, 14, 4, 472–87.

Mol, A., Moser, I., Piras, E.M., Turrini, M., *et al.* (2011) Care in practice: on normativity, concepts, and boundaries, *Tecnoscienza: Italian Journal of Science & Technology Studies*, 2, 1, 73–86.

Moran, A., Enderby, P. and Nancarrow, S. (2011) Defining and identifying common elements of and contextual influences on the roles of support workers in health and social care: a thematic analysis of the literature, *Journal of Evaluation in Clinical Practice*, 17, 6, 1191–9.

NICE (2006) *NICE Clinical Guideline 42: Dementia: Supporting People With Dementia and their Carers in Health and Social Care*. London: NICE/SCIE.

O'Malley, P. (1996) Risk and responsibility. In Barry, A., Osborne, T. and Rose, N. (eds) *Foucault and Political Reason: Liberalism, Neo-Liberalism and Rationalities of Government*. London: UCL Press.

PHI (2009) *Facts: Who are Direct-care Workers?*. New York, NY: Paraprofessional Healthcare Institute.

Royal College of Psychiatrists (RCP) (2013) *National Audit of Dementia Care in General Hospitals 2012–13: Second Round Audit Report and Update*. London: HQIP.

Sabat, S.R. (2001) *The Experience of Alzheimer's Disease: Life through a Tangled Veil*. Hoboken, NJ: Wiley-Blackwell.

Sabat, S.R. (2008) A bio-psycho-social approach to dementia. In Downs, M. and Bowers, B. (eds) *Excellence in Dementia Care: Research Into Practice*. Maidenhead: Open University Press.

Scales, K., Bailey, S. and Lloyd, J. (2011) Separately and together: Reflections on conducting a collaborative team ethnography in dementia care, *Enquire*, 4, 1, 22–44.

Scott, W. (2001) *Institutions and Organizations*. Thousand Oaks, CA: Sage.

Spradley, J.P. (1980) *Participant Observation*. New York: Holt, Rinehart and Winston.

St Pierre, I. and Holmes, D. (2008) Managing nurses through disciplinary power: A Foucauldian analysis of workplace violence, *Journal of Nursing Management*, 16, 352–59.

Twigg, J. (2000) Carework as a form of bodywork, *Ageing and Society*, 20, 4, 389–411.

Webster, J. (2011) Improving care for people with dementia in acute hospital: the role of person-centred assessment, *Quality in Ageing and Older Adults*, 12, 2, 86–94.

Woods, R.T. (1989) *Alzheimer's Disease: Coping with a Living Death*. London: Souvenir Press.

Yeatts, D.E. and Cready, C.M. (2007) Consequences of empowered CNA teams in nursing home settings: a longitudinal assessment, *The Gerontologist*, 47, 3, 323–39.

6

Institutionalising senile dementia in 19th-century Britain
Emily Stella Andrews

The 19th century saw a great proliferation of institutional solutions to social problems. In the UK, they included workhouses for the impoverished, asylums for the insane, prisons for the criminal, and industrial schools for the delinquent. Old people living with dementia were caught in this institutional nexus – in asylums and workhouses – but were never welcome there. Viewed as incurable and unmanageable, the presence of people with dementia in these institutions was decried and (unsuccessfully) resisted. But their presence reveals one of the key functions which these institutions performed: absorbing and containing unmanageable and undesirable behaviour, preserving the order of the outside world, and providing care (often in a very minimal sense) to people whose needs had transcended the financial, practical and emotional capacity of the people around them. These were not institutions designed with the needs of people with dementia in mind, but this did not prevent families and Poor Law authorities from making use of the growing network of institutional provision in Victorian Britain.

This article is about the institutionalisation of poor, old people living with dementia in 19th-century Britain – and particularly, in London. People of all classes and levels of wealth could find themselves institutionalised in this period, but this article examines only those institutions which admitted people who could not afford to pay for their own care: asylums, workhouses and charitable institutions. It also looks at the wranglings which took place at an individual, institutional and national level to try to exclude old people with dementia from these institutions; to deny responsibility for 'the senile'. The belief that old people with dementia represent an intractable policy problem, it will demonstrate, predates the current 'dementia crisis' by over a century.

It is impossible to say how common it was for old people with dementia to be institutionalised in this period, although some documents point us towards proxy indicators. In the second half of the 19th century, half of London's workhouse inmates were reportedly aged 60 or over (Lees 1990: 76). In the year 1880, 509 people in England and Wales were newly admitted to an asylum with 'senile dementia'; in 1900, there were 935 new senile dementia admissions (Commissioners in Lunacy, 1881; 1901). We cannot say how many of these would today be given a diagnosis of dementia. In trying to investigate the historical reality of contextually-understood mental experiences, historians themselves face 'psychiatry's knowledge problem – the elusiveness of certainty' (Lunbeck 1994: 4). Here, a pragmatic approach has been taken, one which focuses on the contemporary categories of 'senile dementia' and 'senility' and the people who were described using those terms.

Ageing, Dementia and the Social Mind, First Edition. Edited by Paul Higgs and Chris Gilleard.
Chapters © 2017 The Authors. Book Compilation © 2017 Foundation for the Sociology of
Health & Illness/Blackwell Publishing Ltd.

This article will examine institutionalisation from the perspective of one institution in particular – the asylum. In 1808, the County Asylums Act empowered local justices of the peace to build asylums for the care and treatment of their pauper lunatics – people certified as insane who could not afford their own care. In 1845, another County Asylums Act made this provision compulsory. At the same time, a national overseeing body for all institutions housing lunatics – the Commissioners in Lunacy – was set up, and their annual reports form a key part of the source base for this article. By 1854 there were 37 county lunatic asylums in England, rising to 63 in 1884 and reaching 97 in 1914 (Scull 1993: 369). After the workhouse, the asylum was the most important public institution in the lives of the Victorian working class. Unlike the workhouse, it generated rich documentation, which offers a unique depth of insight into the lives of people who encountered it. This extends to their lives beyond the walls of the institution (Wright 1997). Much of the evidence in this piece is drawn from a larger case study of one particular asylum's records – 1st Middlesex County Asylum at Hanwell in North-West London. This sample consists of every patient (381 in total) whose age was recorded as 60 or over, and was admitted in the years 1851–1852, 1871–1872, 1891–1892 and 1911–1912.

These documents offer insights into other institutions, including two (Tooting Bec Imbecile Asylum, and the charitable St Joseph's Home for the Aged Poor) which were unique to the capital. Thus, some of its conclusions speak to a very specific place: the sprawling metropolis of Victorian London. The city's large and dense population, and great but unevenly spread wealth, stimulated new approaches to the problems of poverty and dependency. The 1867 Metropolitan Poor Act created more pan-metropolitan poor law institutions, and created a Common Poor fund to alleviate the burdens of poorer unions by redistributing money from the wealthier ones (Green 2010). By the early 1890s, 82 per cent of London's paupers were relieved in the workhouse, compared with 34 per cent in the rest of England. This unusually high rate of institutionalisation provided fertile conditions for more specialised institutions to proliferate (Boyer and Schmidle 2009: 262). Other parts of England had different institutional mixes and faced different challenges. For example, in contrast to the increasingly centralised administration of lunacy in London, the distinctive administrative units which made up the rural county of Devon each took very different approaches to the institutionalisation of their pauper lunatics (Melling and Forsythe 2006). In industrial Lancashire – second only to London in the scale of its system of confinement – large workhouse lunatic wards provided relief to the pressured asylum system (Cox and Marland 2015). This article seeks to situate the London experience in a national narrative, drawing from medical texts and administrative reports covering different parts of the UK, but a different geographical case study may produce a revealingly different picture.

Professionally and intellectually, British psychiatry in the 19th-century encompassed all the individual nations. The Medico-Psychological Association of Great Britain and Ireland (forerunner to the Royal College of Psychiatry) was a UK-wide network whose leading members tended to come from England and Scotland (Renvoise 1991). Edinburgh, and the asylum at Morningside, was a hub of psychiatric education and research whose approaches and alumni often crossed the border (Beveridge 1991). Administratively, however, the UK asylum system was split into distinctive national systems. The Commissioners in Lunacy, with whom this article is concerned, had responsibility only for England and Wales. Scotland had its own Board of Lunacy Commissioners, and a rather different system which promoted the 'boarding out' of some certified lunatics into private homes (with relatives or strangers). Sturdy and Parry-Jones (1999: 86) have estimated that up to 25 per cent of all Scotland's lunatics were housed in this way in the second half of the 19th-century. The experience of people with dementia under this system may have been quite different and is ripe for further investigation – but is beyond the scope of this piece.

The presence of people with dementia in lunatic asylums in the 19th-century often surprises people in the 21st. Although it was not uncontroversial, the admission of 'senile dements' to an asylum for the insane was entirely congruent with the way senile dementia was understood, and the way that those institutions functioned. This article will therefore begin by outlining the place of 'senile dementia' in 19th-century psychiatry. It will then, in turn, discuss the asylum, the workhouse and charitable institutions; explaining how old people with dementia came to be there, but particularly how the administrators and managers of those institutions tried to rhetorically and physically exclude them.

Senile dementia

Dementia was a key category in 19th-century psychiatry and senile dementia was one of its variants. John Charles Prichard was the first Anglophone psychiatrist to use the term senile dementia in 1835. Prichard, like most British psychiatrists of the mid-19th century, was heavily influenced by ideas from France, particularly in his understanding of dementia. Loss was at the centre of this understanding. Dementia, Prichard suggested, would always progress through four stages, each characterised by the loss of a different mental function: the first by loss of memory, the second by loss of reason, the third by loss of comprehension and the last by loss of instinct. A dement in the first stage – 'forgetfulness' – would be unable to form or retain new memories, but would still be able to reason correctly using any memories they already held, or regarding matters immediately in front of them. In the second stage – 'irrationality' – their loss of energy, which had already halted the retention of new impressions, would begin to impact on their ability to concentrate. Unable to follow a train of thought, a dement in the second stage would be unable to reason. In the third stage – 'incomprehension' – the sufferer would be unable to comprehend and engage with the world around them, and would sink into blank inactivity or the ceaseless repetition of old habits. Finally – in a state of 'inappetancy' – even the deepest, 'instinctive' functions would be lost, rendering the sufferer barely able to control their own movements or 'obey the calls of nature'. Not all cases would reach this final stage – due to recovery, plateau, or death – but any progression would always occur in this way (Prichard 1835: 88–9). Dementia, then, was a regular, determined, dismantling of the mind, through which the sufferer lost their mental faculties in a hierarchical fashion. Eventually, they would lose their mind entirely, reduced to 'mere … physical existence' (Bucknill and Tuke; 1858: 124).

Over the next 80 years, the precise definition and psycho-pathological explanation of dementia shifted with the prevailing orthodoxies and fashions of psychiatry, but the essential elements remained the same: dementia was viewed as a progressive loss of mental function, which caused the sufferer to regress down the mental hierarchy. A loss of energy – causing the mind's activities to slow and weaken, and its physical structures to disintegrate – was present explicitly or implicitly in all of these accounts. Old age fit neatly into this aetiological framework, but it did not dominate it. Dementia could occur in different forms at all stages of life. The loss of energy leading to dementia could be caused by physical or mental trauma or exertion, a long struggle with a more energetic form of insanity, excessive or prolonged consumption of alcohol, the distinctive pathology of general paralysis, or simply the exhaustion of living a long life. 'Secondary dementia' – when someone suffering from another form of insanity fell into (usually) irretrievable mental collapse – was often held to be the prototypical form (Clouston 1883: 271). Senile dementia was similarly sequential, coming after many years of living.

Just as senile dementia was not the only form of dementia in 19th-century psychiatry, dementia was not the only form of senility. Around the middle of the century, psychiatrists across Europe became frustrated with 'symptomatic' classifications of insanity, and sought to create taxonomies and categories which were based on the somatic disorder underlying the mental symptoms. With few resources available to make these underlying physical realities visible, psychiatric classification based on stages of the life cycle became popular (for example, Skae 1863, Clouston 1883). Thus 'senile insanity' came to be used as an umbrella term for all mental disorders which could arise from the physical structure of the ageing body, of which senile dementia was one. 'The student … is too apt to assume,' advised one psychiatrist, 'that all varieties of mental ailments in the aged issue in senile dementia … Senile insanity … connotes a very large class of symptoms, embracing between them all the varied forms of insanity usually differentiated' (Bevan Lewis 1889: 405–6). According to Bevan Lewis, this included senile mania, melancholia, epilepsy and convulsions – and senile dementia. Indeed, in spite of his protestations, his instruction highlights the prevalence and importance of senile dementia as a category.

The conceptual link between dementia and an inevitable, inescapable ageing process was strong throughout the century. Prichard (1835) described senile dementia as 'the change which time alone will perhaps sooner or later bring on, in those who long survive the allotted duration of man's days'. These links became particularly strong towards the end of the century, when psychiatrists began conceptualising both dementia and ageing as a form of de-evolutionary decline (Andrews 2014). But it would be a mistake to claim that – in this time before Alzheimer's 'disease' – the status of dementia as a 'natural' part of ageing was settled. British psychiatrists of this period struggled with the relationship between natural ageing and pathological dementia. Most settled for an explanation which encompassed both: a 'normal senility', which could intensify into pathological senile dementia. In the words of one psychiatrist, 'dotage is simply senile dementia in a mild form, and senile dementia is advanced dotage' (Crichton Browne 1874: 601). The problem came in trying to locate the boundary between the two – 'betwixt the ordinary second childishness of old age, and the dementia resulting from the senile atrophy of disease' (Bevan Lewis 1889: 413). This remained, into the early twentieth century, 'the question that cannot be answered' (Stoddart 1908: 340).

While this relationship between natural ageing and the pathological insanity of dementia was mired in uncertainty, senile dementia remained a persistent feature of classificatory taxonomies of insanity. Whether a psychiatrist chose to organise their taxonomy by symptom, aetiology, or physical state, 'senile dementia' was a constant presence from Prichard onwards. Theoretically speaking, then, 19th-century psychiatrists were happy to pronounce senile dementia a form of insanity, or were at least convinced that it was a mental condition which rightfully belonged to their expert domain. But while this theoretical framework legitimised the presence of people with dementia inside the Victorian asylum, it does not explain it. To understand how people living with dementia came to be admitted to asylums, one needs to look beyond the walls of that institution.

The asylum

Entry to a lunatic asylum was a legally encoded process, involving a certificate filled out by a doctor, and usually the assent of a magistrate (Wright 1998). Crucially, the asylum itself had no role in this process: asylum doctors did not certify patients, and were obliged to admit the properly certified lunatics they were presented with. Local Poor Law officials often played an important role in instigating and organising the process of certification and removal (Bartlett 1999). But it is the role of the family which has received the most attention from recent historians of the asylum admissions. In most cases, it was a family member who made the initial approach to the authorities to set the process of certification in motion. Their testimony was key to legally establishing their relative's insanity, providing the 'facts' of the case for the medical certificate. Thus, it was the family, not the medical authorities, who turned a person into a 'patient' (Suzuki 2006: 1).

Historians and sociologists of the 1960s and 70s stressed the utility of the asylum as an instrument of 'social control'; a place to contain deviant and disruptive behaviour (Foucault 1965, Doerner 1977, Mellett 1982). Sociologist Andrew Scull (1980) famously described the asylum as a 'convenient place to get rid of inconvenient people'. In Scull's (1979: 37) account, the proliferation of asylums offered time-poor wage-earners of industrialised Britain relief from the burden of caring for unproductive and troublesome relatives. A 'counter-revisionist' strain of asylum historiography emerged in opposition to this account, and is now the dominant approach (Melling 1999). Counter-revisionists are primarily social historians, who have attempted to humanise our understanding of the asylum admissions process through empirically rich studies of the documentation it left behind. Their accounts stress the many years of home care prior to institutionalisation which are often described in these documents, and the significant strain placed on stretched, impoverished families coping with mental disorder. They argue, as Walton (1985: 141) put it, that asylum admittees 'were not so much "inconvenient" people, in Scull's terminology, as impossible people in the eyes of families, neighbours and authorities'.

The difference between these two positions can be overstated (Brown 1994). They place different emphases on the emotional dynamics of an institutionalisation event, but ascribe it to the same root cause: in both accounts, it is the 'manageability [of the person's behaviour] rather than the nature of the individual's mental defect' which was decisive in leading to a person being sent to an asylum (Scull 1999: 300). What mattered most in determining an asylum admission was how much difficulty a person's behaviour caused to the people around them, and the 'capacity and willingness' of those people to contain, direct, tolerate and bear such behaviour (Melling et al. 1999: 153). Asylum admission occurred when the 'boundary of tolerance' dictated by the patient's particular circumstances was breached (Smith 1999: 96). It was therefore a social event more than a medical one.

In this legal and social context, the admission of people with dementia to asylums is unsurprising. The case notes of people admitted to Hanwell with 'senile dementia' offer insight into the dynamics of home care prior to admission, and the tipping points which triggered institutionalisation. Examples of medical expertise being engaged outside the asylum do appear in the case notes – one sixty-five year old man admitted in 1852 had been subjected to leeching, blistering, mustard poultices and other medicines before he was admitted – but they were not common (Hanwell Asylum 1851–1852: 300). Instead, most families concentrated on containing and managing their relatives' behaviour. The Hanwell case notes contain occasional references to mechanical restraint: Thomas Alcock, admitted to Hanwell in 1852, was 'strapped down to his bed to prevent him from wandering about in a state of nudity' (leaving him with notable bruising on his legs) (Hanwell Asylum 1851–1852: 280). References to surveillance and persuasion are more common. Elizabeth Dyer's daughter, for example, explained that her mother had previously wandered out of the house and got lost, so that now she was 'afraid to leave her alone' (Hanwell Asylum 1872.2: 5). John Auger's daughter explained that she had 'prevailed upon' him to dress, to wash, and to remain within the home, although she had not been successful (Hanwell Asylum 1871–1852: 71). In all of these examples, significant strain was placed on the carer, their lives limited by constant watchfulness and frequent intervention.

If a person had exhibited symptoms of mental dissolution for some time, violent behaviour could be the trigger for institutionalisation. Henry Arnold's violence frightened his daughter, and she told the certifying doctor, 'He threatens to strike us. He is not safe at home' (Hanwell Asylum 1891: 517). This statement carries a dual meaning. Henry Arnold's violence made him an unsafe person within the household, which in turn put his own safety in danger. His daughter both feared him and feared for him. Other forms of disturbance, while less dramatic, could also be extremely disruptive. Harriet Staples's daughter sent her to the workhouse because she was 'very restless and noisy at night, so that it was impossible to have any rest' (Hanwell Asylum 1891.2: 154). Lucy Ward was similarly reported to be 'very sullen at night, [and] had to be continually watched' (Hanwell Asylum 1891.2: 142). Elizabeth Grey had been looked after in her son's home for five years, but when she began to 'wander in the streets', and had to be 'constantly watched' to keep her out of 'mischief', she was finally sent to the infirmary (Hanwell Asylum 1892: 34). As well as these specific descriptions of disruptive behaviour, a general, unspecified unmanageability or troublesomeness was often cited as a reason to institutionalise someone. Benjamin Clark 'was sent to the workhouse for being quite unmanageable at home', while Emma Casswell had previously become 'so excited and troublesome that it was found necessary to send her to [the asylum]' (Hanwell Asylum 1851–1852: 74, 1891.2: 172). 'Unmanageable' and 'troublesome' are words which describe the effect of the individual on the people around them; they demand or refuse to be managed, they cause trouble to others. The frequent use of these terms underlines the fact that a patient's institutionalisation was determined by the limitations of environment from which they came, at least as much as the form and severity of their symptoms. It was, then, not so much the patient's behaviour itself, as the effect it had on others, which led to institutionalisation.

Present-day ethnographic literature on the decision to admit someone into residential care stresses the psychosocial burden on caregivers and the difficulties they face in navigating it, as well as the practical and financial limitations on providing care and comfort to people with persistent needs (Armstrong 2000, Gaugler *et al.* 2009). As the examples above show, the same factors motivated families (and, less often, friends) to send a relative with dementia to the asylum. It was by no means a pleasant option, but in the 19th century, the asylum was one of the only institutions – besides the workhouse – which was available to relieve such pressures. This option was legitimised by the consistent inclusion of senile dementia in the texts of 19th-century psychiatry, but it was not governed by it. The theoretical wranglings over whether senile dementia should be considered a form of insanity was fairly meaningless in the face of these practical considerations. At the same time, the primarily social decision to admit a person with dementia into an asylum had legal and medical subjectifying effects: that person gained the new legal status of 'lunatic', and became a patient.

In the years immediately following the passage of the 1845 Lunacy and County Asylums Acts, the administrators of the county asylums were largely keen to see 'senile dements' included within the ranks of the insane. In 1848, the Lunacy Commissioners complained that '"imbecile" persons, having been so from birth, or become so from senility' were not always included within the ranks of people 'of unsound mind'. While perhaps not 'ordinary lunatics', they were 'incapable of managing their affairs in an efficient manner' and thus required 'in effect nearly the same protection'. That same year, the Commissioners wrote an urgent letter to the Lord Chancellor clarifying their position on the institutionalisation of such people: 'it is of vital importance that no mistake or misconceptions should exist … that according to the law, any person of unsound mind, whether he be pronounced dangerous or not, may legally and properly be placed in a county asylum' (Commissioners in Lunacy 1847–1848: 34).

In the decades which followed this pronouncement, however, the asylum system came under unexpected and unbearable pressure, and the Commissioner's attitudes towards the 'senile' changed. Over the course of the 19th century, the number of people reported as 'insane' increased every single year. Contemporary commentators debated whether this apparent 'increase in insanity' was epidemiological fact, or a consequence of improved record keeping and the incentive to legally certify insanity wrought by the increasing availability of asylum care (Commissioners in Lunacy 1895). This debate has carried over into the historical literature (Hare 1983, Scull 1984). Whatever the reason, the continuous growth in the number of people housed in asylums in the second half of the 19th century is undeniable: between 1850 there were 7,000 patients in county asylums in England and Wales; by 1890 there were 53,000. In the same period, the average number of patients in an asylum rose from 300 to 800 (Commissioners in Lunacy 1851, 1901). As the county lunatic asylums became ever more crowded and miserable, the administrators of lunacy at a national and local level sought explanations for this apparent failure of the asylums project. The Commissioners had originally been occupied with ensuring that all people certified were removed promptly to an asylum, and admonished the workhouses for failing to send their parish's lunatics to the asylum in a timely manner. In the latter part of the century, however, they began to qualify their demands, and to talk about the asylum population of 'desirable and undesirable' cases (Murphy 2002). The aged and senile fell decisively into the latter category.

The people who managed and oversaw the care and treatment of lunatics accused intolerant families and parsimonious Poor Law officials of offloading unsuitable cases onto the asylum and, in doing so, of expanding the meaning of certifiable insanity. 'A change of feeling has undoubtedly occurred in the poorer classes', the Commissioners reported in 1894, 'which now leads them, without reluctance, to see placed in asylums insane and mentally worn-out members of their families whom they would formerly have retained in their homes' (Commissioners in Lunacy 1894: 6). Poor Law officials in particular were criticised for certifying unsuitable patients for the sake of extra government funding (the four-shilling grant of 1874) that they attracted (Jones 1993, Ellis 2006). As a result of this grant, one psychiatrist claimed, 'Parish and workhouse officers willingly saw lunacy in forms of imbecility and illness in which they would never have dreamt at one time of doing so' (Maudsley 1877: 51). In 1886, the medical superintendent of Morningside Asylum in Edinburgh was faced with growing numbers of new patients over 60. In the *British Medical Journal*, he responded to the suggestion that this was caused by a general increase in mental deficiency in the aged population: 'This would be fallacious. We believe that more people in their restless and troublesome dotage … are now sent to asylums, and so come under the category of technical insanity, than formerly' (Clouston 1886: 91).

The administrators of lunacy responded by asserting their own, restricted definitions of insanity and senility. They described the senile as a group whose mental infirmity was incurable, manageable and, crucially, natural. The Commissioners undermined the legitimacy and severity of old-age mental infirmity by describing it as '*mere* senile dementia [emphasis added]' (Commissioners in Lunacy 1875, 1894, 1896). They complained about 'aged persons who are not properly lunatics, but suffering only, or principally, from the decay of faculties incident to old age'. The fact that their behaviour was caused by the 'natural decay' of ageing rather than 'an active form of insanity', they argued, excluded them from a claim to asylum care (Commissioners in Lunacy 1881: 236, 264). These attempts to restrict asylum admissions by policing the boundary between insanity and senility had little effect. In 1880, when the Commissioners' first started collecting figures, 509 people were admitted to asylums with a diagnosis of 'senile dementia' (in England and Wales). By 1900, the figure had risen to 906. This was because – as the psychiatrists and Commissioners recognised – it was the practical definition of insanity based on manageability which governed the asylum admissions process, not a medical definition based on aetiology. As Hanwell's case notes show, people living with dementia often fell within this practical definition.

The workhouse

It was workhouse officials who received the bulk of the Commissioners' ire for using the asylum to ease their own burdens. In the 1840s and 1850s, the Lunacy Commissioners had been extremely critical of the standard of care offered on workhouse lunatic wards. As they looked increasingly to promote the workhouse as a site of care for certain types of lunatic, however, they began to paint these wards in a more positive light, publishing this glowing assessment of them in 1909:

> It is impossible not to be struck with the happiness and contentment that prevails amongst the older inmates of these houses … It would be hard to find more suitable accommodation than is provided in many of the workhouses for certified patients of the inoffensive type. (Commissioners in Lunacy 1909: 68)

Thus, the care of aged and incurable lunatics in the workhouse ward had gone from being an unfortunate, but sometimes unavoidable evil, to a key strategy in the relief of the overcrowded asylum. Crucial to this strategy, was the representation of patients they wished to see excluded from the asylum as easy to care for. Aged and unsuitable patients were sent to them, they said, because they were 'simply garrulous and restless from old age' or 'a little troublesome and difficult to manage' (Commissioners in Lunacy 1878: 25, 1880: 116).

But the view from the workhouse – even of the same individual patients – was very different. In November 1869, Sarah Jarman, 'age said to be 80', was admitted to Hanwell from the workhouse of Westminster Union. On admission, she was reported to be 'very feeble and emaciated [and] not likely to live long'. In the opinion of James Murray Lindsey, Medical Superintendent of the female department of Hanwell, she 'ought not … to have been sent to the Asylum in her weakly and aged condition'. The Hanwell Visitors wrote to the Westminster Guardians to 'express [their] regret … that such a case should have been thought justifiable to expose the Patient to the trial of the journey'. Their comments, and the report from Murray Lindsey which they enclosed, focused entirely on Jarman's physical condition, and made no reference to her mental state, other than to say that her 'restlessness and noise' had prevented them for conducting a thorough examination of her physical ailments. The Westminster Guardians responded with a report from J. G. French, the medical officer of their infirmary:

> she was admitted into the Workhouse on no ground other than her insanity and the inability of her relatives to take proper care of her. In the Workhouse she was noisy and restless, perpetually moving about, and therefore requiring personal restraint. The Medical Officer deemed this to be the case which the law imperatively required to be removed to a Lunatic asylum, in order to protect the inmates of the Workhouse from annoyance. (Hanwell Asylum 1869: 17–23)

French replied to none of the Hanwell Visitors' concerns about Jarman's physical condition and focused instead on her mental state and behaviour. Thus, while Lindsey and the

Hanwell visitors viewed Jarman primarily as an old, infirm case, French and the Westminster Guardians saw her primarily as a lunatic. Sarah Jarman, and other people like her, was caught in between the classificatory schema used by different welfare institutions. Her physical state excluded her from the asylum (or from being seen as an appropriate asylum case), and her mental state excluded her from the workhouse. Sarah Jarman's case suggests that the unclassifiable nature of the senile sharpened the very contours of what the administrators of lunacy imagined them to be. For both Drs French and Lindsey, the essential facts of Sarah Jarman's case corresponded to the ways in which she failed to adhere to the norms of their institutions.

At the beginning of the twentieth century, workhouse medical officers made their responses to these continued complaints and accusations more public, placing articles and letters in the medical press. In 1908, C.T. Parsons, medical officer of the Fulham Infirmary, wrote letters to both the *British Medical Journal* and *The Lancet*, putting forward his perspective on 'The difficulty of dealing with cases of senile insanity'. His use of the term 'senile insanity' was as strategic and loaded as the use of 'mere senile dementia' by the Lunacy Commissioners. His argument focused on the 'grave accusation' implicit in the complaints about senile admissions to the asylum: 'that not only are patients being sent to these asylums illegally, but that they are also being detained illegally' (Parsons 1908: 1720). The law was quite clear, he knowingly suggested: if an individual was not a fit case for the asylum, then they could not legally be certified. The unspoken corollary, of course, was that any person who was being detained under a certificate of lunacy must, therefore, be insane. Like the administrators of lunacy, then, C. T. Parsons and other Poor Law officials manipulated the uncertainty around what constituted insanity to their own ends. Both asylum and workhouse officials appealed to an objective and externally-verifiable definition of a 'true' lunatic in their arguments about the senile, but their experience showed that the only meaningful definition of insanity in this context was a practical one, dictated by the type of behaviour different institutions were prepared to tolerate and type of the care they were willing to provide.

Of course, it is likely that very many people living with dementia did remain in workhouses – particularly in the workhouse infirmary wards which were set up in more populous areas to offer very basic medical care to paupers (Green 2002). Old people were especially likely to end up in these institutions if they fell ill, as charitable hospitals could choose to admit only patients they were confident could be cured (Edwards 1999, Gorsky *et al*. 2006). Workhouses kept far sparser records than asylums, and it is much harder to gain any insight into what life may have been like there – particularly for people living with dementia. In 1850, Charles Dickens (1850: 260) wrote an account of a workhouse with 'longer and longer groves of old people, in up-stairs Infirmary wards, wearing out life.' He did not so much describe dementia, as people living with the depression and hopelessness of potentially ending their days in a punitive and sparse workhouse environment: 'A sullen or lethargic indifference to what was asked, a blunted sensibility to everything but warmth and food, a moody absence of complaint as being of no use, a dogged silence and resentful desire to be left alone'.

So long as people remained in this quiet and apathetic state, they were able to remain in the workhouse. But – as the medical certificates of asylum admissions who had previously resided in the workhouse show – patients with dementia could disrupt the order of the workhouse by failing to perform the role of docile dependents. Several of the medical certificates in this sample mention the trouble caused by aged patients who refused to stay in bed. The head nurse at the Paddington Infirmary complained that she 'had great difficulty keeping [Mary] in bed, by night or day' (Hanwell Asylum 1872.2: 69). John Auger, who entered the workhouse apparently for the first time at the age of 79, 'walked about the ward, rattled and knocked at doors [and] asked why he should go to bed' (Hanwell Asylum 1871–1872: 71). Martin Bates 'cut the head [of a workhouse nurse] open in two places [who was] endeavouring to make him comfortable in his bed' (Hanwell Asylum 1872.3: 167). These patients not only presented the challenge of needing to be looked after, but resisted the attempts of those around them to meet this challenge.

If asylums were often forbidding places, they were at least staffed by people used to dealing with residents who were agitated, distressed, or unable understand their surroundings. Asylums were also equipped with medical supplies to attend to the physical needs of their patients, which could be acute amongst the older inmates (Andrews 2014). By contrast, crowded workhouse wards – even lunatic wards – were entirely unsuitable for people with advanced dementia. The nurse of St George's workhouse informed the certifying doctor that Ann Allcock 'scream[ed] and shout[ed] often at night for hours at a time, disturbing everybody in the house at a long distance from the ward' (Hanwell Asylum 1872: 215). Rebecca Brookman '[did] not allow […] any of the inmates of the ward to sleep with her continual vociferations' (Hanwell Asylum 1891: 322). Other patients physically spread their disruption about the ward by 'interfering' with other patients. Ann Foley 'constantly undressed herself [and] wander[ed] about the house and premises, [got] out of bed at night, pull[ed] the clothes off other beds and frighten[ed] the people' (Hanwell Asylum 1872: 211). George Connington took this one step further, 'throw[ing] off his bedclothes' and 'get[ting] into other patients beds' (Hanwell Asylum 1891: 50). These were uncontained people, whose disruption and disorder leaked beyond the boundaries of their own person and rendered the people around them as disturbed as they were. If their symptoms could not be contained within their person, or within a more appropriate time of day, then they were sent to have their symptoms contained within the walls of the asylum.

Other institutions

In 1903, Tooting Bec Asylum opened its doors. Legally, it had the status of a workhouse rather than an asylum, and was one of the specialised Poor Law medical institutions set up by the London Metropolitan Asylums Board (MAB) (Ayers 1971). Its opening was the result of decades of complaint on the part of the other MAB 'Imbecile Asylums' that they were being sent too many patients who were suffering 'merely from the helplessness and childishness incidental to advanced age', or 'only from the form of Dementia incidental to Senility' (MAB 1882–1883: 44, 1880–1881: 1034). These imbecile asylums had themselves been inspired by the Lunacy Commissioner's suggestion in the 1860s that 'intermediate asylums' could be provided more cheaply for the care of 'harmless and demented' patients (Commissioners in Lunacy 1867). In 1892, the MAB finally declared that 'the Managers should no longer delay the provision of … an Asylum Infirmary in or within easy distance of the Metropolis for the reception of aged, helpless and enfeebled persons of unsound mind is expedient and desirable' (MAB 1892–1893: 582). This, then, was to be an institution expressly for the care of aged people 'of unsound mind', whose presence in other institutions was so decried.

There were almost ten years of wrangling over cost and bed numbers before these plans finally came to fruition. But once it finally opened, Tooting Bec was nowhere near large enough to meet the scale of the problem: in 1906, the MAB had to install another 207 beds in addition to their original 855 (MAB 1907: 202). Faced with the challenging and costly reality of an asylum infirmary for people with dementia, the MAB turned away from the group of people for whom Tooting Bec had originally been conceived. In 1908 the chairman of the MAB told a Royal Commission that the presence of 'old men and women suffering from senile decay' at Tooting Bec was 'a great mistake'. 'In my opinion,' he continued, 'the proper place for this class of patient would be an infirm ward in the workhouse infirmary ... The cost would be less' (Royal Commission on the Care and Control of the Feeble-Minded 1908: 67).

As well as the public institutions of asylums and workhouses, there were charitable initiatives which provided support to the aged deserving poor. These could be similarly unwelcoming for people living with dementia. One Hanwell patient passed through two different philanthropic institutions – the Chesham Alms Houses and the Norfolk Home – before her arrival at the asylum. In both cases, she was expelled for 'quarrelling with the matron' (Hanwell Asylum 1891–1892: 505). In neither instance was her quarrelsomeness taken as a sign of insanity. Nevertheless, her exclusion underlines the desire for a certain level of discipline and order in charitable homes, which made them ill-suited venues for the care of the aged mentally infirm.

Several older patients came to Hanwell from St Joseph's Home for the Aged Poor, in Notting Hill. St Joseph's was opened in 1869 by the Little Sisters of the Poor, a French order of nuns who were established specifically to care for the aged. By the early 1870s, it was quite an operation, housing over 200 inmates, and 'giving an impression of a large workhouse hospital'. In spite of its mission as a home for the aged, one contemporary journalistic account suggests that it was largely populated by the healthy, younger aged, with the very old confined to the infirmaries, presenting 'truly a terrible sight' (Anon 1884). Historian Carmen Mangion (2012) argues that Catholic homes such as St Joseph's were prepared to offer physical medical care to the type of decrepit and incurable patients who would not have been admitted to voluntary hospitals. The case notes of one Hanwell patient, however, suggest that the Little Sisters' tolerance for mental infirmity and behavioural disruption was rather more limited.

Agnes Ryder was admitted to Hanwell in 1911, at the age of 62, from Kensington Infirmary, having been sent there from St Joseph's. Her medical certificate stated that she was 'constantly talking nonsense, singing, and disturbing others'. Upon her admission, however, the asylum doctors found her to be quite rational and calm, and soon wrote to St Joseph's, asking that she might return. They replied that she could not, fearing that she would deteriorate again as others had done in the past. 'We had an old man for a time,' they wrote, 'who also got well, but did not last long and got quite bad again in very short time.' Agnes was discharged, a month after her admission to Hanwell, to the workhouse infirmary – not back to St Joseph's (Hanwell Asylum 1911–1912: 101). Philanthropic and charitable institutions, then, could offer material necessities, treatments for physical ailments, and a level of personal care, but they relied on the submission of a docile population, willing and able to receive this care without challenge. The letters regarding Agnes Ryder's case suggest that those who did not conform to this dependent role were considered unsuitable. By apparently manifesting mental symptoms – even if they had entirely disappeared by the time she arrived at Hanwell – Agnes had transcended her status as a member of the deserving, dependent aged poor.

Conclusion

Victorian policy-makers repeatedly identified 'the senile' as a group whose needs were significant, and who could not be appropriately provided for by any of the existing health or welfare services. But those aged and infirm patients were described as a problem to be solved, or an encumbrance to be rid of; rarely as a group whose particular needs should be catered for. 'The senile' were a perpetual classificatory residuum in the bureaucracy of 19th-century health and welfare: too weak and unresponsive to adhere to the norms of the asylum regime, yet too challenging in their behaviour to conform to that of the workhouse, or the charitable home.

The case of the senile highlights a contradiction at the heart of 19th-century welfare policy and rhetoric: a group which embodied the 'deserving poor' in almost every way – old, incapable, and mentally troubled – was one for which no public institution was prepared to take unequivocal responsibility. This could offer a salient lesson for modern policy-makers. Nineteenth-century Britain was not an 'ageing society'. Indeed, because of the decline in infant mortality during this period, the proportion of the population aged over 60 was in fact historically low (Thane 2000: 3). Yet, as this article has shown, the treatment of the older population as a burden – specifically old people with dementia – predates the increase in longevity by several decades. It was therefore less the intractable fear of growing numbers, but rather the seeming intractability of dementia itself which turned health and welfare providers away from the challenge of providing adequate care, let alone a life of dignity. Ambivalence towards people living with dementia is in the very roots of the welfare state.

References

Andrews, E.S. (2014) Senility before Alzheimer: Old age in British Psychiatry, C. 1835–1912. Thesis submitted for the degree of Doctor of Philosophy in History. Coventry: University of Warwick.

Anon (1884) Little sisters. *All the Year Round*, 33, 788, 159.

Armstrong, M. (2000) Factors affecting the decision to place a relative with dementia into residential care, *Nursing Standard*, 14, 16, 33–7.

Ayers, G.M. (1971) *England's First State Hospitals and the Metropolitan Asylums Board 1867–1930*. London: Wellcome Institute for the History of Medicine.

Bartlett, P. (1999) *The Poor Law of Lunacy: The Administration of Pauper Lunatics in Mid-nineteenth-century England*. London: Leicester University Press.

Bevan Lewis, W. (1889) *A Text-book of Mental Disease: With Special Reference to the Pathological Aspects of Insanity*. London: Charles Griffin.

Beveridge, A. (1991) Thomas Clouston and the Edinburgh School of Psychiatry. In Berrios, G.E. and Freeman, H. (eds) *150 Years of British Psychiatry*. London: Gaskell.

Boyer, G. and Schmidle, T. (2009) Poverty among the elderly in Late Victorian England, *The Economic History Review*, 62, 2, 249–78.

Bucknill, J.C. and Tuke, D.H. (1858) *A Manual of Psychological Medicine*. Philadelphia: Blanchard and Lee.

Brown, T.E. (1994) Dance of the dialectic? Some reflections (polemic or otherwise) on the present state of nineteenth-century asylum studies, *Canadian Bulletin of Medical History*, 11, 2, 267–95.

Clouston, T.S. (1883) *Clinical Lectures on Mental Diseases*. London: J & A Churchill.

Clouston, T. (1886) Decrease of general paralysis, and increase of insanity at advanced ages, at Edinburgh, *British Medical Journal*, 1, 1323, 901.

Commissioners in Lunacy (1847–1912) *[XX]th Report of the Commissioners in Lunacy to the Lord Chancellor*. London: HM Stationery Office.

Cox, C. and Marland, H. (2015) A burden on the county: Madness, institutions of confinement and the Irish patient in Victorian Lancashire, *Social History of Medicine*, 28, 2, 263–87.

Crichton Brown, J. (1874) Clinical lectures on mental and cerebral diseases; – V, senile dementia, *The British Medical Journal*, 1, 697, 601–3.

Dickens, C. (1850) A walk in the workhouse, *Household Words*, 25 May, 204–7.

Doerner, K. (1977) *Madmen and the Bourgeoisie: A Social History of Insanity and Psychiatry*. Oxford: Blackwell.

Edwards, C. (1999) Age-based rationing of medical care in 19th-century England, *Continuity and Change*, 14, 2, 227–65.

Ellis, R. (2006) The asylum, the Poor Law and a reassessment of the four-shilling grant: Admissions to the county asylums of Yorkshire in the 19th Century, *Social History of Medicine*, 19, 1, 55–71.

Foucault, M. (1965) *Madness and Civilization: A History of Insanity in the Age of Reason*. London: Tavistock.

Gaugler, J.E., Yu, F., Krichbaum, K. and Wyman, J.F. (2009) Predictors of nursing home admission for persons with dementia, *Medical Care*, 47, 2, 191–8.

Gorsky, M., Harris, B. and Hinde, A. (2006) Age, sickness and longevity in the late nineteenth and early twentieth centuries: Evidence from the Hampshire Friendly Society, *Social Science History*, 30, 4, 571–600.

Green, D.R. (2002) Medical relief and the new Poor Law in London. In Grell, O., Cunningham, A. and Juette, R. (eds) *Health Care and Poor Relief in Eighteenth and Nineteenth-century Northern Europe*. Aldershot: Ashgate.

Green, D.R. (2010) *Pauper Capital: London and the Poor Law, 1790–1870*. Farnham: Ashgate.

Hanwell Asylum (1851–1852) Case book males No. 2 [Manuscript]. London Metropolitan Archive. H11/ HLL/B/20/002. London.

Hanwell Asylum (1869) Annual report of the Committee of Visitors of the County Lunatic Asylum at Hanwell [Manuscript]. London Metropolitan Archive. H11/HLL/A5/007. London.

Hanwell Asylum (1871–1872) Case book males No. 11 [Manuscript]. London Metropolitan Archive. H11/HLL/B/20/011. London.

Hanwell Asylum (1872) Case book females No. 22 [Manuscript]. London Metropolitan Archive. H11/ HLL/B/19/022. London.

Hanwell Asylum (1872.2) Case book females No. 23 [Manuscript]. London Metropolitan Archive. H11/ HLL/B/19/023. London.

Hanwell Asylum (1872.3) Case book males No. 12 [Manuscript]. London Metropolitan Archive. H11/ HLL/B/19/012. London.

Hanwell Asylum (1891) Case book males No. 12 [Manuscript]. London Metropolitan Archive. H11/ HLL/B/20/021. London.

Hanwell Asylum (1891.2) Case book female No. 13 [Manuscript]. London Metropolitan Archive. H11/ HLL/B/19/036. London.

Hanwell Asylum (1891–1892) Case book females No. 14 [Manuscript]. London Metropolitan Archive. H11/HLL/B/19/037. London.

Hanwell Asylum (1892) Case book females No. 15 [Manuscript]. London Metropolitan Archive. H11/ HLL/B/19/038. London.

Hanwell Asylum (1911–1912) Case book females No. 39 [Manuscript]. London Metropolitan Archive. H11/HLL/B/19/062. London.

Hare, E. (1983) Was insanity on the increase? The fifty-sixth Maudsley Lecture, *The British Journal of Psychiatry*, 142, 5, 439–55.

Jones, K. (1993) *Asylums and After: A Revised History of the Mental Health Services from the Early Eighteenth Century to the 1990s*. London: Athlone.

Lees, L. (1990) The survival of the unfit: Welfare policies and family maintenance in nineteenth-century London. In Mandler, P. (ed) *The Uses of Charity: The Poor on Relief in the Nineteenth-century Metropolis*. Philadelphia: University of Pennsylvania Press.

Lunbeck, E. (1994) *The Psychiatric Persuasion: Knowledge, Gender and Power in Modern America*. Princeton: Princeton University Press.

MAB (1871–1909) Minutes of the Metropolitan Asylums Board, Vols. V–XLIII. London.

Mangion, C.M. (2012) Faith, philanthropy and the aged poor in nineteenth-century England and Wales, *European Review of History*, 19, 4, 515–30.

Maudsley, H. (1877) The alleged increase of insanity, *Journal of Mental Science*, 23, 101, 51.

Mellett, D.J. (1982) *The Prerogative of Asylumdom: Social, Cultural and Administrative Aspects of the Institutional Treatment of the Insane in Nineteenth-century Britain*. New York: Garland.

Melling, J. (1999) Accommodating madness: New research in the history of insanity and institutions. In Melling, J. and Forsythe, B. (eds) *Insanity, Institutions and Society 1800–1914*. London: Routledge.

Melling, J. and Forsythe, B. (2006) *The Politics of Lunacy: The State, Insanity and Society in England 1845–1914*. London: Routledge.

Melling, J., Forsythe, B. and Adair, R. (1999) Families, communities and the legal regulation of lunacy in Victorian England: Assessments of crime, violence and welfare in admissions to the Devon Asylum 1845–1914. In Bartlett, P. and Wright, D. (eds) *Outside the Walls of the Asylums: The History of Care in the Community, 1750–2000*. London: Athlone Press.

Murphy, E. (2002) The Lunacy Commissioners and the East London Guardians 1845–1867, *Medical History*, 46, 4, 495–524.

Parsons, C.T. (1908) The difficulty of dealing with cases of senile insanity: Where are they to be accommodated?, *The Lancet*, 172, 4449, 1706–7.

Prichard, J.C. (1835) *A Treatise on Insanity and Other Disorders Affecting the Mind*. London: Sherwood, Gilbert and Piper.

Renvoise, E. (1991) The Association of Medical Officers of Asylums and Hospitals for the Insane, the Medico-Psychological Association and their presidents. In Berrios, G.E. and Freeman, H. (eds) *150 years of British psychiatry*. London: Gaskell.

Royal Commission on the Care and Control of the Feeble-Minded (1908) *Report of the Royal Commission on the Care and Control of the Feeble-Minded*, Vol. VIII. London: HM Stationery Office (Cd 4215).

Scull, A. (1979) *Museums of Madness: The Social Organization of Insanity in Nineteenth-century England*. New York: St. Martin's Press.

Scull, A. (1980) A convenient place to get rid of inconvenient people: The Victorian lunatic asylum. In King, A.D. (ed) *Buildings and Society: Essays on the Social Development of the Built Environment*. London: Routledge.

Scull, A. (1984) Was insanity increasing? A response to Edward Hare, *The British Journal of Psychiatry*, 144, 4, 432–6.

Scull, A. (1993) *The Most Solitary of Afflictions: Madness and Society in Britain 1700–1900*. New Haven: Yale University Press.

Scull, A. (1999) Rethinking the history of asylumdom. In Melling, J. and Forsythe, B. (eds) *Insanity, Institutions and Society 1800–1914*. London: Routledge.

Skae, D. (1863) A rational and practical classification of insanity, *Journal of Mental Science*, 9, 47, 309–19.

Smith, L. (1999) *Cure, Comfort and Safe Custody: Public Lunatic Asylums in Early Nineteenth Century England*. *London*: Leicester University Press.

Stoddart, W.H.B. (1908) *Mind and its Disorders: A Text-book for Students and Practitioners*. London: H. K. Lewis.

Sturdy, H. and Parry-Jones, W. (1999) Boarding out of insane patients: The significance of the Scottish system 1857–1913. In Bartlett, P. and Wright, D. (eds) *Outside the Walls of the Asylums: The History of Care in the Community 1750–2000*. London: Athlone Press.

Suzuki, A. (2006) *Madness at Home: The Psychiatrist, the Patient and the Family in England 1820–1860*. Berkeley: University of California Press.

Thane, P. (2000) *Old Age in English History: Past Experiences, Present Issues*. Oxford: Oxford University Press.

Walton, J. (1985) Casting Out and Bringing Back in Victorian England: Pauper Lunatics, 1840–70. In William, B.F., Roy, P. and Michael, S. (eds), *The Anatomy of Madness: Essays in the History of Psychiatry*.

Wright, D. (1997) Getting out of the asylum: Understanding the confinement of the insane in the nineteenth century, *Social History of Medicine*, 10, 1, 137–55.

Wright, D. (1998) The certification of Insanity in nineteenth-century England and Wales, *History of Psychiatry*, 9, 35, 267–90.

7

Dichotomising dementia: is there another way?
Patricia Mc Parland, Fiona Kelly and Anthea Innes

Introduction: a dichotomised view

In Western society, the last 50 years have seen a gradual shift in our understandings of dementia as academic, policy and popular discourses on the condition have evolved (Downs *et al.* 2006). Up until the early 1970s, experiences of symptoms associated with dementia were linked to and categorised by age, for example, Alzheimer's disease, established in 1907, was categorised as an exclusively pre-senile dementia, in contrast to the already existing senile dementia (Fox 1989, Lyman 1989). Holstein (1997) documents the historical move to eliminate the demarcation between these two previously separate conditions so that by the 1970s they were together labelled as the single greatest killer disease in the USA. Over time dementia has come to be used as an umbrella term for a range of symptoms that can occur as a result of the deterioration in brain functioning caused by a variety of conditions, including Alzheimer's disease (World Health Organization 2012). Biomedical approaches continue to dominate understandings of dementia, with an explicit focus on loss of function, decline and death; fuelling what has come to be known as a 'tragedy discourse'. The tragedy discourse also dominates carer experiences and stories (Behuniak 2011, Fontana and Smith 1989, Gillies 2011), and continues to be a primary tool of the media (Bartlett and O'Connor 2010, Johnstone 2013, Van Gorp and Vercruysse 2012). However more recently, a move to challenge the tragedy discourse has seen the emergence of the 'living well' discourse, where the emphasis has shifted from loss and decline to supporting remaining strengths and recognising enduring personhood.

Dementia is a complex and challenging condition that will be experienced differently depending on one's age, class, gender, other health conditions, life experiences and a plethora of other social differences (Innes 2009, Kitwood 1997). Hulko (2004) talks about the intersectionality of the experience of dementia. This is a useful way to understand that the experience of dementia relates closely to the social differentiation present in society. Dementia means different things to different people depending on their social context but it is also experienced across a spectrum of care and support needs, and thus, rather than understanding it as a dichotomised experience of tragedy or living well it must be understood within wider social constructs and contexts. In the tragedy discourse there has been little room for any alternative experience at any point in a person's journey with dementia and

Ageing, Dementia and the Social Mind, First Edition. Edited by Paul Higgs and Chris Gilleard.
Chapters © 2017 The Authors. Book Compilation © 2017 Foundation for the Sociology of
Health & Illness/Blackwell Publishing Ltd.

this is also reflected in stereotyping language used about dementia or to describe someone with dementia. Critiques of such language used in discourse about dementia suggest that the themes of animalism (Mc Parland 2014), zombies (Behuniak 2010) and social death (Sweeting and Gilhooley 1997) continue to be perpetuated. Thus, language does more than acknowledge the potential tragedy of living with such a condition; it facilitates the labelling of a person with dementia as 'other' (Goffman 1963, Hughes *et al.* 2006, Kitwood 1997), setting them apart as deviant in some form and different from other members of society. Bruens (2014) suggests that dementia has throughout history been used as a term to identify those considered to be outside normal society, that it remains the most terrifying of conditions, and that a widespread response is to treat those with the condition as though 'they are no longer people' (2014: 84).

The move from a social death (Sweeting and Gilhooly 1997) to a living well discourse (DoH 2009) reflects both a challenge to the previous discourse and a push towards the inclusion of the previously absent voices of people living with dementia (Scottish Dementia Working Group 2016, Swaffer 2011, Taylor 2008). Such developments highlight the possibility of living well with the condition and place an emphasis on social inclusion and positive ongoing life experiences (Dupuis *et al.* 2012). Campaigning organisations are working to shift public perceptions and remove stigma through public awareness drives (Alzheimer Society Canada 2013, Alzheimer Society Ireland 2015, Department of Health [DoH] 2012). It is also interesting to note that the language of policy has shifted with the title of the DoH's (2009) English national dementia strategy 'Living well with dementia', offering a strong indication of a shift in discourse to how we can support, enable and promote living rather than dying with dementia.

In addition, this challenge to the tragedy discourse raises important questions about what we think we know about dementia (Whitehouse and George 2008) and how this impacts on diagnosis, policy, practice, theory and both academic and common sense knowledge. Worldwide dementia policy influencers (Alzheimer's Disease International 2012) have shifted their focus away from loss to supporting strengths, and this is also true of UK policy directives (DoH 2009, 2012, 2015). This can be contextualised within a broader ageing well policy landscape (Walker and Maltby 2012), with an emphasis on individuals taking responsibility for their health. In the media, images of engaged older people participating in sports and leisure abound, and these healthy older people are recognised as being consumers who have time and money to spend. However, there is little in policy or the media that acknowledges the role of socioeconomic factors or power relationships on whether a person is able to participate in this healthy older age agenda.

To shift current perceptions it is essential to provide an alternative image of what it means to live with dementia; one that offers possibility and even hope. However, such an approach also has limitations in that it risks disenfranchising those with complex comorbidities and extreme cognitive difficulties; that is, those who are most vulnerable and who are living with dementia.

It is against such a backdrop that this article considers the predominately western 'successful ageing' paradigm and its implications for dementia. We discuss the tragedy and living well discourses and the dichotomy between the two, before moving on to argue for the need to move away from a dichotomised approach to one that accepts the complex nature of dementia, with the multiple and myriad experiences that may occur along the trajectory of living with this condition. We argue that efforts to normalise people living with dementia risk further exclusion of the most vulnerable and even division among those affected by this condition, and that the acceptance of a living well agenda as a positive move in the dementia discourse must be problematised.

Ageing paradigms

Successful ageing (Havighurst 1961, Rowe and Kahn 1997) is synonymous with terms including 'active ageing', 'ageing well' and 'healthy ageing' and has at its core an emphasis on individual agency and control, the value of independence and the necessity of avoiding dependence, the value of remaining physically and cognitively active and, ultimately, efforts to deny the deleterious aspects of the ageing process. Lamb (2014) offers a useful discussion on the emergence of and rationale for the successful ageing movement originating in the USA and adopted in other Western countries, including Europe and Australia. This movement has been the subject of much debate among critical gerontologists (Biggs 2004, Calasanti 2003, Holstein and Minkler 2003) who argue that one of the consequences of such a paradigm is discrimination against those who are not in a position to engage with active agency in old age or to be productive in a traditional sense. While it is not within the remit of this article to engage with this debate, it does set the scene for our discussion. Older age is associated with dementia, both in real terms, as the risk of dementia increases with age and conceptually, as it remains a condition that continues to be understood by many as part of the ageing process. Indeed 95 per cent of those living with dementia are over the age of 65 (Alzheimer Society 2014). This article thus focuses on dementia as a condition associated with older age but it is worth noting that it is not an attempt to deny the equally challenging experience of living with an early onset dementia. We argue that the very diagnosis of dementia when one is younger has the potential to conceptually catapult the younger person into the terrain or imagery associated with the most vulnerable old.

Higgs (1995) suggests that in the field of health care, older people are presented with two images of ageing: one of the active, healthy person who works to deny old age (the third ager) and the other who is frail and dependant (the fourth ager). Maintaining good health or 'the will to health' is central to third agers' pursuit of a lifestyle in which they have control over their ageing. Thus autonomy is central to third agers and loss of autonomy defines the fourth age (Higgs *et al.* 2009). Dohmen (2014) argues that 'with impairment and decline considered antonyms of successful ageing, the "fourth age" is automatically deemed "unsuccessful" by means of its proximity to illness and death' (2014: 66), while Pickard (2013), in an interrogation of clinical literature on the discourses of senescence and frailty, links the meaning derived from the third age as an opposition to frailty, with the intention of avoiding it. The linking of frailty with the fourth age is further developed by Higgs and Gilleard (2014) who suggest that although frailty is synonymous with the fourth age (the 'frailing' of the fourth age), the overwhelming fear is of an imagined future incapacity and the dread of 'going into care' with the isolation, reduction of autonomy and othering this is perceived to bring. From the point of view of those in the third age working to maintain health and lifestyle, the fourth age 'appears as a horrific apparition that dramatises lack in a rather potent way' (West and Glynos 2016: 230).

Greenberg *et al.* (2002) suggest that non-old people manage their terror of this potential future by regarding older people as intrinsically different from them. Branelly (2011) also suggests that younger, healthier people distance themselves from older, incapacitated people, while Jönson (2013) argues that non-old people, using a temporal construction of old age, contrast their future selves as essentially different from old people of today. This crucially, permits the justification of practices, such as substandard care in care homes, that would not be seen as acceptable to non-old people's future old selves. The fourth age, then, is for others: 'the necessarily distant negative horizon that cannot be allowed to intrude upon third age positivity and control', thus it becomes 'a horizon we can only dread' (West and Glynos 2016: 231).

A tragedy discourse

If we accept that the paradigm of successful ageing is established, particularly among Western societies, we then need to interrogate where people with dementia are socially located. Van Dyk (2014: 96) suggests that older people who are dependent on care, or have dementia or other severe chronic conditions are 'as marginalized and stereotyped as ever, probably even more so'; in the context of 'successful ageing' they are the 'failed ones' because they have not worked hard enough to maintain a third age status.

Mc Parland (2014), in her study of the general public's response to dementia, suggests that the stigma attached to dementia is made up of a complex interplay of many jeopardies (Brooker 2003, Hulko 2004) and labels (Hughes *et al.* 2006, Link and Phelan 2001) but it is also associated with existing perceptions of care, feelings of hopelessness or futility, and a profound fear of developing a condition that appears utterly arbitrary and totally beyond the control of the individual or the world of science and medicine. She argues this 'dementiaism' is driven not only by the social location or labelled identity of the person with dementia, but also by the emotional responses of others to this social location and labelling, with the public visualising a potential future that symbolises loss of control, loss of self, living in poor care and being viewed as 'mad'. Bond *et al.* (2004) have also described the denial of practical citizenship to people with dementia due in part to others' (including family members') negative attributions of their remaining ability to choose their preferred lifestyles. This, they claim is stigmatising, exclusionary and ultimately, diminishing for the person with dementia exposed to such responses.

Zeilig (2014) details the myriad of emotionally charged metaphors used to describe or discuss dementia in policy and general discourse; all of which evoke a general sense of calamity and have the power to terrify us and make us feel powerless. She points to the ways in which frequently used metaphors shape our consciousness about dementia, frailty and dependency. Bartlett and O'Connor (2010) argue that society continues to respond to people with dementia in a deeply stigmatising way, viewing them as 'tragic, weak and completely incapable' (2010: 98). In an effort to distance themselves from such a potential future, the public regards the person with dementia as 'other', creating a social and psychological distance between themselves and this terrifying prospect (Deitrich *et al.* 2004, Greenberg *et al.* 2002, Mc Parland 2014, Werner and Davidson 2004). This is exacerbated by the growing public profile of dementia as the disease of the century, with Ballenger (2006) arguing that the efforts to inform and educate the public that dementia is a disease and thus not the responsibility of the person, fail to understand the true nature of stigma, described as 'the amount of anxiety surrounding the boundary between the normal and the pathological' (Ballenger 2006: 114). The stereotypical picture, among the public, of a person with dementia is of a much older person, living in care and entirely dependent on others for their daily living activities (Mc Parland 2014), closely aligned with the construct of the fourth age as a location without agency or autonomy (Gilleard and Higgs 2010).

The context of these understandings of dementia as a location of frailed, unsuccessful ageing creates the opportunity for society to exclude those affected by the condition, creating different rules, different systems and locations of care and affording others the right to make decisions for people with dementia that they would not consider for their own future selves. In the context of ageing, Baars and Phillipson argue that 'processses of socialisation often carry cultural messages of familiarity versus strangeness that imply practices of inclusion and rejection' (2014: 16). In the case of dementia, this rejection is often complete, when the person with dementia, now regarded as 'other', moves into care, literally making the transition from one world to another. Care homes have been, and to a great extent still are, regarded as a last resort (Townsend 1962); the place where people with dementia must go when they have moved beyond manageable boundaries in our world. Indeed Gilleard and Higgs (2010) suggest that nursing homes have become as terrifying as the workhouses once were. At their most cognitively impaired and thus most vulnerable, people with dementia are not regarded by the general public as 'of our world', nor considered to be bound by the same rules, nor are their human or citizenship rights respected to the same extent as those without dementia (Graham 2004, Kelly and Innes 2013). In the context of the successful ageing paradigm, those with dementia who are most frail have failed the living well test.

Living well – a positive discourse

A diagnosis of dementia inevitably threatens personal identity, roles and expectations for a person's future, and language such as zombie, patient, disease, sufferer, dementing or demented does little to allay fears about such losses. In a movement to counter the impact of such positioning language and its negative consequences, Kitwood (1997) argued that it was possible, and imperative, to support those with dementia to live meaningful lives and that this could be achieved by supporting their personhood; their unique sense of their personal identity, through interactions that have at their core the goal of meeting the individuals' needs for comfort, attachment, inclusion, occupation, identity and, ultimately, love. Sabat (2001) developed this understanding to encompass notions of enduring selfhood that, although contingent on recognition and support from others (Kelly 2010), enable the person with dementia to live well. Kontos (2005) takes this further by applying the meaning this has for the experiences and delivery of care and support, demonstrating that the conceptual understandings of dementia have a very real impact on lived experiences (Kontos and Naglie 2009). This approach to giving voice to people with dementia has been extended to using creative approaches to present the views and experiences of those living with dementia. Killick (2014) has worked using creative media to challenge the public's fear and helplessness associated with dominant medical conceptualisations of dementia; by using poetry to give voice (Goldsmith 1996) to insights of living with dementia. His work is visionary in that it seeks to de-mystify the experience of living with dementia and to illustrate that living with dementia can also be joyous, humorous or creative. Snyder's work highlights the power of language and extra-linguistic communication via body language, facial expression or vocal tones in impacting on intercommunication. She calls on us to regard people with dementia as our teachers: 'we must listen to them as if the well-being of humanity depended on our understanding' (Snyder 2006: 274). This resonates with Post's (2006: 225) proposal that society must affirm the 'continuing moral status of the deeply forgetful'.

Research on positive approaches to dementia has included cognitive rehabilitation (Clare and Woods 2001), coping strategies used by people with dementia (Clare 2002) and self-management (Toms et al. 2015); all part of a body of work countering the nihilism of a tragedy discourse. Genoe et al. (2010) discuss the ways in which people with dementia actively work to maintain their personal identity and social roles and describe how family carers use mealtimes to honour the identity and humanness of the person with dementia: emphasising their strengths, respecting their dignity, their uniqueness as individuals and their common bonds as members of a family. Genoe and Dupuis (2011), drawing on Sabat's work, show that experiences of threat and loss in dementia were resisted by adapting and recreating identity through leisure, illustrating the work that people with dementia do themselves to counter the challenges of living with dementia. Although a movement in the right direction towards hearing the voice (Goldsmith 1996) of people with dementia, research into their experiences remains disproportionate, potentially excluding the experiences and voices of those who are most cognitively impaired and most frail. Indeed, Bruens suggests that the subjective experience of people with dementia in formal care settings 'is still very rarely heard' (2014: 92).

The positive or living well discourse has gradually developed in academia and policy but has yet to have a significant impact on public discourse (Bartlett and O'Connor 2010, Bruens 2014, Mc Parland 2014); instead, this discourse remains primarily one of tragedy, as seen in the literature, media representations and personal accounts. Policy ambitions and campaigning organisations are working to move this living well discourse into public awareness in their efforts to remove the stigma reported by people with dementia and their family carers. Recent campaigns (Alzheimer Society Ireland 2015) are using images of people living well with dementia; images of people continuing to participate in 'normal' life, who are articulate and physically able. Highlighting the normality (Baars and Phillipson 2014) of the life of the person with dementia, these campaigns challenge previously established notions of the 'empty shell' or 'living dead'; and offer an alternative image to the dominant stereotypical image of the most vulnerable and frail person with dementia. This living well discourse has, perhaps for the first time, allowed our understanding of dementia to move towards the successful ageing paradigm.

Dichotomising dementia

We have shown that there are two opposing discourses constructing understandings of dementia; the tragedy discourse and the living well discourse. However, we suggest they are neither co-existing successfully, nor offering a happy marriage that might create a discourse that is more reflective of lived reality. Efforts to include the voice of the person with dementia have seen people living with this condition participating in research, presenting at conferences and featuring in campaigns to shift public understandings. In these instances they are often younger and well educated, usually, and often of necessity, not living with the most challenging aspects of this condition. Page and Keady (2010) suggest that there remains a tendency to privilege male and middle class voices over poorly educated female ones. There is scant literature on the expressed experiences of people living with dementia in non-Western cultures (Mazaheri *et al.* 2013), and as already stated the argument we present here is grounded in a Western perspective and draws on Western literature. However Mazaheri *et al.* suggest that 'the core experience of people with dementia is to some extent universal, despite differences in cultural and political contexts and with different religious beliefs or confessions' (Mazaheri *et al.* 2013: 3037).

Perhaps in line with the successful old, those arguably living well or successfully with dementia could in many respects consider themselves still residing in the third age; agents in creating their own future. Thus, it would appear that the positive, living well discourse does not generally include those living with the most severe cognitive and physical challenges; people with dementia who are usually living in institutional care. We suggest that, currently, rather than being viewed as differing aspects of the same experience, these two voices on the discursive continuum of dementia are potentially competing with each other. If we consider some of the earlier arguments, it is perhaps not surprising they have initially emerged in this competitive form.

A further paradox relates to the voices of people living with dementia in the public forum, whether at conferences, via blogs or in campaigning activities. Many do not draw attention to the more frightening potential future they may face; the fourth age. They concentrate their efforts on encouraging society to recognise people with dementia as normal people living with a difficult condition; they are fighting for inclusion and recognition. This is an entirely legitimate and powerful discourse that is intended to move people with dementia out of the shadows and ensure that they are included as full members of society. In the context of ageing, Van Dyk (2014: 14) refers to the fruitless dichotomy of sameness ('they have to be like us') and difference ('they are the others'). We take this further and question whether people with dementia should have to aspire to be the same, as this still potentially positions them as different if their condition progresses to a point where they are unable to articulate their needs or where they require assistance with all their daily living activities. The risk of a tragedy or living well dichotomy is that it divides people with dementia into those who are living well or successfully with dementia and those who are no longer able to maintain society's notion of living well, and are thus living in the shadows.

Offering the opportunity for new ways of living with dementia and the potential for more acceptance is a tantalising possibility but, similar to Van Dyk's (2014) description of the active ageing paradigm, it in fact offers a new set of social expectations. Furthermore, it is an opportunity that is available only to those meeting certain criteria. Critical gerontologists have raised ethical objections to the idea of anti-discrimination and re-valuation based on achievement and outcome. They criticise the attempt to challenge negative stereotypes of old age with the assertion that older people do contribute to society and are thus worthy and valuable (Martinson and Halpern 2011). Based on these criteria, some people living with dementia will no longer be among this group of the valued and worthy. Lamb asks if the Western paradigm of successful ageing comes at:

> the expense of coming to meaningful terms with late-life changes, situations of (inter)dependence, possibilities of frailty, and the condition of human transience? – setting up for 'failure' embarrassment, or loss of social personhood those who face inevitable bodily or cognitive impairments and impending mortality. (Lamb 2014: 42)

In a thoughtful interrogation of others' perceptions of her mother, living with dementia in a care home, Taylor (2008) also challenges notions of social death (Sweeting and Gilhooly 1997) and the denial of recognition as friend and fellow human being of a person with dementia.

A shadow reality, on the edge of society, continues to be the daily experience of many people living at the most extreme end of dementia. Our concern is how to remember and respect this most vulnerable group of people in the context of the new imagery associated with living well or successfully with dementia. While the newly visible group of people living well with dementia strive to convince society that they are part of its normality, the more vulnerable group of people living with advanced dementia continue to epitomise deviance, differentness or 'otherness'. Baars and Phillipson suggest that 'normality is an elusive concept that invariably serves specific interests' (2014: 11), and struggles on the part of people with dementia to be accepted as part of normality may prove equally elusive. Moving society towards a respectful acceptance and inclusion of the most vulnerable living with dementia is a difficult endeavour, for this group continue to represent that most primal, transcendental fear: 'loss of self'. In our hyper-cognitive society (Post 1995), loss of cognitive ability is closely aligned to assumptions of loss of self, and the physical frailty and diminishing control over bodily functions that often accompany it act to further enhance the fear of this condition. The fear related to dementia is primarily of where we might be socially located as a result of the condition, and that location is within the fourth age, stripped of choice, autonomy and self-expression (Gilleard and Higgs 2010); no longer viewed as a 'real' or 'complete' person.

At a philosophical level dementia arguably represents the human struggle with life and death and our lack of control over these states. Bavidge (2006) has challenged our views of life, death and dying, asking why we view the cognitive impairments that may occur as we grow older as pathological, yet not view the cognitive impairments associated with childhood and adolescence as pathological. A child who does not speak but simply smiles and watches the world go by, responding to touch, sound and smell, is regarded with joy and valued by virtue of their presence in the world. A person with dementia who does the same is regarded with dismay and, if viewed as no longer contributing to society in a meaningful way, is not valued or at least not valued equally.

If we fail to challenge and redress the current dichotomy of these discourses, the risk is that, rather than changing the script around dementia we have simply shifted the boundaries so that some people will live with acknowledged difficulties, accepted and, it is hoped, valued in society for longer periods of time, but some will not. We risk a discourse that urges those living with dementia to fight to continue to meet society's definition of a life that is normal and has value, rather than challenging the very definitions of normality and value. For some, the progression of the condition may mean they never reach what has been described as the fourth age before death. However for many, dependence and potentially care-home life will become a reality at some point in the trajectory of their condition. Unless we challenge societal responses to this life, then the best that can be hoped for with the living well discourse is to delay this frailing life. Furthermore, the group of people living at an earlier point in their dementia and struggling to resist or even deny the most frightening potential of their condition are perhaps the most likely to 'other' this vulnerable group in their efforts to create a social and psychological distance from their potential future. Such a discourse, in effect, means that while some progress has been made in that some of the people living with dementia will be better included in our society for longer, others inevitably no longer will be.

Conclusion

Dementia is a condition that society has been unable to overcome. It is also a condition primarily associated with ageing and Baars and Phillipson suggest that 'modern cultures of ageing often have difficulty acknowledging and dignifying limitations that cannot be overcome but must be successfully integrated in ways of living' (2014: 26). It could be argued that society continues to deny the multiple and complex realities of dementia, albeit in a new form; the living well discourse. Efforts to shift policy and public perceptions through a positive discourse may potentially contribute to the further exclusion of the most vulnerable living with dementia. Rather than this discourse addressing the cultural and societal responses to an undeniably challenging condition, it may instead perpetuate divisive public perceptions and indeed create division among people with dementia themselves. We argue that discourse should recognise the myriad of experiences and the inherent complexity of living and dying with dementia. The notion of living well with dementia has been a necessary response to counter the previous tragedy discourse. However, it could be argued that in many ways it is just as discriminatory, placing new social expectations and criteria on those living with dementia. We argue that it is time to challenge the idea of living well, particularly in the context of active ageing; to challenge the notion of normality and of value in the ongoing dementia discourse. Baars and Phillipson (2014: 26) suggest that 'celebrating ageing as a vital part of life implies recognition of the potentials *and* limitations, the pleasurings and sufferings, the continuing vitality, competence *and* vulnerability of ageing'. Applying such a celebration to dementia would mean accepting that the discourses of living well and tragedy are equally compelling aspects of living with dementia, and that the denial of one or the other is disingenuous. Dementia discourse must acknowledge the limitations associated with this condition, while discovering the remaining pleasures. At the core of both discourses exist some of the truths inherent to experiences of dementia. Unpicking and facing other truths and realities; both the frightening and the joyous, the painful and the liberating, offers the opportunity to produce a future discourse that would more accurately reflect and support the multiple realities of dementia, reduce the risk of marginalisation and create the opportunity for social inclusion.

References

Alzheimer's Disease International, (2012) World Alzheimer Report 2012. Available at http://www.alz.co.uk/research/world-report-2012 (Last accessed 7 October 2015).

Alzheimer Society (2014) Demography. Available at http://www.alzheimers.org.uk/site/scripts/documents_info.php?documentID=412 (Last accessed 14 April 2016).

Alzheimer Society Canada (2013) See me, not my disease. Lets talk about dementia. Available at http://www.alzheimer.ca/chathamkent/~/media/Files/chapters-on/chathamkent/Newsletter%20-%20 Winter% 202013.pdf (Last accessed 5 July 2013).

Alzheimer Society Ireland (2015) Forget the stigma. Available at http://alzheimer.ie/Get-Involved/Campaigning/Forget-the-Stigma.aspx (Last accessed 7 July 2015)

Baars, J. and Phillipson, C. (2014) Connecting meaning with social structure: theoretical foundations. In Baars, J., Dohmen, J., Grenier, A. and Phillipson, C. (eds) *Ageing, Meaning and Social Structure; Connecting Critical and Humanistic Gerontology*. Bristol: Policy Press.

Ballenger, J.F. (2006) The biomedical deconstruction of senility and the persistent stigmatization of old age in the United States. In Leibing, L. and Cohen, L. (eds) *Thinking about Dementia: Culture, Loss and the Anthropology of Senility*. New Brunswick: Rutgers University Press.

Bartlett, R. and O'Connor, D. (2010) *Broadening the Dementia Debate; Towards Social Citizenship*. Bristol: Policy Press.

Bavidge, M. (2006) Ageing and human nature. In Hughes, J.C., Louw, S.J. and Sabat, S.R. (eds) *Dementia, Mind, Meaning and the Person*. Oxford: Oxford University Press.

Behuniak, S.M. (2011) The living dead? The construction of people with Alzheimer's Disease as zombies, *Aging & Society*, 31, 1, 70–92.

Biggs, S. (2004) New ageism: age imperialism, personal experience and ageing policy. In Daatland, S.O. and Biggs, S. (eds) *Ageing and Diversity*. Bristol: Policy Press.

Bond, J., Corner, L. and Graham, R. (2004) Social science theory on dementia research: normal ageing, cultural representation and social exclusion. In Innes, A., Archibald, C. and Murphy, C. (eds) *Dementia and Social Inclusion*. London: Jessica Kingsley.

Branelly, T. (2011) Sustaining citizenship: people with dementia and the phenomena of social death, *Nursing Ethics*, 18, 5, 662–7.

Brooker, D. (2003) What is person-centred care in dementia? *Reviews in Clinical Gerontology*, 13, 3, 215–22.

Bruens, M.T. (2014) Dementia; beyond structures of medicalisation and cultural neglect. In Baars, J., Dohmen, J., Grenier, A. and Phillipson, C. (eds) *Ageing, Meaning and Social Structure; Connecting Critical and Humanistic Gerontology*. Bristol: Policy Press.

Calasanti, T. (2003) Theorizing age relations. In Biggs, S., Lowenstein, A. and Hendricks, J. (eds) *The Need for Theory: Critical Approaches to Social Gerontology*. New York: Baywood.

Clare, L. (2002) We'll fight it as long as we can: coping with the onset of Alzheimer's disease, *Aging and Mental Health*, 6, 2, 139–48.

Clare, L. and Woods, R. (eds) (2001) *Cognitive Rehabilitation in Dementia: A Special Issue of Neuropsychological Rehabilitation*. Hove: Psychology Press.

Deitrich, S., Beck, M., Bujantugs, B., Kenzine, D., *et al.* (2004) The relationship between public causal beliefs and social distance towards mentally ill people, *Australian and New Zealand Journal of Psychiatry*, 38, 5, 348–54.

Department of Health (DoH) (2009) *Living Well with Dementia: A National Dementia Strategy.* London: Department of Health.

DoH (2012) Prime Minister's challenge on dementia: delivering major improvements in dementia care and research by 2015. London: Department of Health.

Dohmen, J. (2014) My own life: ethics, ageing and lifestyle. In Baars, J., Dohmen, J., Grenier, A. and Phillipson, C. (eds) *Ageing, Meaning and Social Structure; Connecting Critical and Humanistic Gerontology*. Bristol: Policy Press.

Downs, M., Clare, L. and Mackenzie, J. (2006) Understandings of dementia: explanatory models and their implications for the person with dementia and therapeutic effect. In Hughes, J., Louw, S. and Sabat, S. (eds) *Dementia: Mind, Meaning and the Person*. Oxford: Oxford University Press.

Dupuis, S.L., Wiersma, E. and Loiselle, L. (2012) Pathologizing behavior: meanings of behaviors in dementia care, *Journal of Aging Studies*, 26, 2, 162–73.

Fontana, A. and Smith, R. (1989) Alzheimer's disease victims: the unbecoming of self and the normalization of competence, *Sociological Perspectives*, 32, 1, 35–46.

Fox, P. (1989) From senility to Alzheimer's disease: the rise of the Alzheimer's disease movement, *Millbank Quarterly*, 67, 1, 58–102.

Genoe, R. and Dupuis, S. (2011) 'I'm just like I always was': a phenomenological exploration of leisure, identity and dementia, *Leisure/Loisir*, 35, 4, 423–52.

Genoe, R., Dupuis, S., Keller, H., Schindel Martin, L., *et al.* (2010) Honouring identity through mealtimes in families living with dementia, *Journal of Aging Studies*, 24, 3, 181–93.

Gilleard, C. and Higgs, P. (2010) Aging without agency: theorising the fourth age, *Aging and Mental Health*, 14, 2, 121–8.

Gillies, B. (2011) Continuity and loss: the carer's journey through dementia, *Dementia*, 11, 5, 657–76.

Goffman, E. (1963) *Stigma: Notes on the Management of Spoiled Identity*. New York: Prentice Hall.

Goldsmith, M. (1996) *Hearing the Voice of People with Dementia: Opportunities and Obstacles*. London: Jessica Kingsley.

Graham, R. (2004) Cognitive citizenship: access to hip surgery for people with dementia, *Health*, 8, 3, 295–310.

Greenberg, J., Schimel, J. and Martens, A. (2002) Ageism: denying the face of the future. In Nelson, T.D. (ed) *Ageism, Stereotyping and Prejudice Against Older Persons*. Cambridge: MIT Press.

Havighurst, R.J. (1961) Successful aging, *Gerontologist*, 1, 1, 8–13.

Higgs, P. (1995) Citizenship and old age: the end of the road? *Ageing & Society*, 15, 4, 535–50.

Higgs, P. and Gilleard, C. (2014) Frailty, abjection and the 'othering' of the fourth age, *Health Sociology Review*, 23, 1, 10–9.

Higgs, P., Leontowitsch, M., Stevenson, F. and Jones, I.R. (2009) Not just old and sick – the 'will to health' in later life, *Ageing & Society*, 29, 5, 687–707.

Holstein, M. (1997) Alzheimer's disease and senile dementia, 1885–1920: an interpretive history of disease negotiation, *Journal of Aging Studies*, 11, 1, 1–13.

Holstein, M.B. and Minkler, M. (2003) Self, society and the 'new gerontology', *Gerontologist*, 43, 6, 787–96.

Hughes, J.C., Louw, S.J. and Sabat, S.R. (2006) *Dementia, Mind, Meaning and the Person*. Oxford: Oxford University Press.

Hulko, W. (2004) Social science perspectives on dementia research: intersectionality. In Innes, A., Archibald, C. and Murphy, C. (eds) *Dementia and Social Inclusion*. London: Jessica Kingsley.

Innes, A. (2009) *Dementia Studies: A Social Science Perspective*. London: Sage.

Johnstone, M. (2013) *Alzheimer's Disease, Media Representations and the Politics of Euthanasia: Constructing Risk and Selling Death in an Ageing Society*. Farnham: Ashgate.

Jönson, H. (2013) We will be different! Ageism and the temporal construction of old age, *Gerontologist*, 53, 2, 198–204.

Kelly, F. (2010) Recognising and supporting self in dementia: a new way to facilitate a person-centred approach to dementia care, *Ageing & Society*, 30, 1, 103–24.

Kelly, F. and Innes, A. (2013) Human rights and citizenship in dementia care nursing, *International Journal of Older People Nursing*, 8, 1, 61–70.

Killick, J. (2014) *Dementia Positive*. Edinburgh: Luath.

Kitwood, T. (1997) *Dementia Reconsidered: The Person Comes First*. Buckingham: Open University Press.

Kontos, P. (2005) Embodied selfhood in Alzheimer's disease: rethinking person centred care, *Dementia*, 4, 4, 553–70.

Kontos, P. and Naglie, G. (2009) Tacit knowledge of caring and embodied selfhood, *Sociology of Health & Illness*, 31, 5, 688–704.

Lamb, S. (2014) Permanent personhood or meaningful decline? Toward a critical anthropology of successful aging, *Journal of Aging Studies*, 29, 41–52.

Link, B.G. and Phelan, J.C. (2001) Conceptualizing stigma, *Annual Review of Sociology*, 27, 363–85.

Lyman, K. (1989) Bringing the social back in: a critique of the biomedicalization of dementia, *Gerontologist*, 29, 5, 597–605.

Mc Parland, P. (2014) Dementia: what comes to mind? PhD thesis. Available at http://dspace.stir.ac.uk/ handle/1893/20411#.VaKbuPlViko (Last accessed 6 June 2015).

Martinson, M. and Halpern, J. (2011) Ethical implications of the promotion of elder volunteerism: a critical perspective, *Journal of Aging Studies*, 25, 4, 427–35.

Mazaheri, M., Eriksson, L., Heikkila, K., Nasrabadi, A., *et al.* (2013) Experiences of living with dementia: qualitative content analysis of semi-structured interviews, *Journal of Clinical Nursing*, 22, 3032–41.

Page, S. and Keady, J. (2010) Sharing stories: a meta-ethnographic analysis of twelve autobiographies written by people with dementia between 1989–2007, *Ageing and Society*, 30, 3, 511–26.

Pickard, S. (2013) Frail bodies: geriatric medicine and the constitution of the fourth age, *Sociology of Health & Illness*, 36, 4, 549–63.

Post, S. (1995) *The Moral Challenge of Alzheimer Disease*. Baltimore and London: John Hopkins University Press.

Post, S. (2006) Respectare: moral respect for the lives of the deeply forgetful. In Hughes, J., Louw, S. and Sabat, S. (eds) *Dementia: Mind, Meaning and the Person*. Oxford: Oxford University Press.

Rowe, J.W. and Kahn, R.L. (1997) Successful aging, *The Gerontologist*, 37, 4, 433–40.

Sabat, S. (2001) The Experience of Alzheimer's Disease: *Life through a Tangled Veil*. Oxford: Blackwell.

Scottish Dementia Working Group (2016) About us. Available at http://www.sdwg.org.uk/ (Last accessed 14 April 2016).

Snyder, L. (2006) Personhood and interpersonal communication in dementia. In Hughes, J., Louw, S. and Sabat, S. (eds) *Dementia: Mind, Meaning and the Person*. Oxford: Oxford University Press.

Swaffer, K. (2011) Creating life with words: inspiration, love and truth. Available at http://kateswaffer.com/ (Last accessed 14 April 2016).

Sweeting, H. and Gilhooly, M. (1997) Dementia and the phenomenon of social death, *Sociology of Health & Illness*, 19, 1, 93–117.

Taylor, J. (2008) On Recognition, Caring, and Dementia, *Medical Anthropology Quarterly*, 22, 4, 313–35.

Toms, G., Quinn, C., Anderson, D. and Clare, L. (2015) Help yourself: perspectives on self-management from people with dementia and their caregivers, *Qualitative Health Research*, 25, 1, 87–98.

Townsend, P. (1962) *The Last Refuge: a Survey of Residential Institutions and Homes for the Aged in England and Wales*. London: Routledge and K. Paul.

Van Dyk, S. (2014) The appraisal of difference: critical gerontology and the active-ageing-paradigm, *Journal of Aging Studies*, 31, 93–103.

Van Gorp, B. and Vercruysse, T. (2012) Frames and counter-frames giving meaning to dementia: a framing analysis of media content, *Social Science & Medicine*, 74, 8, 1274–81.

Walker, A. and Maltby, T. (2012) Active ageing: a strategic policy solution to demographic ageing in the European Union, *International Journal of Social Welfare*, 21, 1, S117–30.

Werner, P. and Davidson, D. (2004) Emotional reactions of lay persons to someone with Alzheimer's disease, *International Journal of Geriatric Psychiatry*, 19, 4, 391–7.

West, K. and Glynos, J. (2016) 'Death talk', 'loss talk' and identification in the process of ageing, *Ageing & Society*, 36, 2, 225–39.

Whitehouse, P. and George, D. (2008) *The Myth of Alzheimer's: What You Aren't Being Told About Today's Most Dreaded Diagnosis*. New York: St Martin's Griffin.

World Health Organization (2012) *Dementia: A Public Health Priority*. Geneva: World Health Organization International. Available at http://www.who.int/mental_health/publications/dementia_report_2012/en/ (Last accessed 14 April 2016).

Zeilig, H. (2014) Dementia as a cultural metaphor, *Gerontologist*, 54, 2, 258–67.

8

When walking becomes wandering: representing the fear of the fourth age

Katherine Brittain*, Cathrine Degnen*, Grant Gibson, Claire Dickinson and Louise Robinson

Background

Wandering and dementia

Dementia, although a contested category (Moreira and Bond 2008), is on the increase (Department of Health 2009). Dementia is an umbrella term encompassing a number of sub-types of cognitive impairment (including vascular, Lewy body and fronto-temporal) that have been linked with a series of specific behavioural changes as the 'disease' progresses. One such behavioural change is 'wandering'. Wandering is a behaviour that occurs frequently (Chan *et al.* 2003, Klein *et al.* 1999); one in five people with dementia are said to wander (Wick and Zanni 2006). It has often been labelled agitation or agitated behaviour (Cohen-Mansfield 1986) and is viewed in dementia care as the most challenging event to manage (Lai and Arthur 2003). It has also been shown to cause considerable carer distress and it can often trigger early institutionalisation (Balestreri *et al.* 2000, Phillips and Diwan 2003).

While wandering is viewed as carrying a significant risk of harm to the person with dementia, the actual level of risk of a significant injury (or death) has been shown to be around 5 per cent. For instance, out of 615 reported incidents of people with dementia in the state of Florida becoming 'lost', four died (three from hypothermia and one from a train accident) and a further 30 people sustained significant injuries (including skin and head injuries, dehydration and hypothermia) (Rowe and Glover 2001). However, although the percentage of people with dementia harmed from wandering is low, families and carers of people with dementia experience intense anxiety about their risk of becoming lost. Indeed, people with dementia who have talked about feeling lost have also reported their own fears of this behaviour (Brittain *et al.* 2010). 'Losing oneself', figuratively and literally, is often evoked in everyday discourse as a marker of when 'real' old age can be said to begin (Degnen 2012), the onset of the feared 'fourth age' (Gilleard and Higgs 2011).

We propose that understanding how and why some behavioural changes are perceived as problematic or challenging is a crucial issue in the current discussions over what is termed 'behavioural psychological symptoms of dementia'. The 'voices of those who have experiential expertise of dementia and wandering' are neglected and are needed to shape future research and practice (Dewing 2006: 239). Our exploration of when walking comes to be understood as wandering adds to these discussions in precisely this way, focusing on experiential and everyday perspectives on these matters.

*These authors are joint first authors

Ageing, Dementia and the Social Mind, First Edition. Edited by Paul Higgs and Chris Gilleard.
Chapters © 2017 The Authors. Book Compilation © 2017 Foundation for the Sociology of
Health & Illness/Blackwell Publishing Ltd.

What does wandering mean?

Wandering has been discussed in the healthcare literature since the 1970s (Halek and Bartholomeyczik 2012: 406). In earlier years of these debates, wandering was defined as 'a tendency to move about, either in a seemingly aimless or disoriented fashion, or in pursuit of an indefinable or unobtainable goal' (Snyder *et al.* 1978: 272). This definition and others that focus on the aimlessness of the wandering have however come under increasing scrutiny (Algase 1999, Algase *et al.* 1997, Halek and Bartholomeyczik 2012, Lucero 2002). Indeed, not only is 'the aetiology of wandering poorly understood' but it also 'remains an unresolved riddle' (Cipriani *et al.* 2014: 137). Although wandering is clinically recognised, there is no standard definition of it (Cipriani *et al.* 2014), and in review 70 different definitions used in this research field are identified (Dewing 2006: 241).

Attempts made to define wandering, however, fall mostly into one of two broad camps. As noted by Halek and Bartholomeyczik (2012) in their review of the state of the field, these are, firstly, a person-centred care approach, where wandering is viewed as derogatory; and secondly, an approach that views wandering as a normal human activity. In the latter case, wandering is argued to be understandable and to be a 'consequence of a search for something familiar, safe and pleasant' (Coltharp *et al.* 1996, cited in Halek and Bartholomeyczik 2012: 406). Attempts to define specifically what wandering is are further hampered by the complexity of the behaviour attributed to it (Lai and Arthur 2003, White and Montgomery 2014) as well as difficulties in articulating appropriate theoretical frameworks for analysis. Indeed Algase (2006), a leading figure in debates over wandering, reports that over half the research published in this area lacks any theoretical framework at all (2006).

Evident in these ongoing debates is thus the complexity of how to define precisely what wandering is, the kinds of wandering that occur, the behaviour associated with it, the usefulness of the term itself, and appropriate theoretical tools to analyse it. There also is no agreement over the issue of the intentions of the person with dementia, and wandering is seen to be both aimless and directed: the 'extent [to which] wandering is random and aimless or goal-oriented and planned cannot be clarified' (Halek and Bartholomeyczik 2012: 407). Some have sought to differentiate between normal walking and wandering by classifying wandering in four ways: lapping, pacing, random travel and direct travel (Algase *et al.* 1997) while others have argued for the need to reconceptualise wandering as 'a natural form of activity', positing the possibility of 'generating other forms of theoretical descriptions and explanations' (Dewing 2006: 245) via 'the meshing of research with other disciplines such as human geography, architectural and environmental design' (Dewing 2006: 240). Wandering is thus a notoriously tricky category to pin down, one that eludes easy categorisation in the healthcare literature. As such, it may not be surprising that the term wandering itself is viewed by some as completely outdated (Maher 2001).

Walking: more than just exercise

In stark contrast to the negative associations around wandering is 'walking'. Walking is viewed as an activity that brings numerous health benefits, and it is included in recommended guidelines on how beneficial exercise is for older adults (Nelson *et al.* 2007). But walking is also valorised in a growing social science literature focusing on mobilities. This literature includes researchers in human geography, anthropology and sociology, with scholars considering walking from a variety of perspectives. (See Middleton (2011) and Andrews *et al.* (2012) for valuable summaries). Lessons from this literature include, for example, the importance of walking for producing an experience of place (Middleton 2011) and in turn enhancing a sense of place attachment and facilitating everyday sociality (Bean *et al.* 2008). This emergent body of literature makes it clear that pedestrian activity should not be dismissed as a banal form of transport from one point to another, nor is walking simply an issue of health, but instead it is linked to people's relationships with each other and with place.

Also revealing are popular understandings of walking in Western[1] societies, understandings that have a long history of moralising. On the one hand, walking has been perceived as 'tedious and commonplace, a view that lingers in the residual connotations of the word "pedestrian"' (Ingold 2004: 321); on the other hand, walking, when done 'properly' (see Edensor 2000: 87–99), has long been attributed with the power to free the mind to higher planes of contemplation, permitting the 'connections between human mind and sublime nature' (Michael 2000: 110). Additionally, some kinds of walking are understood to be appropriate and others, not: schoolchildren travelling between school and home, commuters and the *flâneur's* 'leisurely stroll' all are seen as legitimate, in contrast with 'the slow wanderings of the unemployed and homeless' (Edensor 2010: 69). So, in sum: walking can be done both 'correctly' and 'incorrectly'. When not done properly, walking is socially stigmatising, and some incorrect walking becomes wandering.

But this still leaves us with the question we set out with: when does walking become wandering? In a partial response, we say that some – but not all – wandering is seen to be respectable. Correct walking is understood to be mindful, rational, controlled and cultured: all characteristics that epitomise the modern subject. Respectable forms of wandering are also perceived to be 'cultured', such as that of the *flâneur* and the tourist. However, stigmatised wandering is often signalled in relation to problematic forms of temporality and problematic forms of embodiment. This stigmatised form of wandering is perceived as childlike, unthinking, non-rational and closer to a state of nature where the body takes over the mind.

While the walking and mobilities literature is bourgeoning, accounts of non-normative, everyday pedestrian activity are still absent from it (Andrews *et al.* 2012, Middleton 2010), including wandering. We posit that wandering is one of these forms of non-normative walking that requires careful attention. We seek to explore how these non-normative forms of pedestrian activity reveal the ways in which 'mobility and movement are entangled with relations of power, identity and embodiment' (Spinney 2010: 7, cited in Middleton 2011), which have too often been ignored in the case of people with dementia and which demand a fuller account. For instance, Western understandings of pedestrian activity contain the notion that walking and thinking are connected. Rhythms of walking are understood to be bound up with thinking, and different rhythms of walking can generate different ways of thinking (Middleton 2009, cited in Edensor 2010: 73). That walking is linked with the thinking, modern self (Edensor 2000: 84) but wandering by the person with dementia is not, and should be associated with a pathological mind-body relationship, is, we suggest, incidental. This is a point to which we will return.

Aim

In this article we pose the question 'when does walking become wandering?' We draw on qualitative research with carers of people with dementia, investigating a series of interrelated issues on the fourth age and the social representation of dementia when a perceptible shift occurs. In this context, understandings of walking change from viewing it as a healthy activity and something that is aspired to in 'successful' ageing to behaviour that is viewed with fear and that comes to have deeply negative consequences in terms of care. This shift further marginalises people with dementia from the ability to participate in the 'emancipatory capacities of city spaces' (Middleton 2011: 93) and the social networks and place attachment facilitated by walking (Bean *et al.* 2008), characteristics that are linked with an enhanced sense of well-being. As a corrective to these cultural assumptions about pedestrian activity for people with dementia, we focus on how carers 'produce' pedestrian activity as wandering. Our article describes – from the perspective of carers – narratives on wandering and stories of the individual with dementia becoming lost. These narratives, we argue, in actual fact challenge the notion of aimless, unthinking or non-purposeful walking during the fourth age precisely because they highlight ties to specific areas where people with dementia walk to. We attend to the importance of place, as signalled above by Edensor and Bean *et al.*, asking what happens to the relationship between body and place when the focus in carer's accounts shifts from walking to wandering. This permits us to contribute to evolving debates on the behaviour of people with dementia. Our material problematises and unsettles the terms and normative perspectives on such behaviour; calls attention to the broader cultural issues that underpin and reinforce assumptions about wandering and opens up space to consider other perspectives on the question of when a behaviour is a 'challenging' or 'problematic' one.

Methods

This article is based on qualitative data derived from two studies that explored the experience of carers of people with dementia and the use of assistive technology, within and outside of the home. The interviews touched on their views of accessing outside spaces and whether or not they used technology to support the person with dementia to carry on with activities in and outside the home. The results from these individual studies have been published previously (Brittain *et al.* 2010, Gibson *et al.* 2015), but here we draw on as yet unpublished narratives of carers. This article specifically focuses on the carers' experiences of managing getting out and about with the person with dementia. Although the carers' narratives are not specifically about 'wandering' or 'place attachment', both these concepts repeatedly appeared in their accounts. As such, they offer valuable insights into both the experiences of carers and people with dementia that help unpack and critically examine the ideas underlying the perceived transformation from walking to wandering.

An inductive approach to data collection was adopted in both studies, using the constant comparative method (Glaser 1965) and deviant case analysis. In total, there were three focus groups with 11 carers and 26 one-to-one interviews with carers. Both the focus group discussions and interviews lasted approximately 1 hour, and all were digitally recorded, transcribed verbatim and anonymised. The focus groups were held in familiar surroundings to ensure a sense of continuity and familiarity for the participants. These were facilitated by Brittain, and took place in different settings in the community (such as church, the residential home, the Alzheimer's Society). Participants were recruited from two local branches of the Alzheimer's Society in two North of England coastal towns. The interviews took place in a room on the university campus or the person's home, depending on what was most convenient for the interviewee. All recruitment strategies and interaction with participants have followed strict ethical guidelines, complying with the British Society of Gerontology's (2008) guidelines on ethical research. Participation was voluntary and participants were told that they could opt out at any stage of the research process. Ethical approval for both studies was sought and given through the university ethics committee.

In this article we have explored the question 'when does walking become wandering' and highlight both the tension surrounding the fear that the person being cared for might get 'lost' and the recognition that those being cared for want to participate in outside activities. In answering this question Brittain and Degnen undertook a secondary analysis of the two datasets, by revisiting previously coded sections of data that specifically related to wandering or walking from the perspective of carers of people with dementia. We call this a secondary analysis, as the research design and data previously collected (by Brittain) was revisited and analysed by two of the authors (Brittain and Degnen). One of the challenges of carrying out secondary analysis within qualitative research is retaining the original context of the data collected when new questions are asked of it (see van den Berg 2008 for an in-depth discussion). In this instance we believe the risk of decontextualisation was mitigated by Brittain's personal involvement in the research design, data collection and analysis of the original studies.

Findings

Fear of losing them

Carers were explicit about the responsibility and generalised sense of worry they often experienced as they became more aware of the potential of losing the person with dementia. This is something they fear deeply:

> I know other people have had to worry about people who have gone missing, but it's when you actually live through it and you think 'God, what's happened to him', and he had completely forgotten within 5 minutes that he had been missing, but I hadn't, I still, even when he is just at his day care, I am on edge the whole time, because I am thinking, 'is he going to get out when they don't notice him?' (Joan, wife)

Even when the person with dementia was not able to leave the site, carers still lived with the fear that they might disappear in the night:

> I mean, the way she used to wander through the night, and we were in separate rooms then, but I have always been a light sleeper, and if she got up, I was up as well, so I wasn't getting any rest … I was constantly watching her … when she was in the house, the door was always locked, and then it ended up, I got a little dog for her and that seemed to help her because the dog would bring her back, but she would only go across the road, and we have got a little green, and she used to sort of, go round the green, but the dog would drag her back. (Bill, husband)

Indeed, as we have reported previously, sometimes it is the fear of the carers that stops the person with dementia being independent in accessing the outside spaces that they enjoy (Brittain *et al.* 2010).

Another carer spoke about how the family had to make a decision about the care of her grandma because she was constantly 'getting out', and because she did not have any recollection of her husband, she did not want to go back 'home' to him:

> She got to the point where she was getting out and she didn't know who my granddad was, so she then refused to go back home … a couple of times she got out and she would just flee, basically, and then … she'd end up in, like, the neighbours. Who thankfully knew her, they knew my granddad, and she was just like, 'I'm not going back to that house, there's an old man in that house and I don't know who he is' … I think it must have been awful because there would have been that fear of, kind of, that natural fear to, kind of, flight, 'cause, like, 'I'm in a situation, I don't know where I'm at, I need to get out'. But equally it's kind of like 'you, you can't get out because it's not safe for you to be wandering around'. (Sarah, granddaughter)

The extent and frequency of wandering behaviour is thus often a crucial factor in how carers evaluate if the person with dementia can be cared for at home, or if they need residential care. In the case of Sarah's grandmother, the family decided ultimately that for her own safety, to mitigate the risk of 'her getting out', and for her husband's safety, as she had started to be aggressive towards him, that 'settling' her into a residential home was the best decision for all.

These fears of the person with dementia 'getting out' were profoundly linked with the perceived safety of the person with dementia:

> She used to ask about her dad quite a lot, and she used to talk about her home in a different place … things got bad, I think – bad, whatever that means – when she started getting stressed, but also when she started doing night time walks. That was when things got really concerning … the police came round once as well. They'd found her, one occasion, out, you know, in, in an inappropriate state of dress in very cold conditions. So that – I think that's when it started getting really worrying, and when we really felt that we needed to do a lot more. And, and I think that was – those reports were the beginning of the time when we really started seriously thinking about residential care. (Kate, granddaughter)

Interesting differences are also evident, however, if we contrast Sarah's experiences with Kate's. In her narrative above, Kate used the phrase 'night walks' for the instances when her grandma walked to her house in the night; note that she does not classify this as 'wandering':

> Night walks were, yeah. I mean, and I, I imagine I have no idea just how regular they were … but then there would be, often, nights where she'd show up at 3 o'clock in the morning, with her [to your house?] – yeah, with her nightie on. So she'd always get in my house – well, I think. She got in my house on a number of occasions … she'd show up with her nightie on at 3 o'clock in the morning, you know. And – or, the neighbours might kind of tell us that they'd seen her going out – they'd ring us – so we'd have to go looking for her. (Kate, granddaughter)

This same woman, once she had moved into the residential home, remained active:

> She helped the cleaners … she would kind of keep herself busy pottering about the place … she pottered about the corridors and they would often kind of be – direct her back to her bed. But, you know, pottering about your corridors … and sleeping in your chair, you know, the next day, it doesn't really matter. It's wandering about in a state of undress when it's minus something outside, in the middle of the night, that is the worry, isn't it? And, and, what happens if you don't manage to get back somewhere? Corridors, what you gonna do? Where are – you're harmless. (Kate, granddaughter)

Kate recounts how her grandma 'pottered around the corridors' and makes a clear distinction between 'pottering' which is 'harmless' and 'wandering' in thin, 'inappropriate' clothes outside in the cold which is a 'worry'. The form of pedestrian activity might be the same, but it is the time, place and conditions under which they occur that make the carer's interpretation of this mobility shift from walking to wandering.

The use of technologies to prevent the person with dementia being able to 'wander'

Many of the carers recounted examples of times when they did not know where the person they cared for was. Sometimes this transformed their behaviour outside the home or changed the ways in which they managed within the home, such as ensuring that doors were locked. There was a common thread in the narratives of how carers used locks, the removal of keys, and alarms to ensure that the person with dementia did not get out, particularly at night:

> But my Alan … in the early stages he used to do some wandering, and I had to get bolts on both sides of the side trellis doors so that he couldn't get out, you know, and it was long time when I had to lock the doors and hide the keys and everything, but somehow or other, he used get himself out, and we live right near the seafront at Rowton[2] and I used to think, 'oh God if he gets onto that main road he would just cross the road', he wouldn't have any traffic sense at all … so that's how I, I had to lock the doors, I had to stop him getting out … [Once when he was in respite care and escaped] the neighbours realised he must be from the [respite] home and they brought him back, which was very worrying because that was so near a very main road. (Eileen, wife)

> So the, the door alarm is sort of for us, gave us peace of mind that we knew that she wasn't out wandering, that she wasn't gonna get lost and stuff like that. (Cath, daughter)

Joan talks about her husband Fred 'loving to get out' and how he loved walking but that it got to the stage where she simply could not keep up:

> He can't go anywhere on his own … I mean, he'd just be lost, but he wants to go out the whole time; I mean I get no peace and I have got very bad arthritis so I find it difficult. So if we have been for one walk, I mean a walk of a mile or two mile, that's my limit for that day. But Fred doesn't think so, I mean he will come in, have a cup of tea, and then the sun is still shining so he's putting his coat on, 'come on then, are we going for a walk' … and the only way I can get him to stay in is to give him a can of beer, then he will stop in. (Joan, wife)

As Fred increasingly became 'lost' from the club that he used to go to, Joan made the decision to move to a place that she felt was more pleasant to walk around, instead of where they had lived before which to her was just 'streets':

> Before Fred reached this stage, before we moved here, he used to go to the club every day for a pint, and it got to the stage where he forgot the way home and then he forgot how long he had been out and what not, and that was when I decided it was time to move to a different location, because that wasn't conducive to the rest of our lives to live where there was just streets to walk round, so we come down here where it is pleasant to walk, but he can't go anywhere on his own, he has to, that, I mean, he'd just be lost, but he wants to go out the whole time. (Joan, wife)

A different carer spoke about how, even within the early stages of dementia, her mother became distressed when she was unable to get home. She was away all day before being found in a nearby field:

We looked frantically all over the place; again we weren't expecting her to get lost, we thought she is just next door ... so hours passed and we got the police and they got the dogs out and we were frantic, thought you know, because she was so vulnerable and it was getting ... quite cold and she just, she had, she didn't have a cardigan on or anything and where she was found ... on the field just around the, behind the back garden, in the school field where the long grass [is] ... and she was crouched down in the grass when they found her, sort of rocking backwards and forwards, she was very, very distressed. (Angela, daughter)

Taken together, the examples here give some sense of the complexity that carers faced. For instance, Angela, the respondent in the extract above, highlights later in her interview the impracticality of existing technologies for finding her mother. Identity cards or bracelets, she points out, would have been ineffective because of her mother's distressed state and the way she was crouched down in a field, making it difficult for her to be seen. The lasting impact that this had on this family and the person with dementia was the sharp curtailment of activities because all (including the mother herself) were 'terrified of (her) going out'. Cath, on the other hand, gets peace of mind from the door alarm technology in order to monitor her mother's movements, but Fred's wife's account clearly demonstrates that locks and keys are not always sufficient technologies for carers to control the urge of the person with dementia to be on the move. Strategies used include improvising with everyday household items at hand, in this case beer, and in the section above, the family dog who is relied upon for help, but also more radical changes such as moving home, as in the case of Joan who, recognising the changes in her husband, sought a 'better' place for him to walk in.

Families thus rely on a range of strategies to manage, but more explicit forms of technology have often been viewed as a solution to challenging behaviour such as wandering. In the example below, the use of a mobile tracking technology became the reason why Liz's husband was prevented from getting out and about. The technology made Liz aware of how far her husband was travelling and this in turn prompted Liz to replace the tracking technology with a door alarm to warn her when he was trying to get out. Although the tracking technology proved useful when he wandered locally, such as into town, it caused fear when on one occasion he got on a bus out of the area. Although she knew where he was through the tracking device and she informed the police, Liz felt that he was now wandering too far to be safe. This example shows that the success of the technology, making visible the distances her husband travelled, actually led to its failure. This is because the tracker technology is meant to enable independence, not determine when independence should be curtailed (as it seemed to be in this case):

It was in that sort of in between stage when we first, first time he just missed the house and disappeared onto the moor. And we found him on the top. Police were very concerned 'cause one day last year, or the year before, a lad was, died on the moor with hypothermia. So this last time, the last time I lost him just sort of locally, he just got out of the house ... Found him on the High Street in the end ... the tracker in the early stages was a comfort, you know, I did like to know where he was at any time. But it always the drawback of what do you do when you do find out where he is? You know, you find he's in the middle of the town moor it's not, it's not easy to know which bit to start looking. They're not exact enough. (Liz, wife)

Thus, in a variety of ways, technologies shape carers' behaviour and decision-making. The use of technologies has implications for independent living (which is highly culturally valued) in that they can both facilitate it and extend it in the home space. But the goal of maintaining independent living is constantly being weighed up by carers against their fears (both perceived and real) about the safety of the individual with dementia, and also powerful cultural norms of familial responsibility when people with dementia can no longer 'be trusted' with their own behaviour.

When wandering is linked to place, including 'home'
Carers also spoke about places that are known to the person with dementia, whether these are places in their earlier lives or places they loved to visit. Joan below talks about why they moved to the coast and how her husband Fred loved Rowton, because they always used to go there for holidays. Fred on one occasion escaped from his respite care home and journeyed via train to the coast where Joan lived in a flat, but unfortunately 'he had turned the other way and wandered through' past her street. This had worried Joan because he would have got to the seafront and 'goodness knows where he would have gone to from there'. As she elaborates:

> The first time my husband was in respite, we lost him and he was missing for 4 hours … eventually it was my own son who was out in his car looking and he found him, he had wandered from [the city] to Rowton [14.5 km]. (Joan, wife)

Similarly, Jenny, another carer, recounts a time where Richard, her husband, was admitted to hospital. He told her when she visited that he had 'been for a walk' but Jenny thought he was 'being silly'; there was no way he could have gone for a walk because he was in hospital. However, the sister on the ward informed them later that he had been out of the hospital and was found walking around the car park. Jenny then went on to speak about the second time this happened. The ward sister rang her at home when Richard had been discovered missing. The sister had said Richard had 'gone walkabout' and that the police had been called, but that she was ringing because 'we thought that if he's walking' she said, 'he might have walked home'. Jenny says that she could not believe this would happen as she lives a substantial distance from the hospital and that Richard did not have any shoes, only slippers. Despite this, Richard did arrive home, on foot, later that day. Jenny says that the first thing she asked him was:

> 'What are you doing?', and he said 'I just wanted to come home' … his dressing gown he had on, but he had that on his, over his shoulders, and his eyes were red, because it was freezing cold, it was a freezing cold day, and when I look down, he had his slippers on … and I thought, they look soaking wet, this whole slipper looked wet, and so we sort of brought him in and put him on a chair and then I said, 'take your slippers off' then we realised, it wasn't water, it was blood. All his feet were just – the skin was hanging off his feet. (Jenny, wife)

Richard had navigated the 10 km walk 'getting home' by using all of the familiar places he remembered:

> He'd gone down through Seacrest … and he said he had walked along and then he said, 'up by the ice cream place we'd go for a coffee', which was the Seafront cafe, you know, and he had come up that way … and then he'd cut through, through Erston because he knew about the church and he says, 'that place where the church is' … so he'd used all the back … all the places he'd known. (Jenny, wife)

Both Joan and Jenny's accounts highlight how walking or wandering in dementia is not always aimless or lacking cognitive capacity, but can be linked to memories of familiar places. While Fred had made a wrong turning when he was nearly at the flat (and had successfully negotiated nearly 15 km before getting disorientated, including a trip on the train), Richard navigated his way on foot, relying on familiar landmarks to arrive back at the family home.

Wanting to go home – to a familiar home
A number of carers mentioned that the person with dementia wanted to go home. This was often linked to home being a familiar place, even if the 'home' they wanted to go to was one from their past. Joan speaks of how her husband, Fred, regularly refers to their home, but by this he means where they lived before the Second World War:

> But then he would get his wallet out and he was looking at his wallet and I said, 'what's the matter, what are you looking for?', he says 'I'm just wondering if I have got enough to get back', I says 'to get back where Fred?', and he says 'well home', and I says 'well this is home', 'no, no' he says, 'I mean' he says, and I says, 'in any case Fred, you don't pay on the bus now, it's now all free on the bus'. I am trying to change the conversation and I said 'put your wallet away, you don't need your money', and he says 'But I have to go, I have to go' and I say 'well look, just go and have a look and you'll see your bedroom, just along there'. 'My bedroom's just along there?' 'Go on, go and have a look at your bedroom, it's just around there', so I'll say 'leave this door open and I'll make sure you go up the right place', so he opens the door, goes out, comes back and he says 'yes, I have slept in that bed before, I recognise that'. (Joan, wife)

Tracy, on the other hand, expains how while she herself worried about her father losing his way, her mother did not share this fear. Instead, she was confident that her husband would make it back home:

> When [my dad would walk to the shop] I worried myself silly, 'Has he got lost?' She never did, she was always confident he would find his way home. And he always did, but it worried the heck out of me because I was thinking, 'Oh my God', you know. (Tracy, daughter)

Tracy continues that 'it took my my mum a long time to sort of understand what he was able to do and what he wasn't able to do', but her mother had a certainty, born out by experience, that her father could navigate successfully home. Similarly, Cath, below, describes the panic she felt when her mother went missing, but she also felt that her mother would be able to get back home because she had always managed to, although on this occasion she didn't make it home but made it back to the spot where she had become detached from her family:

> I was absolutely beside myself, because I didn't know whether she would, she was also always very good at actually getting home. She was, she knew how to get home. So we went down to our old home, because she was at my house, so and stuff like that. But she just wasn't there, but she managed to get herself back to where she started. I don't know how she did it. (Cath, daughter)

'Home' is obviously not a straightforward category. In Fred's case, for instance, the passage of time is collapsed and his desire to go home does not map onto his current residence, but instead onto one from many decades prior. Having said that, all the examples above underline the strength of attachment to a familiar home, and how many carers' recognised this significant relationship as enabling people with dementia to navigate back.

Discussion

Firstly, throughout the narratives around the experience of wandering or the person with dementia becoming lost, the carers demonstrate the importance of a range of intersecting strategies they undertake to enable them to manage and care for their family members who exhibit agitated behaviour associated with dementia. These include assistive technologies such as door alarms, GPS tracking devices and identity cards. But they also include the wider social networks of which the people with dementia are part, so that some neighbours informally monitor their activities and raise alerts. Additionally, there are also the everyday, improvisational domestic resources such as the family dog who 'would drag her back'; and Fred's wife's 'can of beer' when she is not physically able to do a second walk in the same day. As such, what is evident here are the ways in which multiple, intersecting levels of technology are employed to manage both the behavioural characteristics of the person with dementia but also the responsibilities and fears of the carers. Having said that, what is also evident is that these strategies and technologies become part of the process in which the carers identify when walking has become wandering, or when walking has become 'too dangerous' and needs to be curtailed. Unintended consequences can follow from this, whereby technologies meant to extend or facilitate independence end up *limiting* independence by redefining non-normative walking as dangerous, rather than as a manageable activity.

Secondly, what is evident in the carers' narratives about wandering is the specificity of local landscapes and places. On the one hand, this is a source of consternation and fear. Carers talk about a number of topographical features in their accounts above: main roads, road crossings, a school field with long grass, the bus station and the sea front. Many (although not all) of their fears are linked to aspects of place that might make them particulary threatening. But on the other hand, places and travelling between them feature importantly in the trajectories and pedestrain trips the same carers report that the people with dementia undertake. This reoccurring theme of place strikes us as particularly pertinent in our attempts to answer when walking becomes wandering. We return here to Edensor's (2010) point about rhythms, walking and embodied relations with place, and ask if there might be some mileage to be gained by thinking about wandering and embodied relationships with place. On the one hand, it seems to us that carers perceive wandering as threatening due to an apparent lack of rhythm and intent ('aimless', in the healthcare literature), and that it is this they feel tips walking over into wandering. But the accounts above push us to ask if the pedestrian activity of some of these people with dementia also has a rhythm, which is an alternative, non-normative form of rhythm, a rhythm that is linked to place.

Ingold (2004), writing about walking and seeking to escape the Cartesian binary of mind versus body, helps us make this argument. He encourages us to think about walking as a form of intelligence that is not simply in the mind. Instead, he posits an intelligence that is 'distributed throughout the entire field of relations comprised by the presence of the human being in the inhabited world' (Ingold 2004: 332), or as Bean *et al.* put it, how 'walking internalises the relationship between the body and place' (2008: 2837). In a number of instances above, the individuals wander to known places such as their homes or favourite locations. It is precisely this that attests to the 'relational field(s)', the 'embodied capacities of movement' (Ingold 2004: 333) that those with dementia continue to be enmeshed in, despite assumptions that they are no longer able to engage in such sorts of relations. It appears, then, in these cases at least, that the person with dementia does indeed have a walking intelligence, one that 'is not located exclusively in the head' but which is instead part and parcel of the person's relationships with place (Ingold 2004: 332). We must not, however, sugar coat this – we recognise the very real fears about wandering for carers and people with dementia themselves, and also some of its distressing consequences. But we want to claim that our data show how place still matters in these examples of wandering, and how it pushes back against the damning, limited, binary stereotypes about the disappearance of mind and thus of person.

Thirdly, there is the issue of how both wandering and the person with dementia should be associated with a pathological mind-body relationship. We said above that it is not coincidental that walking should be associated with the thinking, modern self and that wandering by those with dementia should be associated with a problematic mind-body relationship. This is inextricably due to Cartesian mind-body dualism that frames western understandings of the world. This binary firstly posits the self as residing in the mind (a *cognitive* model of self) and secondly resists the possibility that self and identity might also be at least partially embodied (a *corporeal* understanding of the self) (Kontos, 2003, 2005). Drawing inspiration from the work of Kontos, we contend that recognising 'the irreducibly embodied nature of human subjectivity and agency' (2003: 152) helps reveal the cultural assumptions at work in the shift when walking comes to be described as wandering. Walking is understood to be possible when the mind and body work together correctly, while wandering is perceived as when the mind is 'lost' and the body takes over. These underpinning assumptions of mind-body dualism are also evident in the healthcare literature in the debates we summarise above about behaviour associated with wandering, and if the movement of the person with dementia is 'aimless' or 'directed' (Algase *et al.* 1997, Halek and Bartholomeyczik 2012, Snyder *et al.* 1978). A good example of how these assumptions are reproduced in everyday life comes from the grandaughter's account above where she describes her grandmother's locomotion as 'night walking' and not 'wandering', seemingly because her grandmother's night walking is intentional and rational as it leads to her grandaughter's house due to the relations and memories lodged there. Similarly, the same grandaughter distinguishes between harmless pottering around and wandering, in that the former is unthreatening and not destabilising or in need of control.

This contrast between walking (with the implicit connotation of a healthy mind-body relationship) and wandering (with an implied pathological mind-body relationship) becomes even clearer if one considers other forms of the 'wrong kind' of walking, such as shuffling: 'adopting a shuffling gait … is widely regarded as a mark of impotence, infirmity or decrepitude' (Ingold 2004: 324). Here, finally, we come to the nub of the matter: the abject figure of the fourth age, the emergent 'event horizon' of 'mindlessness and immobility' (Higgs and Gilleard: 2015: 16–17) in the social imagining of dementia in which the mind is, purportedly, entirely subsumed by the body. This non-normative, 'decrepit' figure is virtually absent from the literature on walking for it is assumed that wandering is in and of itself *evidence* of the no longer mindful state of someone with dementia. This circular logic then becomes nearly impossible to disrupt or challenge, and instead becomes self-fulfilling in the social imaginary.

In conclusion, there are clear parallels between the ways in which the mind-body split is conceptualised when analysing walking and when analysing selfhood in dementia. That is to say, that ideas in the west about walking are clearly bound up in complicated Cartesian dualisms of mind and body. So, too, are ideas on selfhood in people with dementia and the idea of mind being overcome by body. Wandering – a wrong kind of walking – is interpreted as collapsing the division between head and heels,[3] mind and body. Dementia is understood as irretrievably collapsing this divide, with 'body' coming to completely overtake 'mind', and leaving little possibility, in the social imagination, for reclaiming meaning or intentionality, as those are assumed to be simply cognitive matters.

Such cultural assumptions are encoded in understandings of the shift when walking becomes wandering in western cultures. In response, we contend that 'confining what is essential about selfhood to the brain is to overlook how bodily sources of agency, grounded in the pre-reflective level of experience, are fundamental to the constitution and manifestation of selfhood and Alzheimer's disease' (Kontos 2005: 555) and that significance must also be granted to the body and embodied agency in a person-centred approach to dementia (Kontos 2005). The data we present here on the importance of place and embodiment are a corrective to these assumptions about when walking becomes wandering, and are an important consideration of a non-normative form of mobility. As our data demonstrate, wandering is not a term that can easily be dispensed with: it is a concept that carers use in their everyday lives to try and describe and explain behaviour that is very worrying to them. But simultaneously, by using this term, all the associations it conjures up of the person with dementia being 'aimless' and unable to meaningfully travel on foot reinforces the negative and dehumanising notions we have about dementia and about a supposed disappearance of mind and self. Our data, based on the experiences of carers, challenges the simplicity of this equation by highlighting *where* it is that people wander.

Notes

1   While 'Western' is a falsely homogenous category that obscures a great deal of cultural variation, it also provides a useful shorthand for describing some of the shared worldviews shaping this material.
2   All names have been replaced with pseudonyms. However, in doing so we acknowledge the importance of place.
3   We are indebted here to Ingold (2004: 315) for this expression of 'head over heels' in regard to the relationship of mind and body in Western thought.

References

Algase, D.L. (1999) Wandering in dementia, *Annual Review of Nursing Research*, 17, 1, 185–217.
Algase, D.L. (2006) What's new about wandering behaviour? An assessment of recent studies, *International Journal of Older People Nursing*, 1, 4, 226–34.
Algase, D.L., Kupferschmid, B., Beel-Bates, C.A. and Beattie, E.R. (1997) Estimates of stability of daily wandering behavior among cognitively impaired long-term care residents, *Nursing Research*, 46, 3, 172–8.
Andrews, G.J., Hall, E., Evans, B. and Colls, R. (2012) Moving beyond walkability: on the potential of health geography, *Social Science & Medicine*, 75, 11, 1925–32.
Balestreri, L., Grossberg, A. and Grossberg, G.T. (2000) Behavioral and psychological symptoms of dementia as a risk factor for nursing home placement, *International Psychogeriatrics*, 12, 1, 59–62.
Bean, C., Kearns, R. and Collins, D. (2008) Exploring social mobilities: narratives of walking and driving in Auckland, New Zealand, *Urban Studies*, 45, 13, 2829–48.
British Society of Gerontology (2008) British Society of Gerontology Guidelines on ethical research with human participants. Available at http://www.britishgerontology.org/about-bsg/bsg-ethical-guidelines.html (Last accessed 25 August 2016).
Brittain, K.R., Corner, L., Robinson, A.L. and Bond, J. (2010) Ageing in place and technologies of place: the lived experience of people with dementia in changing social, physical and technological environments, *Sociology of Health & Illness*, 32, 2, 272–87.

Chan, D.C., Kasper, J.D., Black, B.S. and Rabins, P.V. (2003) Prevalence and correlates of behavioural and psychiatric symptoms in community-dwelling elders with dementia or mild cognitive impairment: The Memory and Medical Care study, *International Journal of Geriatric Psychiatry*, 18, 2, 174–82.

Cipriani, G., Lucetti, C., Nuti, A. and Danti, S. (2014) Wandering and dementia, *Psychogeriatrics*, 12, 2, 135–42.

Cohen-Mansfield, J. (1986) Agitated behaviors in the elderly. II. Preliminary results in the cognitively deteriorated, *Journal of the American Geriatrics Society*, 34, 10, 722–27.

Degnen, C. (2012) *Ageing Selves and Everyday Life in the North of England: Years in the Making.* Manchester: Manchester University Press.

Department of Health (2009) *Living Well with Dementia: a National Dementia Strategy.* London: Department of Health.

Dewing, J. (2006) Wandering into the future: reconceptualizing wandering 'a natural and good thing', *International Journal of Older People Nursing*, 1, 4, 239–49.

Edensor, T. (2000) Walking in the British Countryside: reflexivity, embodied practices and ways to escape, *Body & Society*, 6, 3–4, 81–106.

Edensor, T. (2010) Walking in rhythms: place, regulation, style and the flow of experience, *Visual Studies*, 25, 1, 69–79.

Gibson, G., Dickinson, C., Brittain, K. and Robinson, L. (2015) The everyday use of assistive technology by people with dementia and their family carers: a qualitative study, *BMC Geriatrics*, 15, 1, 89.

Gilleard, C. and Higgs, P. (2011) Ageing abjection and embodiment in the fourth age, *Journal of Aging Studies*, 25, 2, 135–42.

Glaser, B. (1965) The constant comparison: methods of qualitative analysis, *Social Problems*, 12, 4, 436–45.

Halek, M. and Bartholomeyczik, S. (2012) Description of the behaviour of wandering in people with dementia living in nursing home – a review of the literature, *Scandinavian Journal of Caring Sciences*, 26, 2, 404–13.

Higgs, P. and Gilleard, C. (2015) *Rethinking Old Age: Theorising the Fourth Age.* London: Palgrave.

Ingold, T. (2004) Culture on the ground: the world perceived through the feet, *Journal of Material Culture*, 9, 3, 315–40.

Klein, D.A., Steinberg, M., Galik, E., Steele, C., *et al.* (1999) Wandering behaviour in community-residing persons with dementia, *International Journal of Geriatric Psychiatry*, 14, 4, 272–9.

Kontos, P. (2003) 'The painterly hand': embodied consciousness and Alzheimer's disease, *Journal of Aging Studies*, 17, 2, 151–70.

Kontos, P. (2005) Embodied selfhood in Alzheimer's disease: rethinking person-centred care, *Dementia*, 4, 4, 553–70.

Lai, C.K. and Arthur, D.G. (2003) Wandering behaviour in people with dementia, *Journal of Advanced Nursing*, 44, 2, 173–82.

Lucero, M. (2002) Intervention strategies for exit-seeking wandering behavior in dementia residents, *American Journal of Alzheimer's Disease and Other Dementias*, 17, 5, 277–80.

Maher, L.A. (2001) Wandering. Repaving the way you think, *Contemporary Longterm Care*, 24, 12, 8–10.

Michael, M. (2000) These boots are made for walking … : mundane technology, the body and human-environment relations, *Body & Society*, 6, 3–4, 107–26.

Middleton, J. (2010) Sense and the city: exploring the embodied geographies of urban walking, *Social and Cultural Geography*, 11, 6, 575–96.

Middleton, J. (2011) Walking in the city: the geographies of everyday pedestrian practices, *Geography Compass*, 5, 2, 90–105.

Moreira, T. and Bond, J. (2008) Does the prevention of brain ageing constitute anti-ageing medicine? Outline of a new space of representation for Alzheimer's Disease, *Journal of Aging Studies*, 22, 4, 356–65.

Nelson, M.E., Rejeski, W.J., Blair, S.N., Duncan, S.N., *et al.* (2007) Physical activity and public health in older adults: recommendation from the American College of Sports Medicine and the American Heart Association, *Circulation*, 116, 9, 1094–105.

Phillips, V.L. and Diwan, S. (2003) The incremental effect of dementia-related problem behaviours on the time to nursing home placement in poor, frail, demented older people, *Journal of the American Geriatrics Society*, 51, 2, 188–93.

Rowe, M.A. and Glover, J.C. (2001) Antecedents, descriptions and consequences of wandering in cognitively-impaired adults and the Safe Return (SR) program, *American Journal of Alzheimer's Disease and Other Dementias*, 16, 6, 344–52.

Snyder, L.H., Rupprecht, P., Pyrek, J., Brekhus, S., *et al.* (1978) Wandering, *The Gerontologist*, 18, 3, 272–80.

White, E.B. and Montgomery, P. (2014) A review of 'wandering' instruments for people with dementia who get lost, *Research on Social Work Practice*, 24, 4, 400–13.

Wick, J. and Zanni, G. (2006) Aimless excursions: wandering in the elderly, *Consultant Pharmacist*, 21, 8, 608–18.

Van den Berg, H. (2008) Reanalyzing qualitative interviews from different angles: the risk of decontextualization and other problems of sharing qualitative data, *Historical Social Research*, 6, 1, 179–92.

9

Re-imagining dementia in the fourth age: the ironic fictions of Alice Munro

Marlene Goldman

Illness is the night-side of life, a more onerous citizenship. Everyone who is born holds dual citizenship, in the kingdom of the well and in the kingdom of the sick. Although we all prefer to use only the good passport, sooner or later each of us is obliged, at least for a spell, to identify ourselves as citizens of that other place.

(Sontag 1978: 1)

Introduction

This paper analyses two stories by Nobel-prize-winning Canadian writer Alice Munro to explore how her fiction interrogates the prevailing social imaginary of the fourth age. Munro's fiction eschews the familiar binary opposition between Sontag's infamous kingdoms of the well and the sick, and, more specifically, its current configuration, what the editors of this collection, Chris Gilleard and Paul Higgs, describe in their call for papers as 'a successful, productive and active later life', on the one hand, and 'an unsuccessful, failed and "frailed" old age', on the other. Formally and thematically, Munro's stories rely on irony and surreal imagery to subvert the logic that engenders and normalises the opposition between the third and fourth ages, and, by extension, the disempowerment and social death of people coping with later-life dementia.

As medical anthropologist Michael Lambek (2004: 1) observes, 'there is often something in situations of illness that resembles irony or that brings the recognition of irony to the fore'. In using the term irony, Lambek refers to its most famous classical Greek expressions: Sophoclean tragic irony (also known as situational irony), in which spectators know what is happening but characters are unable or refuse to acknowledge or accept it; and Socratic irony (or verbal irony), a rhetorical stance characterised by turning questions back on the questioner to demonstrate the latter's gaps in ostensibly rational thinking. Fundamentally, irony relies on the possibility of arriving at more than one meaning. For Roman rhetoricians, including Cicero and Quintilian, 'ironia denoted a rhetorical figure and a manner of discourse, in which, for the most part, the meaning was contrary to the words'; indeed, this 'double-edgedness appears to be a diachronic feature of irony' (Cuddon 1991: 458, 460). Verbal irony oscillates between the simultaneous 'perception of the said and the unsaid' (Hutcheon 1994: 39) – between literal and inferred meanings. In general, 'most forms of irony involve the perception or awareness of a discrepancy or incongruity between words and their meaning, or

Ageing, Dementia and the Social Mind, First Edition. Edited by Paul Higgs and Chris Gilleard.
Chapters © 2017 The Authors. Book Compilation © 2017 Foundation for the Sociology of
Health & Illness/Blackwell Publishing Ltd.

Figure 1   *Duck/rabbit*

between actions and their results, or between appearance and reality. In all cases there may be an element of the absurd and the paradoxical' (Cuddon 1991: 460). Visual irony likewise depends on the possibility of two or more interpretations of what at first glance appears to be a single image. By drawing on irony's inherent doubleness (imagine, for example, the figure of the duck/rabbit: see Figure 1), Munro's fiction displaces the hegemonic, gothic view of the fourth age and brings an alternative perspective to the foreground. Ultimately, Munro's fiction does not so much reveal the truth about the fourth age, as expose the reader's complicity in the construction of the prevailing gothic social imaginary.

I begin by analysing 'Dance of the Happy Shades', published in Munro's first collection of the same title in 1968, because this story forcibly underscores her engagement with the historical context in which her narratives were written. More important, this story engages in an attempt to subvert the often unspoken links between cognitive decline and gothic horror. In speaking of the gothic, I am referring to the genre, typically associated with Horace Walpole's (1930) publication of *The castle of Otranto* (1764), known for its evocation of mystery, horror, nightmares, hidden recesses, and the uncanny. As scholars observe, the genre is preoccupied 'with matters of madness, states of fear, extremes of suffering, cruelty, violence, crime, torture, and murder' (Cuddon 1991: 385). As I note elsewhere, in general, both dementia and Alzheimer's, as well as the delegation of blame, culpability, and agency associated with them, are mediated through narratives. But once an illness such as Alzheimer's disease – or a symptom such as dementia or cognitive impairment – is categorised as morally wrong and horrifying, the illness or symptom is, in effect, 'seen through the lens of the gothic, which typically exposes the existence of evil and features monsters and monstrous transformations' (Goldman 2015: 74).[1]

Munro's 'Dance of the happy shades' highlights the similarities and differences between children with Down syndrome and the frail elderly coping with dementia. When the story first appeared in *The New Yorker* in 1961, views of cognitive disability were beginning to shift due to the impact of the de-institutionalisation movement in the late 1960s and children with cognitive challenges were no longer viewed as figures of abjection that should be hidden away in asylums. Whereas 'Dance of the Happy Shades' charts the widening gap between society's treatment of cognitively disabled children and elders, Munro's recent story 'In Sight of the Lake' (2012), which I analyse in the second half of this essay, provides her most powerful counter-argument to date to portrayals of later life as a gothic state of abject 'unbecoming'. As I argue elsewhere, Munro's writings reflect a growing trend on the part of Canadian authors to recognise the legacy of identifying dementia and Alzheimer's disease with the gothic and to contest this social imaginary (Goldman 2015). With respect to Munro's fiction, in contrast to her previous stories, 'In Sight of the Lake' offers insight (pun intended) into the mind of an elderly woman coping with symptoms of dementia. Equally important, the story incorporates surreal elements to bring the reader into the imaginative world of the protagonist. Although 'In sight of the lake' is entirely Munro's surreal fantasy of what goes on in her character's mind, this vision offers an alternative to the paranoid gothic representation of the fourth age. Taken together, the narrative's focalisation and its reliance on surrealism to re-create the experiences of dementia constitute Munro's most profound challenge to date of the gothic metaphor of dementia as what Gilleard and Higgs (2010: 121) have recently termed 'a black hole'.

The Third and Fourth Age as a social imaginary

Invoking the well-known model of the four ages of man, Laslett (1989: 4) was one of the first to identify the third age as 'an era of personal fulfilment' in contrast to a fourth age as 'an era of final dependence, decrepitude and death' (see also Hazan 1996: 11). As Grenier (2012: 57) observes, Laslett's main contribution lies in 'challenging the naturalisation of age by articulating the third age as a time of opportunity and freedom characterised by choice, related not to chronological age, but to potential and possibility'. Unlike more empirically-based models afforded by biomedicine and psychology, Laslett's conception emphasises, as Grenier (2012: 57) points out, the idea of 'lifestyle based on choice and the negotiation of experience' – lifestyle or social features that continue to figure largely in the writings on the topic by Gilleard and Higgs.

To date, there have been many useful elaborations and critiques of both the theory and the concepts of the third and fourth age (see, for example, Calasanti and King 2011, Holstein 2011, Neuberger 2009, Scharf 2009). As a literary critic, my contribution lies in exploring the metaphors that have constellated around the lifestyle paradigm. In particular, I am concerned with the impact of Gilleard and Higg's reliance on the metaphor of the 'black hole' and the attendant metaphor of 'the event horizon' to characterise the fourth age. As they confess, the metaphor of the black hole 'might seem too strong but our object in using it is to convey the inherent unknowability of the fourth age' (Gilleard and Higg 2015: 16). Glossing the term, Gilleard and Higgs (2015: 16) note that in astronomy, 'a black hole creates a massive gravitational pull that sucks in every phenomenon of the "event horizon" which is a point where light disappears completely. Any light emitted from beyond this horizon can never reach the observer'. In essence, these cosmic metaphors align the fourth age with something sublime, mysterious, and dark, but also lifeless and all-consuming – an enormous sphere of nothing, a void that sucks everything around it into itself. Yet, as Lloyd (2015: 262) asserts, in some ways 'it matters less whether the fourth age is 'unknowable' as a cultural concept than that a better understanding of older people's experience of declining health and self-reliance is developed'. I argue further, in keeping with Grenier, that 'defining this period as a void is problematic' (Goldman 2012: 179). As Grenier (2012: 179) suggests, 'liminal spaces from "othered" locations', such as the fourth age, can 'also contain space for redefinition'. In accordance with this insight, in what follows, I offer a close reading of two stories by Alice Munro in an effort to redefine the experience and meaning of the space of the fourth age.

Before turning to Munro's fiction, I want to consider Gilleard and Higgs's suggestion that the metaphor of the black hole best captures the horrors associated with the fourth age. Gilleard and Higgs (2010: 122) maintain that the third age constitutes a cultural field associated with 'the development of generational lifestyles whose origins can be traced to 1960s youth culture with its emphasis on choice, autonomy and self-expression'. They argue further that due to a set of developments which include 'the narrowing of mortality within the life space, the expanding possibilities of not appearing or not performing as 'old', (Gilleard and

Higgs 2011: 138) and the efforts to promote a more positive image of 'normal' aging (Gilleard and Higgs 2014), the fourth age has been increasingly construed as a gothic transformation and associated with a locus devoid of self-consciousness and choice:

> It is when people are no longer 'getting by', when they are seen as not managing the daily round, when they become third persons in others' age-based discourse, within others' rules, that they become subjects of a fourth age. At this point an 'event horizon' is passed, beyond which the everyday round cannot situate a frame of reference from which individual agency is interpreted. It is the combination of a public failure of self-management and the securing of this failure by institutional forms of care that a key boundary is passed. (Gilleard and Higgs 2010: 122)

In their writings on the fourth age, Gilleard and Higgs emphasise the deleterious impact of institutionalisation and the role it plays in creating a gothic social imaginary:

> The irreversibility of nursing home placement, the disappearance of any personal exchange in the processes of admission, and the 'deprivatization of experience' that results from admission (Gubrium and Holstein 1999) create an immense negative force upon both the third age that surrounds but remains imperceptive of it and the general attitude to old age. In short, the fourth age acts as a metaphorical black hole of aging (Gilleard and Higgs 2010: 125).

Gilleard and Higgs invoke the metaphor of the black hole not because it represents the truth, but because it captures society's affective response and fantasies – what they term the 'social imaginary' – associated with later-life. I would argue further that this particular expression of the social imaginary is drawn from high gothic, which, as noted above, emphasises horrifying evil and monstrous transformations.

As Gilleard and Higgs (2011: 140) explain, however, the fourth age 'is neither an inevitable nor an inescapable stage of life'; instead, it can be understood 'as a form of social imaginary, coordinated by our collective understandings of frailty and abjection and realised through the social institutions that develop in response to those understandings'. Rather than view the third and fourth age in the traditional sense as 'stages of life', they suggest they are more properly understood as 'contested cultural spaces', with the latter's social meaning derived from at least two basic societal changes: 'the 'densification' of old age (through general improvements in mortality, institutional policies and practices) and the objectification of frailty and abjection that arises from viewing and/or listening to the narratives of older people in care' (Gilleard and Higgs 2011: 140).

Fiction and the psychological products of fantasy play a central role in the construction of the social imaginary of the fourth age since, as Gilleard and Higgs maintain, it is generated solely on the basis of external perspectives and third-party narratives; in this regard, it mirrors the third-person stance of biomedical models:

> To many people in or approaching 'later' life, the position of those in the fourth age can be likened to that of an object that has strayed too close to the event horizon and has now gone over it, beyond any chance of return. Equally, no light shines back once the event horizon is traversed. In the absence of any reflexive return it becomes impossible to separate what is projected into it and what occurs within it. (Gilleard and Higgs 2010: 125)

As this passage indicates, straying 'too close to the event horizon' describes a shift in narrative perspective such that one becomes the object of third-person narratives and third-party actions, rather than the author of a first-person account that articulates one's own thoughts and desires. Simply put, one is no longer the hero of one's own story. This shift results in one becoming "lost' from citizenship and the "civilized'" (Gilleard and Higgs 2014: 15). I cite Gilleard and Higgs's insights at length because, on the one hand, they recall eighteenth-century philosopher John Locke's view of the 'idiot' as located 'outside language' (Bewell 1989: 57). On the other hand, Gilleard and Higgs also stress the importance of narrative perspective and metaphor – the very terrain on which Munro's fiction contests the prevailing social imaginary of the fourth age as a black hole.

Ironic reversals in 'Dance of the happy shades'

Rather than re-install this gothic social imaginary, which one might expect of a story written in the 1960s, Munro's 'Dance of the happy shades' invokes the anti-gothic motif of rescuing people with cognitive impairment from the land of the dead. It is significant in this regard that the story's title is drawn from the myth of Orpheus and Eurydice, which relates the hero's failed quest to rescue his beloved, who is condemned to live in the underworld.[2] The title of Munro's story, in fact, refers to a far more prosaic allusion to the myth: a piano piece played at a children's music recital by a girl with Down syndrome, a genetic condition associated with both cognitive impairment and Alzheimer's disease (Dalton and Wallace 2011). By relying on this intertext, Munro's narrative underscores the similarities and differences between society's treatment of children living with cognitive impairment and elderly individuals with dementia; initially, both groups are silenced and typically hidden from view – a form of live burial.

Munro's story is set in the first half of the twentieth century when the parents of children with Down syndrome were advised to institutionalise their child at birth, and when physicians routinely informed parents that their child might never talk and could not be taught. As medical historian Mark Jackson (2000: 149) observes, 'permanent segregation of the feeble minded in purpose-built colonies, and the separation of the sexes within those colonies, not only served as a means of effectively limiting the propagation of degenerates, but also crucially established a convenient physical and ideological distance between the healthy middle classes, on the one hand, and the polluted and contaminated 'residuum,' on the other'. The radical challenge posed by 'Dance of the happy shades' is perhaps best understood when one considers when the story first appeared in 1961 in *The New Yorker*, there were few literary models for representing cognitively disabled children. The only serious, literary work in which Down syndrome figured was Faulkner's (1931) portrayal of Benjy Compson in *The Sound and the Fury* (1929).[3] Beyond the realm of literature, Neufeldt (2003: 20) observes, in Canada prior to the 1960s:

> 'Mental retardation,' as it was then known, was characterised by a sense of shame and social stigma felt by families and a lack of concerted interest on the part of both professionals of all kinds and policy makers … The fact that parents of children with intellectual impairments neither knew of each other, nor were emboldened to take collective action until after WWII speaks volumes about the shame and neglect attached to the condition.

Children with cognitive impairments were sent away to live in small residential schools (the first was built in Orillia, Ontario in 1888); and while the 'original intent was laudable, the residential 'schools' rapidly deteriorated into what become 'human warehouses' that were the subject of much attention by advocates in succeeding decades' (Neufeldt 2003: 17). These overarching historical dimensions provide the background for my reading of 'Dance of the happy shades', a domestic narrative that portrays a series of surprising events which transpire at Miss Marsalles's annual piano recital.

The story is related from the perspective of the adolescent, middle-class narrator, who is Miss Marsalles's pupil (as was her mother before her). Early on, readers learn that neither the young performers nor their well-heeled, young mothers are looking forward to the prospect of attending yet another recital at Miss Marsalles's home. Over the years, the elderly Miss Marsalles has moved from her tiny Rosedale home to ever more cramped accommodations. Early on, the narrative draws a parallel between her economic decline and her aging body. The narrator's mother insists that Miss Marsalles is simply getting 'too old' (Munro 1968: 211). She also complains that the last three parties were 'rather squashed' and that this year, Miss Marsalles has moved to an even tinier home in a seedy part of town (Munro 1968: 211). Equally distressing and potentially one of the causes of the economic decline, Miss Marsalles's older sister, once a fixture at her annual recital, is now bedridden following a stroke that has left her unable to speak and profoundly cognitively impaired. Never appearing in the story, the sister remains a haunting, gothic figure of mental and physical age-related degeneration.

The themes of decay and degeneration pervade the story, which highlight society's tendency to stigmatise and expel those experiencing economic, physical, and cognitive decline. Of particular interest is how the story's blurring of these categories reflects shifts that occurred during the first half of the twentieth century when rather than view social pathology as inhering solely in socio-economic conditions – as a problem associated with 'the poor' – the rhetoric was adapted to convey a new conception of a social pathology 'clearly located in the *biological* nature of a distinct "class" of the population' – the newly designated category of the 'feeble minded' (Jackson 2000: 2, my emphasis).

Overarching anxieties concerning mental and physical degeneration and decay are introduced in Munro's story from the start, with the party-goers' concern that the food, which has been set out early in the day, will spoil in the heat. The related threat of cognitive degeneration is explicitly introduced early on when the narrator and her mother meet Miss Marsalles's neighbour, Mrs. Clegg, and the latter whispers that Miss Marsalles's sister will not be joining them. 'Yes, it's a shame', Mrs. Clegg confides, 'She lost her powers of speech, you know. Her powers of control generally, she lost' (Munro 1968: 218). In this instance, the narrative draws attention to those who are rendered mute and whose cognitive fitness has waned – variables that potentially doom individuals to a social death.

Despite her guests' barely veiled desire to be over and done with the dreadful ritual, for reasons that are not immediately apparent, Miss Marsalles insists on making everyone wait. From the start, when she enters the house, the narrator senses that Miss Marsalles 'was looking beyond us as she kissed us; she was looking up the street for someone who had not yet arrived' (Munro 1968: 217). Only when the narrator is playing her piece does the explanation arrive for Miss Marsalles's delay. As the narrator says, out of the corner of her eye, she sees 'a whole procession of children, eight or ten in all, with a red-haired woman in something like a uniform, mounting the front step' (Munro 1968: 220). The narrator remarks further on her sense that something 'has happened, something unforeseen, perhaps something disastrous' (Munro 1968: 221). Only when she returns to her seat is she able to scrutinise the unusual features of the children. Her attention is caught by the singular profile of a boy about nine or ten, who is walking toward the piano. As he looks up at Miss Marsalles, the narrator observes his 'heavy, unfinished features, the abnormally small and slanting eyes' (Munro 1968: 221).

Gazing at the rest of the children, she sees the same profile repeated two or three times – a repetition that enhances the story's emphasis on ironic doubleness and mimicry. Rather than rely on these visual and corporeal stock images to identify the less than human, the narrative's emphasis on these markers of difference in conjunction with evidence of the children's musical ability is used to challenge the reductive visual logic that supported society's decision to banish these children to institutions.

In answer to the narrator's mother's shrill question, 'Who are they?' Mrs. Clegg explains that they are from the class that Miss Marsalles has out at the Green Hill School. 'They're nice little things', Miss Clegg says, 'and some of them quite musical but of course they're not all there' (Munro 1968: 221). Throughout the story, the connection between Miss Marsalles's sister and the children remains implicit. Yet both the elderly woman suffering from cognitive decline and these youngsters are aligned with degeneration (the antithesis of evolution) and are deemed nonpersons: 'unfinished' 'things' who are supposedly 'not all there'. Both groups are also expected to remain hidden, secluded in private bedrooms or asylums, and thereby comply with their social death. In keeping with the theme of degeneration, Miss Marsalles's sister who has lost her powers of speech is etymologically likened to an 'infant', a word derived from the Greek term, meaning 'not-speaking'. By stressing the silence of Miss Marsalles and the children in contrast to the vocal and shaming commentary of Mrs. Clegg and the outraged mothers in the audience, the story underscores who has the power to control the social and affective meanings of cognitive impairment. Yet, by relating events from the more open-minded perspective of the youthful narrator, 'Dance of the happy shades' immediately casts doubt on the adults' deeply entrenched, negative perceptions of both elders and children with cognitive impairment.

The mothers' initial response to the children from Green Hill – a combination of pity and disgust – recalls Jackson's (2000: 1) insight that those 'inhabiting the borderlands of imbecility were both pitied and considered a danger to the State'. When the children from Green Hill first make their appearance, the narrator states that the adults are almost audible in saying to themselves: 'No, I know it is not right to be repelled by such children and I am not repelled, but nobody told me I was going to come here to listen to a procession of little – little idiots for that's what they are' (Munro 1968: 222). Far from imposing a utopian resolution to this moral conflict, the narrative illustrates, instead, that non-violent approaches to dementia have always shadowed the dominant response of fear and revulsion. Both the dissenting views of the narrator and the presence of the accepting and compassionate Miss Marsalles introduce an alternative, ironic approach to cognitive disability within the narrative. Despite the mothers' attempt to stigmatise the children from Green Hill, and thereby create a division between their children and the latecomers, the narrator insists that the latter do not play any worse than the regular students. Nevertheless, she goes on to admit that there is 'an atmosphere in the room of some freakish inescapable dream' (Munro 1968: 222). Her use of the words 'freakish' and 'dream' indicate, however, that from the perspective of the narrator and the mothers, neither Miss Marsalles's sister nor these children occupy the real world.

Within the story, the eruption of surreal elements effectively highlights the limits of representation and society's efforts to master the Other. As philosopher and gender critic Judith Butler (2006: 144) explains, 'for representation to convey the human, representation must not only fail, but it must show its failure. There is something unrepresentable that we nevertheless seek to represent, and that paradox must be retained in the representation we give'. Munro's (1968: 233) narrative exposes this failure most forcibly when it relates how, as they listen to Dolores Boyle perform 'The Dance of the happy shades', the mothers sit speechless, 'caught with a look of protest on their faces, a more profound anxiety than before, as if reminded of something that they had forgotten they had forgotten'. Prior systems of representation explicitly fail because in this uncanny moment, they forget to forget (i.e. they no longer repress their awareness and thus fleetingly remember) that the division between 'feeble minded' and neurotypical individuals was, in fact, 'sheer invention' – a historical artifact of the eighteenth century that, according to Locke's philosophy, designated specific groups as non-citizens who existed outside of the law. Equally relevant, the story's description of the mothers' plight also resonates with common descriptions of advanced dementia, which likewise causes people to 'forget that they have forgotten'. Viewed in this light, the mother's cognitive lapse momentarily aligns them with individuals with dementia, further eliding the division between neurotypical and non-neurotypical behaviour.

In Munro's texts, dreams, dream-like states, and 'other' countries frequently serve as catalysts for irony by highlighting the world of fantasy versus reality and by blurring the boundary between the two. In addition to highlighting the potential ironic inversion of real versus imagined worlds, dreams also prompt Munro's characters to reflect on the supplemental, existential ironies that attend the natural passage of time that renders certain societal views and ways of life obsolete. In 'Dance of the happy shades', a version of this type of ironic, temporal joke is played on the mothers who vainly insist on upholding the distinction between what they deem the real world (in which 'neurotypical' individuals are respected and those deemed 'non-neurotypical' remain hidden in asylums) and the unreal world (in which people with cognitive impairment mingle freely with 'neurotypicals' and are accorded the same respect). In Munro's fiction, life's social rhythms and conventions can change for the better. Ironically, it is Dolores, whose name is from the Latin word for 'sorrows', who conveys the possibility of the freedom of a great unemotional happiness. Although the mystery of her music is never resolved, it offers insight into a non-egocentric form of happiness that is not restricted by the notion of a rational self. In portraying Dolores as an enigma, Munro recalls Wordsworth's representation of the 'Idiot' as a 'figure of mystery, and thus of our own limits of understanding, recalling Renaissance notions of divine folly' (Andrews 1998: 74).[4]

When faced with the mothers' palpable disgust and dismay, however, Miss Marsalles refuses to abide by the implicit rules of the real world. Rather than acquiesce to the social death of people with cognitive impairment, those whom Locke and the mothers term 'idiots', Miss Marsalles says each child's name as if it were 'a cause for celebration' (Munro 1968: 222). Moreover, for her, the bravura performance of Dolores Boyle, in particular, is 'something she always expected, and she finds it natural and satisfying' (Munro 1968: 223). In this instance, her response reflects the changing *Zeitgeist*, specifically, the transformation of the social imaginary that, prior to the 1960s, deemed children with Down syndrome '"lost" from citizenship and the "civilized"' (Gilleard and Higgs 2014: 15).

In considering Munro's ironic aesthetics, it is significant that the story's emphasis on performance, specifically, the parade – figured in 'Dance of the happy shades' as a Bakhtinian, carnivalesque 'procession of little idiots', constitutes one of Munro's signature motifs (Redekop 1992: xiii). In Munro's fiction, the parade allows for an often ironic comparison between two worldviews because it produces a 'tableau effect', in which 'old conventions are briefly held still for us so that we may examine their workings' (Redekop 1992: xiii). Whereas Redekop has focused on how Munro's stories invoke the parade and play with both the masquerade and mimicry to deconstruct the idealised maternal figure, I argue that her stories rely on these elements to challenge socially constructed notions of disability.

According to feminist philosopher Luce Irigaray (1985: 76), the goal of the mimic is to '"make visible" by an effect of playful repetition, what was supposed to remain invisible'. With the introduction of the child named 'Dolores Boyle', a preternaturally gifted musician, 'Dance of the happy shades', 'makes visible' and 'audible' both the outdated views of the mothers and the newly emergent subject position of the Other, a child with Down syndrome. In figuratively and literally staging the appearance of Dolores and by demonstrating her ability, in the mother's eyes, to mimic and, indeed, exceed the musical ability of neurotypical children, 'Dance of the happy shades' offers its most emphatic challenge to gothic representations – the live burial – of people coping with cognitive disability.

By flaunting the demand for the segregation of the 'unfit', and by portraying a child with Down syndrome as a brilliant musician whose abilities far surpass that of neurotypical children, Munro's text signals its debt to the larger disability movements that articulated the rights of people with cognitive disabilities. As scholars observe, the disability movement was founded 'on the transformative and liberation politics of the 1960s new left movements' (Chivers 2008: 307, also see Neufeldt 2003). These changes affected not only people with disabilities but also the meanings and linkages between youth and elderly people coping with disability. As Higgs and Gilleard (2014) observe, in the case of disability organisations, the historical alliance with the youth movements of the 1960s rendered suspect any close alliance with the old. Marshall (2014: 25) observes, for example, that whereas 'a sizable number of people identify with disability-focused alliances', there is 'not a broadly accepted Elder culture with which people connect'. As a result, in specific contexts, 'people with disabilities have a higher level of social visibility than do people of advanced age' (Marshall 2014: 25). Marshall (2014: 26) refers to the 'hyper-visibility of bodies with disabilities'. Moreover, as both disability and chronic illness movements increasingly relied on first-person narratives to contest the dominance of biomedical worldviews, the newly emergent, citizen/subject positions associated with not only disability, but also with older age and chronic illness were gradually disaggregated from the social imaginary of age-related dementia and Alzheimer's disease. People who identified as disabled, as aged but otherwise healthy 'zoomers',[5] or coping with a chronic illness, successfully transformed their objectification through narrative and used their status as oppressed subjects as a platform to claim rights, recognition, and respect. In keeping with these socio-historical shifts, Munro's narrative figuratively rescues the children from the land of the dead, whereas Miss Marsalles's sister and, by extension, citizens coping with age-related dementia remain absent and threatening figures, images of 'final dependence, decrepitude and death' (Laslett 1989: 4).

Ironically, in a narrative that features silent, cognitively challenged children and elderly individuals, at the end of the story, it is the mothers who are rendered speechless. They find themselves in the same position as Miss Marsalles's sister, who, due to a stroke, also lost her powers of speech. More precisely, the women find themselves unable to utter the words 'Poor Miss Marsalles' (Munro 1968: 224). They have lost their 'powers of control generally' and, as a result, they can neither shame Miss Marsalles nor dismiss the revelation afforded by the children from Green Hill School. The story's final sentence highlights the power of art to effect this revelation. As the narrator says, 'It is the Dance of the happy shades that prevents us, it is that one communiqué from the other country where she lives' (Munro 1968: 224). Having witnessed Dolores Boyles's capacity for artistic genius, the mothers can no longer fully control the meaning of dementia nor reduce it to a pathology that eclipses an individual's humanity or her capacity for creative expression.

Despite this ironic reversal, the story nevertheless demonstrates that the meanings attributed to dementia are not the same for the young and old. The narrator's reference, for example, to 'the other country' where the elderly Miss Marsalles lives recalls William Butler Yeats's poem 'Sailing to Byzantium' (1928), whose opening line proclaims: 'That is no country for old men'. Viewed in this light, 'Dance of the happy shades' offers a partial counter-argument to Yeats's resigned acquiescence to enforced exile. On one level, Munro's narrative suggests that people who mistakenly equate genius with wholeness, wealth, and physical and mental perfection may find themselves silenced and exiled from a vital source of human creativity. Although this insight potentially includes both younger and older individuals coping with cognitive decline, as noted above, in the 1960s, later-life dementia became increasingly disaggregated from the positive re-casting of disability, chronic illness, and the third age. In 'Dance of the happy shades' Miss Marsalles's sister has, to borrow Gilleard and Higgs's terms, strayed across the event horizon and is thus 'beyond any chance of return'; in her later writings, Munro playfully contests this facet of the social imaginary, specifically, the conception of dementia as a black hole from which no light escapes.

'In sight of the lake': the joke is on us

The opening sentence of 'In sight of the lake' – 'A woman goes to her doctor to have a prescription renewed' – relies on the diction and cadence of a joke, including the deferred expectation of a punchline.[6] From the start, readers are alerted to the story's central organising principle and its overarching thematic concern with the nature of jokes and tricks. The story offers an account of a woman named Nancy, who has been referred to a specialist due to her memory problems. Rather than make her way to the specialist's office early in the morning, Nancy decides to travel to the nearby village a few days beforehand to avoid running around and getting lost when she is in a hurry to get there in the morning. Due to a series of errors, however, Nancy cannot find the specialist's office. When looking for the doctor's name and address, for example, she discovers that she has misplaced the information. Examining the scrap of paper she finds in her pocket, she realises to her dismay that the only thing written on it is the shoe size of her husband's sister, who is dead. Following this mishap, increasingly strange and surreal phenomena characterise her trip, ranging from the sight of clocks that no longer tell the time, to a boy riding his bicycle backwards, to a strange, lush, private garden filled with flowers that burst from between the paths and from the grass.[7] Nancy, like Alice in Wonderland, has tumbled down the proverbial rabbit hole and she is hopelessly lost. In an attempt to find her way to the doctor, toward the conclusion, she strikes up a conversation with a man who tends the exotic flower garden. When she asks him for directions to the specialist's office, he wisely suggests that she look for the specialist at the Lakeview Rest Home. To her chagrin, however, Nancy realises that rather than respond to him properly, she merely echoes his words. The story concludes with Nancy, who has made her way to the rest home, alone at night in an empty corridor of the institution, hysterically calling for help. In the end, help of a sort arrives. An orderly named Sandy chides Nancy for creating a scene. At this point readers are shocked to discover that Nancy is, in fact, a resident of the home, and that the preceding events were merely her subjective fantasy. 'What are we going to do with you?' says Sandy. 'All we want is to get you into your nightie. And you go and carry on like a chicken that's scared of being et for dinner' (Munro 2012: 232).

As this brief plot summary indicates, the story relies on the clichéd formal ending of 'it was all a dream' to prompt readers to relate to Nancy as a subject rather than the object of the gaze. Indeed, as she embarks on her quest and we follow her on her journey until the final, shocking revelation of her status as a patient in the nursing home, we literally see through her eyes, as she surveys the town and its inhabitants. As Redekop (1992) astutely observes, Munro's principal tactic for subverting the tendency to turn female bodies into objects is to portray them in the act of looking. Redekop (1992: 5) argues further that for the woman who subjects others to her gaze, 'nothing less than the survival of her self is at stake'. Like any confident tourist visiting a small town, Nancy displays all of the markers of robust subjectivity: she makes choices, she generates several hypotheses concerning the most likely location of the specialist and she tests them, she is emotionally attuned to her surroundings, and she expresses her judgments freely.

She is also demonstrably playful, but, understandably, would prefer to be the one making the jokes rather than serving as the butt of other people's jokes. When she first catches sight of the nursing home, for example, she notices that the floor 'is all silvery tiles, the sort that children love to slide on' (Munro 2012: 229). For a moment, 'she thinks of the patients sliding and slipping for pleasure and the idea makes her light-hearted' (Munro 2012: 229). As the narrator explains, she holds an internal colloquy on the topic of whether or not she should give it a try, but, ultimately, decides against it:

'I didn't dare try it myself', she says in a charming voice to somebody in her head, perhaps her husband. 'It wouldn't have done, would it? I could have found myself in front of the doctor, the very one who was getting ready to test my mental stability. And then what would he have to say?' (Munro 2012: 229)[8]

From the start, however, readers recognise that life has already played a trick on Nancy and shamed her because when she goes to see her doctor, the latter is not there. We are told that 'It's her day off. In fact the woman has got the day wrong, she has mixed up Monday with Tuesday' (Munro 2012: 217). Nancy's error pertains to the very issue that she had wanted to raise with her doctor: 'She has wondered if her mind is slipping a bit' (Munro 2012: 212). Anxious about her memory slips, Nancy secretly hopes that her doctor will laugh off her concerns. Instead, the doctor's assistant phones to tell Nancy that an appointment has been made with a specialist. During their conversation, Nancy continues to yearn for reassurance, for someone to understand and, simultaneously, to reduce her anxiety by making light of her problem. When the assistant explains that the specialist 'deals with elderly patients', Nancy replies, 'Indeed. Elderly patients who are off their nut' (Munro 2012: 212). For Nancy, it is a tremendous relief when she manages to get someone to laugh with her rather than at her (Munro 2012: 218).

In addition to highlighting Nancy's desire to remain in control and maintain her independence, the story – which is narrated in the third person but focalised in the first person – affords tremendous insight into Nancy's emotional sensitivity and her desire to avoid being shamed, which creates an empathetic bond between reader and character. Throughout the story, Nancy's emotions, particularly her anxiety, remain palpable. For example, Nancy decides to visit the town prior to her appointment precisely because she wants to ensure that there will be 'no danger of her arriving all flustered or even a little late, creating a bad impression right off the bat' (Munro 2012: 218).[9] Later, when she takes leave of the man who tends the lovely garden and heads off to the Lakeview Rest Home, she worries that she will not be able to find her keys: 'She can feel the approach of familiar, tiresome panic. But then she finds them, in her pocket' (Munro 2012: 228). Finally, as she drives away, she catches sight of the gardener talking to some of the townspeople and wonders if their conversation concerns her: 'Maybe a remark to be made, some joke about her vagueness or silliness. Or just her age. A mark against her' (Munro 2012: 228). As these passages suggest, Nancy desires more than anything to be in control, to be the one 'making a silly joke' (Munro 2012: 227). By conveying Nancy's thoughts as she grows ever more desperate to orient herself and to avoid being mocked, readers appreciate what it must be like not merely to be lost (disoriented), but also 'to have lost face and, as a corollary, in the words of Gilleard and Higgs (2014: 15), to be "'lost' from citizenship and the 'civilised'". When the punchline of the story hits home, readers recognise that despite her persistent worries about being caught 'slipping', all along, Nancy has been in the same position as Miss Marsalles's sister; both are women who, in the eyes of others, have demonstrably lost their 'powers of control' (Munro 1968: 218).

On the one hand, the conclusion demonstrates irrefutably that Nancy's powers are severely restricted since she seemingly cannot put on her own nightie. Equally relevant, throughout the text are clues, most obviously the references to the broken clocks and chipped crockery that serve as objective correlatives for Nancy's status as a broken object. On the other hand, in keeping with the doubled structure of irony, as in the figure of the duck-rabbit, these clues remain in the background while, in the foreground, Nancy focalises her journey through her surreal dream world. In the end, when the perspective shifts, the gothic returns with a vengeance, but its status as a social imaginary and its external origins are highlighted by the fact that it is supplied by the reader. Simply put, readers have more insight into Nancy's abject position within the nursing home than Nancy herself; hence, readers impose a gothic point of view. In her thoughts, Nancy remains a subject who chooses to leave the Lakeview Rest Home. In keeping with the story's reliance on dramatic irony and its emphasis on the external origins of the gothic social imaginary, readers must ignore the awareness of Nancy's sense of personhood and agency to view her as an object.

In light of the story's engagement with the Female Gothic,[10] it is no coincidence that the image of the helpless woman, often garbed only in a nightie, serves as a recurring motif in this story. The pervasiveness of this image of female helplessness and confinement suggests that it is integral to western society's gothic social imaginary of the fourth age. I would argue further that both the figure of the helpless woman and the allusions to hysteria in the closing paragraph of 'In sight of the lake' remind us further that the gothic social imaginary of the fourth age, specifically late-onset dementia, draws on some of the same fears and desires inherent in earlier fears concerning pathological memory loss associated with the late-nineteenth and early-twentieth century hysteria diagnosis.[11]

By juxtaposing hysteria and age-related dementia and linking them to the locus of the asylum, 'In sight of the lake' highlights the origins and structure of the social imaginary of the fourth age, which partly derives its affective power from the ongoing stigma and pathologisation of women's supposedly inherently diseased minds and bodies. Rather than re-install this stigma, 'In sight of the lake' uses Munrovian irony to drive home the awareness that in discussions of later-life dementia, and even in seemingly factual medical accounts, fantasy and storytelling play a crucial role. Equally important, Munro's narrative demonstrates that the voices and insights of the people most affected by our fantasies are missing. 'In sight of the lake' effects a vertiginous shift in perspective that plunges the reader into the world of dreams. In the end, the reader returns to 'the real world' only to realise that she is still within a dream; the ending of the story, which locates the reader in the nursing home, is still part of Munro's fiction.

Rather than serve as a joke solely on Nancy – a mark against her alone – the narrative plays an elaborate trick on the reader by destabilising her sense of what is real and what is imagined and by showing how both are mutually constitutive. Readers are left to consider whether the world we currently live in is, in part, a dream in which we all slip and slide, and where failure and mortality are not accidents, but part of the life course and meaningful components of both personal and social narratives. It is sobering, in this regard, to recognise that one out of two people over eighty-five suffers from cognitive impairment – a fact which raises the perennial question of whether the illness springs from disease or from the natural course of aging.

Far from inviting the reader to dismiss Nancy as a failed or deluded quester, 'In sight of the lake', like the previous short story 'Dance of the happy shades', admits the reader into a larger community of vulnerability, risk, and failure. As Redekop (1992: 237) maintains, the 'backdrop of Munro's comic performances is black'. False comforts 'are seen through, but there is no true comfort simply in debunking the false ones. The comfort, rather, comes from our sense of participating in a community that has mutual fears and desires' (Redekop 1992: 237). Equally crucial, instead of castigating readers for ignoring the real world, like some prim school marm, 'In sight of the lake' relies on a third-person narrator to highlight the complexity and insights afforded by dreams and, more generally, the imagination. 'You must have had a dream', Sandy says to Nancy. 'What did you dream about now?' (Munro 2012: 232). Although these words are addressed to Nancy, they also implicate the reader who has shared Nancy's dream.

Munro's debt to Surrealism

In the final section of this paper, I want to analyse some of the implications of Munro's reliance on dreams and, more precisely, on the elements of surrealism within the tests that figure Nancy's later-life dementia. In brief, Surrealism which began in the 1920s and whose members were initially concentrated in Paris, developed out of the earlier Dada activities, a movement whose beginnings coincided with the onset of World War I. The Dadaists believed that the reason and logic of bourgeois capitalist society had led people into war. They expressed their rejection of that ideology in artistic expressions that appeared to eschew logic and embrace chaos and irrationality. The Surrealists likewise rejected conventional notions of madness and frequently relied on the practices of free association, automatic writing, and dream analysis in their attempts to alter civilisation and liberate the imagination. Although both Dadaists and Surrealists maintained in common the rejection of logic and reason, the followers of both groups eventually separated. Equally important, unlike the Dadaists, the Surrealists were profoundly influenced by the writings of Sigmund Freud, specifically his notion of the unconscious.

On the one hand, the repeated mention of the broken clocks in 'In sight of the lake' may remind some readers of the clock-drawing test used to screen for cognitive impairment and dementia. Such tests transform subjects into numerical scores that determine their 'citizenship', in Sontag's terms, as either impaired or neurotypical, ill or well. On the other hand, for readers with only a passing familiarity with the Surrealist movement, Munro's allusion to broken clocks may also bring to mind Salvador Dali's famous painting of melting clocks, 'The Persistence of Memory' (1931), which features three large clock faces draped over various objects – a tree branch, a table, and what appears to be a white cloth laying on the ground. Similarly, the image of the boy riding backward together with Nancy's internal colloquy recall Dali's equally evocative painting, 'Sentimental Colloquy' (1948). At the centre of this painting is a blue grand piano sitting on what appears to be an immense cream-coloured plank floor that runs from the foreground to the vanishing point. The piano's cracked top board thrusts upward toward the upper edge of the frame. Water pours through the immense crack, transforming the broken instrument into a fountain. In the foreground and the background skeletal figures ride bicycles across the plank floor in neat rows, forming a grid, with their white veil-like capes trailing behind them.

In drawing these associations, I am not suggesting that there is a one-to-one correspondence between the verbal images Munro generates in her narrative and those found in Dali's art. Instead, I am arguing that the narrative's depiction of surrealist images highlights a debt to a movement that prized the individual imagination and famously did not pathologise altered states of consciousness. Far from positing that Munro was conscious of these connections, I am drawing a connection between Surrealism and 'In sight of the lake's rejection of logic and reason in an effort to liberate the imagination to highlight an important alternative to gothic constructions of the fourth age as a black hole.

It is significant in this regard that André Breton (1896–1966), one of the founding fathers of the Surrealist movement, was a physician who trained in psychiatry. During the war, Breton worked in an asylum where he treated soldiers for shellshock, which, according to

Charcot and Freud, was a form of hysteria. In treating his patients, Breton notably listened carefully to their fantasies and prized their imagination. In his first *Surrealist Manifesto* (1924), Breton championed the power of the imagination to liberate individuals from the corrosive impact of shame and from society's deathly rules and conventions. As he states:

> Amidst all the shame we are heir to, it is well to recognize that the widest freedom of spirit remains to us. It is up to us not to abuse it in any serious manner. To make a slave of the imagination, even though what is vulgarly called happiness is at stake, is to fail profoundly to do justice to one's deepest self. Only imagination realises the possible in me, and it is enough to lift for a moment the dreadful proscription. (Breton 1924: n.p.)

Breton also argued that those deemed mad should not be confined within asylums or denied their liberty simply because they had retreated into their imaginations. He argued, instead, that this faculty represents the most vital core of our humanity. Moreover, for people unjustly confined, the imagination provides great solace:

> Everyone knows, in fact, that the mad owe their incarceration to a number of legally reprehensible actions, and that were it not for those actions, their liberty (or what we see as their liberty) would not be at risk. They may be, in some measure, victims of their imagination, I am prepared to concede that, in the way that it induces them not to observe certain rules, without which the species feels threatened, which it pays us all to be aware of. But the profound indifference they show for the judgment we pass on them, and even the various punishments inflicted on them, allows us to suppose that they derive great solace from imagination, that they enjoy their delirium enough to endure the fact that it is only of value to themselves. And, indeed, hallucinations, illusions, etc., are no slight source of pleasure. (Breton 1924: n.p.)

Breton made the equally bold claim that rather than view error as a sign of degeneration, pathology, or a loss of control, it is perhaps more appropriate to see error – which, as noted, Munro's story aligns with losing one's way and slipping and sliding – as fundamental to human creativity and play. 'Is not the possibility of error, for the spirit', Breton asks, 'rather a circumstance conducive to its well-being?' (Breton 1924: n.p.).

Reading 'In sight of the lake' in light of surrealism offers insight into prior moments of resistance to earlier gothic social imaginaries concerning mental illness. From my research on representations of dementia and Alzheimer's disease from the 1850s to the present, broadly speaking, it seems as if western society oscillates between two fantasies – a utopian image of enduring personhood or a dystopian image of a black hole. This tendency toward splitting recalls Sontag's (1978: 1) famous opening to *Illness as Metaphor* cited in the epigraph:

> Illness is the night-side of life, a more onerous citizenship. Everyone who is born holds dual citizenship, in the kingdom of the well and in the kingdom of the sick. Although we all prefer to use only the good passport, sooner or later each of us is obliged, at least for a spell, to identify ourselves as citizens of that other place.

As Munro's stories illustrate, however, both forms of citizenship are determined by societal fears and desires rather than solely on the basis of biomedical fact. As Ingram (2014: 122) insists, there is 'no chasm between normal mental functioning and Alzheimer's disease'.

Instead, 'there is, at best, a blurred line between normal cognition, mild impairment and full-on dementia' (Ingram 2014: 123). Rather than make a compassionate bid to allow those with a 'bad' passport to enjoy the rights and privileges accorded to those blessed with a 'good' passport, 'Dance of the happy shades' and 'In sight of the lake' rely on the tropes of mimicry and irony to undermine the authenticity of both good and bad passports and the efficacy of policing the border between the countries of the well and the sick. As we have seen, 'In sight of the lake' imaginatively reconfigures and, for a time, replaces the prevailing gothic map of the kingdom of the sick, with an alternative, yet equally imaginative map.[12] Thanks to this playful act of substitution, readers can revise their understanding of the fourth age as a black hole populated by 'orphaned bodies'. In Munro's fiction, readers encounter elderly women, many of whom are isolated and anxious, dreaming of more inclusive social imaginaries, towns with gardens where everyone is 'welcome to rest' and where '[e]very soul counts' (Munro 2012: 224, 219). While Munro's stories acknowledge that dreams and the imagination may be false comforts that readers see through, rather than mock the illusion, Munro's fiction invites us, instead, to join a community based on our mutual vulnerability, one bonded by 'mutual fears and desires' (Redekop 1992: 237). In sum, Munro's stories play a profound role in highlighting the social construction of dementia by showing how the supposedly true stories we tell ourselves about the real world are often complicit in consolatory attempts to deny our vulnerability – epitomised by aging and dementia. Paradoxically, Munro's stories also demonstrate that fiction – which, in her hands, serves as a medium for communiqués from other countries and inner worlds to which we currently lack access – remains one of our most powerful tools for bringing us into a more ethical relationship with people coping with dementia and, more broadly, with our own vulnerability and mortality.

Notes

1   Other scholars likewise discuss the gothic in relation to disability studies. See, for example, Couser (2009) and Taylor (2008).

2   The title, 'Dance of the Happy Shades,' refers to a song from *Orphée et Eurydice* (1762), an opera written by the German composer Christoph Willibald Gluck.

3   My references to the story's literary contexts are drawn from the following website: http://mookseandgripes.com/reviews/2013/04/11/alice-munro-dance-of-the-happy-shades/.

4   As Bewell (1989: 54) argues, this type of identification was progressive in Wordsworth's day; I would argue further that it remained progressive, albeit to a lesser extent in the 1960s when Munro wrote 'Dance of the Happy Shades.' Nowadays, of course, portraying people with disabilities akin to Rain Man – 'the autistic savant in Armani descending the escalator to win big at Vegas' – has been broadly critiqued by disability studies theorists (Riley 2005: 84).

5   Moses Znaimer, founder of Zoomer Media, defines a Zoomer as follows: 'The demographic of active people aged 45 plus; "Zoomers". Zoomers; noun. Derived from "Boomers With Zip!" People age 45 plus who enjoy life to the fullest'. Revie (2014).

6   For more information on Munro's reliance on comedy and jokes, see Heble's (1994) and Redekop (1992).

7   The description of the surreal flowers recalls the opening of Atwood's (1996) *Alias grace,* a novel that probes the hysteria diagnosis, and by extension the infamous reference to hysterics as sterile flowers.

8   I emphasise Nancy's capacity to conduct a colloquy because, in the eyes of philosopher Hannah Arendt (2003: 44), the ability to hold this type of inner debate – as opposed to relying on an external authority figure to decide whether or not to pursue a course of action – was what elevated an individual to the category of human.

9   The concern with being late recalls the implications associated with the lateness of the children from Greenhill in 'Dance of the happy shades'.

10   As I note in my essay, (Goldman 2013):

> In recognition of women writers' early and ongoing investment in the Gothic, Ellen Moers coined the term Female Gothic (1976). For Moers, the Female Gothic represents fears about women's entrapment within domestic spaces and anxieties about childbirth. Ultimately, Moers identifies the Female Gothic as ' the mode par excellence that female writers have employed to give voice to women's deep-rooted fears about their own powerlessness and imprisonment within patriarchy' (1976: 5). In *The madwoman in the attic* (1979), Sandra Gilbert and Susan Gubar develop the Female Gothic further, and specifically link the concept to female anxieties about authorship, "the split psyche produced by the woman writer's 'quest for self-definition'" (Moers, 1976: 76) – a doubleness vividly illustrated by the Gothic doubling of Jane Eyre and her monstrous 'Other', the imprisoned first wife Bertha Rochester (Goldman 2012: 230).

11   The hysteria diagnosis casts its shadow over 'In Sight of the Lake' from the moment Nancy sees the flowers bursting from between the flagstones in the dream-like garden and extends to her final panicked realisation that she is incarcerated in the nursing home, which triggers a classic example of the 'hysterical fit'. As the narrator explains, 'She opens her mouth to yell but it seems that no yell is forthcoming. She is shaking all over and no matter how she tries she cannot get her breath down into her lungs. It is as if she has a blotter in her throat. Suffocation'. (Munro 2012: 232). The references in this passage to the 'blotter' in the throat and to 'suffocation' explicitly gesture to the age-old hysteria diagnosis.

As medical historians observe, during the long turn between the nineteenth and twentieth centuries, women were viewed as inherently susceptible to hysteria; the term 'hysteria' originates from the Greek word for uterus, 'hystera', which derives from the Sanskrit word for stomach or belly. According to the ancient Egyptians, the cause of disturbances in adult women was the wandering movement of the uterus, which they believed to be 'an autonomous, free-floating organism, upward from its normal pelvic position' (Micale 1995: 19). These ancient Egyptian beliefs, in turn, provided the foundation for classical Greek medical and philosophical accounts of hysteria. The Greeks adopted 'the notion of the migratory uterus and embroidered upon the connection … between hysteria and an unsatisfactory sexual life' (Micale 1995: 19). In *Timaeus,* Plato famously explains that 'the womb is an animal which longs to generate children. When it remains barren too long after puberty, it is distressed and sorely disturbed, and straying about in the body and cutting off the passage of the breath, it impedes respiration and brings the sufferer into the extremist anguish and provokes all manner of diseases besides' (quoted in Micale 1995: 19). Owing to hysteria's association with choking and loss of air, in the 1600s, it was referred to as 'the suffocation of the mother' (Micale 1995: 47).

12   This process is reminiscent of challenging the fanciful maps of early cartographers who famously wrote the phrases 'Here be Monsters' over swaths of unknown territory.

References

Andrews, J. (1998) Begging the question of idiocy: the definition and socio-cultural meaning of idiocy in Early Modern Britain: part I, *History of Psychiatry*, 9, 33, 65–95.

Arendt, H. (2003) Personal responsibility under dictatorship. In Kohn, J. (ed.) *Responsibility and Judgment*. New York: Shocken.

Atwood, M. (1996) *Alias Grace*. Toronto: McClelland and Stewart.

Bewell, A. (1989) *Wordsworth and the Enlightenment: nature, man, and society in the experimental poetry*. New Haven: Yale University Press.

Breton, A. (1924) *Surrealist manifesto*. trans. A. S. Kline. Available at http://poetsofmodernity.xyz/POMBR/French/Manifesto.htm (Last accessed 4 June 2015).

Butler, J. (2004) *Precarious life: the powers of mourning and violence*. London: Verso.

Calasanti, T. and King, N. (2011) A feminist lens of the third age: refining the framework. In Carr, D. and Komp, K. (eds) *Gerontology in the era of the third age*. New York: Springer.

Chivers, S. (2008) Barrier by barrier: the Canadian disability movement and the fight for equal rights. In Smith, M. (ed.) *Group politics and social movements in Canada*. Broadview: Peterborough.

Couser, G.T. (2009) *Signifying bodies: disability in contemporary life writing*. Ann Arbor: University of Michigan Press.

Cuddon, J.A. (ed.) (1991) *The Penguin dictionary of literary terms and titerary theory*. 3rd edn. London: Penguin.

Dalton, A.J. and Wallace, R.A. (2011) What can we learn from study of Alzheimer's Disease in patients with Down Syndrome for early-onset Alzheimer's Disease in the general population? *Alzheimer's Research & Therapy*, 3, 13. Available at http://www.alzres.com/content/3/2/13> (Last accessed 19 Mar 2015).

Faulkner, W. (1931) *The sound and the fury*. London: Chatto & Windus.

Gilbert, S.M. and Gubar, S. (1979) *The madwoman in the attic: the woman writer and the nineteenthcentury literary imagination*. New Haven: Yale University Press.

Gilleard, C. and Higgs, P. (2010) Aging without agency: theorizing the fourth age, *Aging and Mental Health*, 14, 2, 121–8.

Gilleard, C. and Higgs, P. (2011) Aging, abjection and embodiment in the fourth age, *Journal of Aging Studies*, 25, 2, 135–42.

Gilleard, C. and Higgs, P. (2014) Frailty, abjection and the 'othering' of the fourth age, *Health Studies Review*, 23, 1, 10–9.

Gilleard, C. and Higgs, P. (2015) *Rethinking old age: theorising the fourth age*. London: Palgrave.

Goldman, M. (2012) *Dispossession: haunting in Canadian fiction*. Kingston: McGill-Queen's University Press.

Goldman, M. (2013) Canadian female gothic on the foreign border: Margaret Atwood's bodily harm and Karen Connelly's Burmese lessons, *University of Toronto Quarterly*, 82, 2, 225–41.

Goldman, M. (2015) Purging the world of the whore and the horror: gothic and apocalyptic portraits of dementia in Canadian fiction. In Swinnen, A. and Schweda, M. (eds) *Popularizing dementia: public expressions and representations of forgetfulness*. Bielefeld: Transcript Verlag.

Grenier, A. (2012) *Transitions and the lifecourse: challenging the constructions of 'growing old'*. Bristol: Policy Press.

Gubrium, J. and Holstein, J.A. (1999) The nursing home as a discursive anchor for the ageing body. *Ageing & Society*, 19, 519–38.

Hazan, H. (1996) *From first principles: an experiment in ageing*. Westport: Bergin and Garvey.

Heble, A. (1994) *The tumble of reason: Alice Munro's discourse of absence*. Toronto: University of Toronto Press.

Holstein, M. (2011) Cultural ideals, ethics, and agelessness: a critical perspective on the third age. In Carr, D. and Komp, K. (eds) *Gerontology in the era of the third age*. New York: Springer.

Hutcheon, L. (1994) *Irony's edge: the theory and politics of irony*. London: Routledge.

Ingram, J. (2014) *The end of memory: a natural history of aging and Alzheimer's*. Toronto: HarperCollins.

Irigaray, L. (1985) *This sex which is not one*. trans. C. Porter with C. Burke. Ithaca: Cornell University Press.

Jackson, M. (2000) *The borderland of imbecility: medicine, society and the fabrication of the feeble mind in late Victorian and Edwardian England*. Manchester: Manchester University Press.

Lambek, M. (2004) Introduction. In Lambek, M. and Antze, P. (eds) *Irony and illness: on the ambiguity of suffering in culture*. New York: Berghahn Books.

Laslett, P. (1989) *A fresh map of life: the emergence of the third age*. London: Weidenfeld and Nicolson.

Lloyd, L. (2015) The fourth age. In Twigg, J. and Martin, W. (eds) *Routledge handbook of cultural gerontology*. London: Routledge.

Marshall, L. (2014) Agility studies: the interplay of critical approaches in age studies and disability studies. In Kriebernegg, U., Maierhofer, R. and Ratzenböck, B. (eds) *Alive and kicking at all ages: health, life expectancy, and life course identity*. Bielefeld, Germany: Transcript Verlag.

Micale, M.S. (1995) *Approaching hysteria: disease and its interpretations*. Princeton, NJ: Princeton University Press.

Moers, E. (1976) *Literary women*. Garden City: Doubleday.

Munro, A. (1968) Dance of the happy shades. In Munro, A. (ed.) *Dance of the happy shades*. Toronto: McGraw-Hill Ryerson, 211–24.

Munro, A. (2012) In sight of the lake. In Munro, A. (ed.) *Dear Life*. Toronto: McClelland.

Neuberger, J. (2009) *Not dead yet: A manifesto for old age*. London: HarperCollins.

Neufeldt, A.H. (2003) Growth and evolution of disability advocacy in Canada. In Stienstra, D. and Wight-Felske, A. (eds) *Making equality: history of advocacy and persons with disabilities in Canada*. Toronto: Captus.

Redekop, M. (1992) *Mothers and other clowns: the stories of Alice Munro*. London: Routledge.

Revie, N. (2014) A boomer is a zoomer if they want to be, *Guelph Mercury* 26 June. Available at http://www.guelphmercury.com/opinion-story/4598347-a-boomer-is-a-zoomer-if-they-want-to-be/ (Last accessed 22 January 2016).

Riley, C.A. (2005) *Disability and the media*. Lebanon: University Press of New England.

Scharf, T. (2009) Too tight to mention: unequal income in her age. In Cann, P. and Dean, M. (eds) *Unequal ageing: the untold story of exclusion in Old Age*. Bristol: Policy Press.

Sontag, S. (1978) *Illness as metaphor*. New York: Farrar Straus and Giroux.

Taylor, J. (2008) On recognition, caring, and dementia, *Medical Anthropology Quarterly*, 22, 4, 313–35.

Walpole, H. (1930) *The castle of Otranto*. London: Chatto & Windus.

Yeats, W.B. (1928) Sailing to Byzantium. In Ellmann, R. and O'Clair, R. (eds) *Modern poems: a Norton introduction*. 2nd edn. New York: W. W. Norton & Company.

10

Social class, dementia and the fourth age
Ian Rees Jones

Introduction

> The only known images of Auguste are a series of four asylum photographs taken
> around 1902, the most well known being sepia stained which makes Auguste appear to
> be dirty and her features somewhat swarthy, with a sorrowful expression and dressed in
> the asylum nightshirt she is denied the more modest attire for a lady of the time.
> (Page and Fletcher 2006: 579)

It is now over a hundred years since Alois Alzheimer described Auguste D, a middle-aged
woman, whose symptoms included depression, hallucinations and loss of memory. In their
review of the case, Page and Fletcher (2006) argue that the medical asylum regime under
which she was treated did little to maintain her sense of self. They picture her as a voice-
less victim whose biography is ignored and erased by medical concerns; a criticism that resonates with contemporary critiques of biomedical approaches to dementia (Kitwood and
Benson 1995). In response, they attempt to reconsider the person behind the illness and situate Auguste D as a 51-year-old, working-class Protestant woman who grew up in the class-
driven hierarchical society that, by the time of her death in the opening years of the 20th
century, was a fully formed Imperial Germany. While their ability to reconstruct her social
background and everyday life is constrained by the records available, their work is an important reminder of the need to situate the lives of people suffering from dementia today within
their social context and their own biographies.

The experience of dementia is not a universal process and different sociocultural understandings and conceptualisations have a profound influence over responses to the symptoms
of dementia in different places and at different times. For example, some have argued that
the western emphasis on cognitive skills and capacities leads to particular understandings
of and responses to dementia that may foster stigma and fear among those who suffer from
the illness (Cipriani and Borin 2015). Dementia attacks our memory and thus our capacity
to maintain and build social relations. This suggests that the social and cultural background
to our relationships may be an important prism for understanding the lived experience of
dementia. There is now a strong body of research showing that social interaction (measured
by contacts, participation and networks) is associated with the incidence of dementia in the
general population at a level that is on par with education, physical inactivity and depression

Ageing, Dementia and the Social Mind, First Edition. Edited by Paul Higgs and Chris Gilleard.
Chapters © 2017 The Authors. Book Compilation © 2017 Foundation for the Sociology of
Health & Illness/Blackwell Publishing Ltd.

in later life (Kuiper *et al.* 2015). Research addressing social class and dementia has largely focused on occupational class and other measures of socioeconomic status (SES) as risk factors for dementia; or as potential explanatory factors for observed differences in diagnosis, access to treatment and care and individual understandings of disease and illness. This large and diverse body of work has produced important insights but also contains numerous problems and weaknesses. Research needs to be placed in the context of the radical social transformations that have occurred over the last 40 years or more (Archer 2007, 2010). It is also important to view class in terms of personal trajectories and biographies. While discourses of class may not be explicit, everyday accounts of 'ordinariness' can still reveal the ways in which inequalities and suffering are legitimised and naturalised (Crompton 2006, Skeggs 2011, Skeggs and Loveday 2012). As both ageing and social class have been transformed in tandem with the economic, social and cultural coordinates of late modernity, there are important questions to ask of how practices of distinction are enacted and where inequalities can take root in later life (Jones and Higgs 2013). These changes have particular consequences for individual identities and social relations and consequently impinge on social understandings and individual experiences of dementia. In particular, changes in lay normative responses to both class and dementia will affect how and under what circumstances people value each other (Sayer 2002, 2005).

Following on from the above, this article adopts a critical gaze on research that considers interactions between dementia and social class in three key areas: (i) epidemiological approaches to inequalities in risk; (ii) the role of social class in diagnosis and treatment; and (iii) class in the framing of care and access to care. In doing so the article will argue that in addition to existing conceptual and empirical problems associated with social class in the field of ageing research there are specific issues that relate to dementia research in each of the above areas. One way of addressing these problems is to give greater weight to the changes that have occurred in recent years to normative accounts of class and of ageing. Dementia and class are embedded in social relations and, with this in mind, the article then turns to studies of dementia and social class that focus on lay understandings and biographical accounts of dementia.

Epidemiological approaches to inequalities in risk

The term 'dementia' describes a clinical syndrome that covers a range of difficulties in memory, language and behaviour that lead to impairment. Within this is a range of sub-types, with Alzheimer's disease being the most common, followed by vascular dementia, mixed dementia and dementia with Lewy bodies. But the science of dementia remains open to disagreement (Innes 2009) and this has implications for diagnosis (Robinson *et al.* 2015) and estimates of prevalence (Matthews *et al.* 2013). Bearing this in mind, studies have shown there is a higher risk of Alzheimer's disease and dementia in those with lower SES in a range of settings and countries, including Mexican Americans (Al Hazzouri *et al.* 2011), and older people in Italy (Marengoni *et al.* 2011) and Israel (Goldbourt *et al.* 2007). The evidence, however, is equivocal. For example, a study in a Canadian inner city setting found age and comorbidity were more strongly correlated with a diagnosis of dementia than SES (Fischer *et al.* 2009) and a study of Catholic clergy in the USA found that early life SES was related to cognition in later life but not to the risk of Alzheimer's disease (Wilson *et al.* 2005). One of the key problems here is that SES tends to be an umbrella term for a wide range of indicators, from occupational class, subjective measures of status and hierarchy, to measures of income and wealth at different points in time. Thus, some studies that have examined SES and dementia have concluded there is an inverse association between income and risk of dementia (Yaffe *et al.* 2013), while others have concluded that there is no such association (Kim *et al.* 2012) and yet others suggest the association is confounded by education (Chen *et al.* 2012, Karp *et al.* 2004). These latter studies also indicate that the educational or cognitive capacities effect appears to hold in different cultures and national contexts while the socioeconomic effect may vary cross-culturally. Moreover, studies that focus on income as a measure of SES face the issue of income levels fluctuating over the life course with subsequent fluctuations in the association (Anttila *et al.* 2002).

Life-course epidemiology has started to address the extent to which the socioeconomic environment in childhood and early adulthood may influence the risk of dementia in later life (Norton *et al.* 2011, Tschanz *et al.* 2013). For example, a meta-analysis of 11 prospective cohort studies in the UK based on over 86,000 men and women (Russ *et al.* 2013) found that women who left full-time education early had an increased risk of dementia death. However, this relationship was not apparent for men and indeed, occupational social class was not statistically significantly associated with dementia death in either men or women. An analysis of UK data indicates that, while there appears to be an association with years spent in education, there was no link between social class and dementia (Yip *et al.* 2006). Such studies have also focused on the relationship between cerebrovascular disease and dementia, drawing on evidence linking social class and educational level with cerebrovascular disease through behavioural pathways and making further links to the lowering of dementia risk. An analysis of UK cognitive function and ageing studies (CFAS)[1] data, however, found that, while there were significant differences in risk, the absolute differences based on class and education were small (Brayne *et al.* 2006).

Researchers have postulated a number of explanatory frameworks linking factors in the early life with dementia in later life (Hogervorst and Clifford 2013). Links have been drawn between low SES and harmful lifestyles across the life course with stress and a range of chronic health problems in later life that are also related to dementia (McEwen and Gianaros 2010). Evidence for a link between smoking and risk of dementia in later life is strong (Zhong *et al.* 2015) and there may be cohort effects that are related to variations in declining smoking patterns by social class. One pathway focuses on higher levels of IQ in childhood, providing access to higher levels of social, cultural and economic capital in adulthood that protect against illnesses, including dementia. The pathways are clearly complex and a focus on lifestyles is overly simplistic. Parental social class, for example, may be viewed as important because it may mean a healthier environment in childhood. Moreover, maternal health is viewed by some as an important determinant of child health with concomitant effects in mid-life. Risks are transferred across generations and there is an increasing focus on the role of epigenetics in foetal and child development, influencing pathways to dementia in later life.

As previously noted however, studies often suffer from problems of measurement, confounding and reverse causality (Deaton 2013, Lynch *et al.* 2004). A key problem for scholars studying dementia is that SES and education are interrelated, making it difficult to untangle both their relative effects and causal properties. The association between income and dementia in later life may reflect 'hidden' dementia in mid-life affecting individual earning capacities (Anttila *et al.* 2002). Education may have an independent protective effect against the development of dementia and in many studies what initially appear to be strong class effects tend to disappear when a measure of educational status is introduced into regression analyses (Staff *et al.* 2016). Karp *et al.* (2004) found that while low education levels and low SES were individually associated with Alzheimer's and dementia, only education remained a risk factor when they were examined simultaneously. These authors argue that the relationship between low education and increased risk of Alzheimer's was not mediated by SES and they concluded that early life factors may be particularly relevant in developing a risk of dementia. So, while the relationship between low education levels and high risk of dementia is well documented (Evans *et al.* 1997) the evidence remains unclear. A recent review of studies examining the relationship between dementia and education found lower educational levels to be associated with greater risk of dementia in many but not across all studies and the relationship was more consistent in studies where the measure of education level reflected cognitive capacity (Sharp and Gatz 2011). An analysis of CFAS data (Muniz-Terrera *et al.* 2009) showed associations between a range of socio-demographic variables and cognitive performance but education was not related to the rate of cognitive decline (in this case measured by the mini-mental state examination [MMSE]^2). Indeed, higher levels of education were not found to protect against cognitive decline; though the use of MMSE in diagnosis may lead to those with lower education being diagnosed earlier with dementia. This is a controversial area but it has been established for some time now that social and psychological factors contribute substantially to cognitive test scores and thus assessment procedures in epidemiological surveys of dementia need to be treated with caution (O' Connor *et al.* 1991).

The theory of cognitive reserve suggests that levels of intelligence and associated educational or occupational attainments may lead to a 'reserve' of skill sets or repertoires that may help prevent the onset of dementia and act as a buffer to help individuals with dementia cope better with their symptoms (Meng and D'Arcy 2012, Stern, 2002, 2012, Tucker and Stern 2011). In the preventative sense this is sometimes crassly referred to as a 'use or lose it' model, where the brain is viewed as a muscle that, like any other muscle, needs regular exercise. Within such a model education is seen as a strong predictor of a later age at onset of dementia symptoms but a faster rate of decline once these are present (Andel *et al.* 2006, Esiri and Chance 2012). Analysis of US data indicates that the main determinant of ethnic and socioeconomic disparities in cognitive function in older Americans is the level of peak cognitive performance achieved earlier in the life course (Karlamangla *et al.* 2009). Nevertheless, occupational class may still be relevant because of the cognitive requirements for different jobs, with some studies indicating that complexity of work tasks is associated with better cognitive performance in later life, independent of age, schooling, income and duration of occupation (Ribeiro *et al.* 2013). Complex tasks and work activities have been identified as a source of cognitive reserve (Kroger *et al.* 2008), while the positive protective effects of work settings has been identified both in terms of physical activity (Rovio *et al.* 2007) and psychosocial benefits (Seidler *et al.* 2004). Other studies, however, show no such protective effect from occupation-based SES (Helmer *et al.* 2001, Karp *et al.* 2004) and indeed, no evidence of SES in early life being associated with cognitive reserve (Wilson *et al.* 2005).

A prospective study of over 45,944 Norwegian men who were over 30 years of age found no association between mid-life income and dementia mortality risk but lower educational attainment was significantly associated with dementia risk. These authors concluded that their study supported the cognitive reserve hypothesis, emphasising that it was mental activity and capacity, not access to material resources, that determined dementia risk (Strand *et al.* 2015). Despite such findings, the cognitive reserve model does encounter problems and criticisms in terms of the role of educational level in influencing the initial diagnosis and in determining the rate of cognitive decline that might be attributed to dementia. Education may have an independent protective effect through promoting knowledge of healthier lifestyles and providing the basis for health-promoting activities (Karp *et al.* 2004). At the same time, education may also promote cognitive resources through access to a wider vocabulary and through coping styles that enable individuals to solve problems.

A study of lifetime principal occupation and risk of Alzheimer's disease (Qiu *et al.* 2003) found that manual work appeared to increase the risk of dementia. While these researchers argue that their findings are consistent with the theory of cognitive reserve they equally accept that their results may be affected by a tendency for earlier diagnosis, at least of clinical Alzheimer's, among people with lower levels of education. Furthermore, they state that a strong role for occupational status in developing forms of dementia cannot be dismissed. There is some, disputed, evidence that the mechanisms for this may be found in occupational exposure to biomaterial hazards (Koeman *et al.* 2015, Santibanez *et al.* 2007); for example, from exposure to electro-magnetic fields (García *et al.* 2008, Qiu *et al.* 2004, Vergara *et al.* 2013) and pesticides (Hayden *et al.* 2010) and from psycho-social stress at work (Wang *et al.* 2012). Such studies are an indication of the continued need to take account of those social, environmental and economic factors that are related to social class, when we consider the aetiology of dementia. They also suggest that a political economy of dementia can offer further insights into the social context of illness and provide further questioning of what is taken for granted about causal accounts of dementia and its treatments (Innes 2009). In this sense, it is important to examine the role of social class in the diagnosis and care of people with dementia.

The role of social class in diagnosis and treatment

A number of studies have highlighted the potential role that different forms of social location, including social status, class, ethnicity and educational background may have in determining diagnosis and access to treatment and care for people with dementia. A recent study of general practice (GP) patients in England (Connolly *et al.* 2011) found that fewer than half of the expected numbers of patients with dementia were identified in the GP dementia registers. This under-diagnosis of dementia appears to vary with practice characteristics, indicators of socioeconomic deprivation for practice areas and between administrative bodies responsible for commissioning health care. There is also evidence of social determinants playing a role in the prescription of drugs. An analysis of CFAS data (Matthews *et al.* 2007) indicated that the uptake of cholinesterase inhibitors was biased towards individuals with more education and higher social class, though it should be noted that this was in the early period of prescribing these drugs.

Prescription was also an issue in a study of people with dementia living independently (Cooper *et al.* 2010a), which found that owning ones' own home was a strong predictor of being prescribed drugs. The same study, however, did not find barriers to access to treatment for socioeconomically disadvantaged people when controlling for dementia severity. Inequalities in access to treatment and services may be more closely related to the status of having a dementia diagnosis whatever one's social background. For example, a cross-sectional study of patients in British general practice found that people with dementia were less likely than those without dementia to receive routine care measurements for vascular diseases. Within the group who had dementia the most disadvantaged appeared to be women, individuals living in care homes and those with fewer comorbid physical conditions and medications (Connolly *et al.* 2013).

Before considering the role of class and socioeconomic context, however, we need to recognise that the reasons for low levels of diagnosis are complex and traditional insights of medical sociology on diagnosis and referral processes are pertinent here (Stimson and Webb 1975), as well as research indicating that class plays a key role in health-seeking behaviour (Young 2004). In the case of dementia such processes may cut across traditional class distinctions. It may be that subtle changes in memory, behaviour and cognitive abilities go unnoticed or are dismissed as a normal part of growing old and that this is related to class and occupational histories. Even where problems are noticed individuals may delay taking action, may hide their problems or seek alternative advice to medical professionals. Where medical advice is sought this may not lead directly to diagnosis. There may be an element of professional avoidance of diagnosis for a variety of reasons including avoiding distress and stigma. Delaying diagnosis may also be related to the wider context of health and social care provision. Where there is a sense that service levels are low or inadequate, or there are long waiting lists, this may influence professional responses and decisions that follow rationing pathways of denial, delay, deflection, deterrence and dilution (Klein *et al.* 1996). In the UK concerns have been raised about the impact of government cuts to social care budgets and their potential consequences, in terms of inequalities in access to care and treatment (qualitywatch.org.uk).

Overviews of research on health-seeking behaviour and dementia highlight a preference for seeking help from close relatives in the first instance coupled with low levels of knowledge and the presence of stigma and fear of diagnosis. But existing studies also appear to lack theoretical and conceptual insights (Werner *et al.* 2014). Here it may be useful to draw on understandings from related areas. We know, in the field of mental health services, that talking therapies are underused by those in lower socioeconomic groups despite higher rates of common mental health problems among such groups (Eaton and Muntaner 2010). Furthermore, while there is evidence of an underuse of talking therapies, this is coupled with a higher use of prescription medication (Anderson *et al.* 2009). While such patterns do not directly translate to inequalities in access and use of dementia treatment and care it is useful to reflect on attempts to explain difference in uptake of treatments in mental health. These have a long legacy and in the past have tended to focus on working-class 'mind sets' as a problem; for example the expression of short-term preferences for immediate treatment (orientation to the future) rather than the longer term perspectives of therapeutic approaches (Hollingshead and Redlich 1958). Others have viewed the problem in terms of low expectations of professional services among working-class groups (Lorion 1974). More recent research has focused on the dissonance between middle-class therapeutic professionals and mental health users from working-class backgrounds (Sue and Sue 2003). While it is important to avoid the trap of viewing working-class people as stereotypically fatalistic (Bennett 2007, Bourdieu 1984), differences in linguistic expression and in values may be important in terms of social class differences in speech systems. Interestingly, Cicourel (2013) uses the term 'reverse socialization' to refer to how adult capacities weaken over time leading to loss of sense of self, a sense of others and a decline in routine practices. Cicourel argues that this is 'differentiated' and that caregivers 'scaffolding practices' (Vygotsky 1978) in socio-cultural interaction are designed to maintain their own identity in response to the person with dementia. There is not enough research into the ways in which class may influence the management of changes in behaviour associated with dementia and how social relations are 'maintained' or 'repaired.' Such research could provide important clues to class differences in diagnosis, health-seeking behaviour, access and responses to treatment and care in the field of dementia.

Class in the framing of care and access to care

The lack of awareness of dementia has been seen, from a dominant biomedical perspective, as a symptom reflecting underlying biological conditions. However, in a series of articles Clare (2002, 2004, Clare *et al.* 2012) has argued that in early stage dementia expressions of awareness or unawareness (anosognosia) are strongly related to socio-psychological factors. Drawing on in-depth interviews, her work shows that this is not an either/or situation.

While cognitive impairment clearly affects awareness, there are also instances when individual understandings are moulded by social and psychological factors. Here the context in which individuals talk about their lives becomes important. The expression of attitudes and beliefs may be related to a host of different factors including societal attitudes, avoidance of stigma, individual coping styles, forms of denial, relationships with partners, health services and health professionals and a host of other influences that in turn may be related to aspects of social location, including class and SES.

These influences have a knock-on effect in terms of the uptake of dementia services and may be reflected in the demographic patterning of patients and carers attending services such as memory clinics (Bruce and Paterson 2000, Johnston *et al.* 2011). Research has identified important disparities in uptake among black and minority ethnic populations (Cooper *et al.* 2010b, Mukadam *et al.* 2011a, 2011b) as well as communication issues between professionals and patients (Bruce *et al.* 2002). The reasons for refusing or not seeking services are clearly complex but one possible explanation, from a carers' perspective, is that of 'ambiguous gain' or a mismatch between the logic of bureaucratic systems and everyday domestic 'lifeworlds' (Lloyd and Stirling 2011). Once a person begins to encounter a healthcare system as a person with dementia there may also be barriers and obstacles that may or may not be related to socioeconomic and cultural factors.

Work by Peel and Harding (2014) offers a view of carers not, as is often assumed, as individuals 'failing' to engage, but as individuals attempting to navigate a complex system that is often more difficult and time consuming than the day to day caring work they undertake. In their sample of middle-class and working-class carers they found that although the carers diverged in terms of class background, funding status and location of care they shared a central frustration with services, which they commonly referred to as 'the system.' While this suggests there may be systemic problems that cut across issues of class and class identity, other researchers have identified forms of multiple disadvantage that impact on the negotiation of pathways through mental health services for particular groups (Kovandzic *et al.* 2011).

Work by Koehn *et al.* (2014) has drawn on the 'candidacy' framework (Dixon-Woods *et al.* 2006) to illustrate potential barriers to dementia diagnosis and to services. They found that forms of social and cultural capital were important in conferring disadvantage on all people with dementia as levels of social capital declined, but they also conferred a potential advantage for some groups in terms of identifying a problem, having a diagnosis and accessing services.

It is also important to acknowledge potential inequalities in access to research studies, for example, ensuring diversity of recruitment onto drug trials (Cooper *et al.* 2010a) and low levels of participation among working-class groups in studies of social aspects of dementia (Bunn *et al.* 2012). Further research is required to explore the possible mechanisms for disadvantage, drawing on understandings from the general health inequalities literature (Abel 2008, Abel and Frohlich 2012) of the ways in which different forms of capital (social capital and cultural capital) interact with access to assets and resources to contribute to disadvantage in accessing dementia services (Clare *et al.* 2014).

Dementia, class and social relations

Following critiques of biomedical approaches (Kitwood 1997, Sabat *et al.* 1999) dementia is increasingly viewed as both a consequence of neuropathological processes and the social relations that influence the way people are perceived and treated. MacRae (2008, 2011) has shown the significance of social context and the ways in which positive social interactions can help address the potentially negative impact of dementia and how access to economic resources and educational capital may enable more privileged individuals to respond positively to adversity. Responses to dementia may range from fear of a 'social death' (Sweeting and Gilhooly 1997) to its incorporation into ideas of normal ageing (Peel 2014). Such responses are related to the biographies of individuals, their social context and changing social norms. For Hulko (2009), expectations of ageing that develop through socialisation (that forms and is formed by the habitus) play a key role in constructions of dementia. Moreover, she suggests that memory loss is more difficult to cope with and adapt by privileged groups, where memory and intellectual capacities are viewed as a key component of their social status.

Despite the problems associated with class and dementia outlined earlier in this article, therefore, class identities may have an important role to play in individual responses both to the experience and the conceptualisation of dementia. Indeed, careful and detailed observational research has illustrated the ways in which etiquette, manners and bodily dispositions, derived from identity and class relations, reflect a habitus that is carried by individuals through their lived experience of dementia (Kontos 2012). This body of work has highlighted how signifiers of class and gender retrain their power and influence for the person with dementia and their carers (Kontos and Martin 2013, Kontos et al. 2011). Building on these insights, Twigg and Buse (2013) show how dementia disrupts the everyday practices of dressing and washing and the everyday work of maintaining bodily appearance. Such 'disruptions' can have different meanings for the person with dementia, their family, their friends and professionals. Crucially, Twigg and Buse argue, forms of social location, including gender and class, influence the different ways in which dress maintains and disrupts embodied identity. In a similar vein, Peet has argued that individual and specific responses to dementia are understood in the context of structures of social class and gender that shape everyday meanings (Peet 2014).

In an attempt to capture the effects of different forms of social location, some writers in the past have drawn on the idea of double or multiple jeopardy in relation to dementia (Innes et al. 2004). More recently, researchers have drawn on the concept of intersectionality where categories of social relations are understood in terms of interlocking sets of power relations (Dressel et al. 1997). Work in this field has attempted to show how relationships between multiple dimensions and modalities of social relationships and subject formations, including those of age, class, gender and ethnicity, contribute to individual and group advantage and disadvantage. The concept has had an important influence in recent years in the field of ageing (Calasanti 2004, 2010, Krekula 2007, Levy 1988). Indeed, some researchers have embraced this approach to argue that people 'do age' in the context of age-specific and gendered process that are shaped by class-based values, ideals and practices (Pietila and Ojala 2011). However, while work of this nature contributes to perspectives that emphasise the importance of social location and social context, there are significant problems with the approach in terms of method and subjectivity. In particular, researchers have criticised intersectionality in terms of how interactions are judged and analysed and how decisions are made on priority and emphasis (Massey et al. 2014, McCall 2005).

Conclusion

This article began with a description of Auguste D that tried to set what little we know of her life in the context of a hierarchical imperial Germany as a means of highlighting the need to situate the lives of people suffering from dementia in the present day within their own social context and biographies. While research appears to show that education and cognitive capacity play a key role in relation to class and the aetiology of dementia across the life-course, there is some evidence from epidemiology, health research and sociology that indicates that forms of distinction based on class may have a role to play in the diagnosis of dementia, in access to treatment and care, and in the social relations that underpin the lived experience of dementia. Sociological research in this area has explored the ways in which individual and group responses to dementia develop in the context of the larger structural processes that shape everyday meanings.

Much work remains to be done, therefore, and in particular work needs to focus on class relations that are part of the lives of people with dementia and their carers in the context of wider social change. We know, for example, that contemporary societies place a high value on cognitive skills, intellectual capacities and associated forms of accreditation. Consequently, the impact of dementia is likely to be devastating for individuals in terms of the loss of status that might accompany a spoiled identity or the threat of a spoiled identity. Such losses may be associated with educational status and aspects of social and cultural capital that are strongly related to class.

Research on occupational and class differences in health can only get us so far in this respect. If we are to understand the relationship between class identity and the impact of dementia we need to explore lay normative responses to both class and dementia and start to unpick how, and under what circumstances, people value themselves and others. In relation to the themes addressed in this special issue, closer attention is needed to the way that feelings of shame, embarrassment and contempt, as well as notions of compassion, dignity and respect, are closely tied up with class relationships, if we are to better understand the attitudes to frailty and cognitive decline that are part of the social imaginary of the fourth age. In short, rather than seek to insert class into an aetiological model of dementia, it may be more productive to bring to bear a class perspective on the social relations that initiate, support and maintain the capacity of people to live well with dementia.

Acknowledgements

The research for this article was undertaken as part of the IDEAL study funded by the Economic and Social Research Council and the National Institute for Health Research through grant ES/L001853/1, 'Improving the experience of dementia and enhancing active life: living well with dementia'. The investigators are L. Clare, I.R. Jones, C. Victor, J.V. Hindle, R.W. Jones, M. Knapp, M.D. Kopelman, A. Martyr, R.G. Morris, S.M. Nelis, J.A. Pickett, C. Quinn, J.M. Rusted, N.M. Savitch and J.M. Thom. Thanks also to the anonymous reviewers and to Chris Gilleard and Paul Higgs for their constructive criticisms and suggestions.

Notes

1   The CFAS studies are population based studies in the UK of individuals aged 65 years and over living in the community, including institutions.
2   The MMSE is a 30-point questionnaire that is used extensively in clinical and research settings to measure cognitive impairment. It is recognised that demographic factors may affect the score.

References

Abel, T. (2008) Cultural capital and social inequality in health, *Journal of Epidemiology and Community Health*, 62, 7, e13.
Abel, T. and Frohlich, K. (2012) Capitals and capabilities: linking structure and agency to reduce health inequalities, *Social Science & Medicine*, 74, 2, 236–44.

Al Hazzouri, A., Haan, M., Kalbfleisch, J., Galea, S., *et al.* (2011) Life-course socioeconomic position and incidence of dementia and cognitive impairment without dementia in older Mexican Americans: results from the Sacramento Area Latino Study on Aging, *American Journal of Epidemiology*, 173, 10, 1148–58.

Andel, R., Vigen, C., Mack, W., Clark, L., *et al.* (2006) The effect of education and occupational complexity on rate of cognitive decline in Alzheimer's patients, *Journal of the International Neuropsychological Society*, 12, 1, 147–52.

Anderson, S., Brownlie, J. and Given, L. (2009) Therapy culture? Attitudes towards emotional support. In Park, A., Curtice, J., Thomson, K., Phillips, M., *et al.* (eds) *British Social Attitudes, the 25th Report*. London: National Centre for Social Research.

Anttila, T., Helkala, E., Kivipelto, M., Hallikainen, M., *et al.* (2002) Midlife income, occupation, APOE status, and dementia – a population-based study, *Neurology*, 59, 6, 887–93.

Archer, M. (2007) *Making Our Way through the World, Human Reflexivity and Social Mobility*. Cambridge: Cambridge University Press.

Archer, M.S. (2010) Routine, reflexivity, and realism, *Sociological Theory*, 28, 3, 272–303.

Bennett, T. (2007) Habitus clivé: aesthetics and politics in the work of Pierre Bourdieu, *New Literary History*, 38, 1, 201–28.

Bourdieu, P. (1984) *Distinction: A Social Critique of the Judgement of Taste*. London: Routledge.

Brayne, C., Gao, L., Dewey, M., Matthews, F., *et al.* (2006) Dementia before death in ageing societies – the promise of prevention and the reality, *Plos Medicine*, 3, 10, 1922–30.

Bruce, D. and Paterson, A. (2000) Barriers to community support for the dementia carer: a qualitative study, *International Journal of Geriatric Psychiatry*, 15, 5, 451–7.

Bruce, D., Paley, G., Underwood, P., Roberts, D., *et al.* (2002) Communication problems between dementia carers and general practitioners: effect on access to community support services, *Medical Journal of Australia*, 177, 4, 186–8.

Bunn, F., Goodman, C., Sworn, K., Rait, G., *et al.* (2012) Psychosocial factors that shape patient and carer experiences of dementia diagnosis and treatment: a systematic review of qualitative studies, *Plos Medicine*, 9, 10, e1001331.

Calasanti, T. (2004) Feminist gerontology and old men, *Journals of Gerontology Series B*, 59, 6, S305–14.

Calasanti, T. (2010) Gender relations and applied research on aging, *Gerontologist*, 50, 6, 720–34.

Chen, R., Ma, Y., Wilson, K., Hu, Z., *et al.* (2012) A multicentre community-based study of dementia cases and subcases in older people in China – the GMS-AGECAT prevalence and socio-economic correlates, *International Journal of Geriatric Psychiatry*, 27, 7, 692–702.

Cicourel, A. (2013) Origin and demise of socio-cultural presentations of self from birth to death: caregiver 'scaffolding' practices necessary for guiding and sustaining communal social structure throughout the life cycle, *Sociology*, 47, 1, 51–73.

Cipriani, G. and Borin, G. (2015) Understanding dementia in the sociocultural context: a review, *International Journal of Social Psychiatry*, 61, 2, 198–204.

Clare, L. (2002) Developing awareness about awareness in early-stage dementia: the role of psychosocial factors, *Dementia*, 1, 3, 295–312.

Clare, L. (2004) Awareness in early-stage Alzheimer's disease: a review of methods and evidence, *British Journal of Clinical Psychology*, 43, 2, 177–96.

Clare, L., Nelis, S., Martyr, A., Roberts, J., *et al.* (2012) The influence of psychological, social and contextual factors on the expression and measurement of awareness in early-stage dementia: testing a biopsychosocial model, *International Journal of Geriatric Psychiatry*, 27, 2, 167–77.

Clare, L., Nelis, S., Quinn, C., Martyr, A., *et al.* (2014) Improving the experience of dementia and enhancing active life – living well with dementia: study protocol for the IDEAL study, *Health and Quality of Life Outcomes*, 12, 164. doi:10.1186/s12955-014-0164-6.

Connolly, A., Campbell, S., Gaehl, E., Iliffe, S., *et al.* (2013) Under-provision of medical care for vascular diseases for people with dementia in primary care: a cross-sectional review, *British Journal of General Practice*, 63, 607, E88–96.

Connolly, A., Gaehl, E., Martin, H., Morris, J., *et al.* (2011) Underdiagnosis of dementia in primary care: variations in the observed prevalence and comparisons to the expected prevalence, *Aging and Mental Health*, 15, 8, 978–84.

Cooper, C., Blanchard, M., Selwood, A. and Livingston, G. (2010a) Antidementia drugs: prescription by level of cognitive impairment or by socio-economic group?, *Aging and Mental Health*, 14, 1, 85–9.

Cooper, C., Tandy, A., Balamurali, T. and Livingston, G. (2010b) A systematic review and meta-analysis of ethnic differences in use of dementia treatment, care, and research, *American Journal of Geriatric Psychiatry*, 18, 3, 193–203.

Crompton, R. (2006) Class and family, *Sociological Review*, 54, 4, 658–77.

Deaton, A. (2013) *The Great Escape: Health, Wealth, and the Origins of Inequality*. Princeton: Princeton University Press.

Dixon-Woods, M., Cavers, D., Agarwal, S., Annandale, E., *et al.* (2006) Conducting a critical interpretive synthesis of the literature on access to healthcare by vulnerable groups, *BMC Medical Research Methodology*, 6, 35.

Dressel, P., Minkler, M. and Yen, I. (1997) Gender, race, class, and aging: advances and opportunities, *International Journal of Health Services*, 27, 4, 579–600.

Eaton, W.W. and Muntaner, C. (2010) Socio-economic stratification and mental disorder. In Schend, T.L. and Brown, T.N. (eds) *Handbook for the Study of Mental Health: Social Contexts Theories and Systems*. Cambridge: Cambridge University Press.

Esiri, M. and Chance, S. (2012) Cognitive reserve, cortical plasticity and resistance to Alzheimer's disease, *Alzheimers Research and Therapy*, 4, 2, 7.

Evans, D.A., Hebert, L.E., Beckett, L.A., Scherr, P.A., *et al.* (1997) Education and other measures of socioeconomic status and risk of incident Alzheimer disease in a defined population of older persons, *Archives of Neurology*, 54, 11, 1399–405.

Fischer, C., Yeung, E., Hansen, T., Gibbons, S., *et al.* (2009) Impact of socioeconomic status on the prevalence of dementia in an inner city memory disorders clinic, *International Psychogeriatrics*, 21, 6, 1096–104.

García, A.M., Sistemas, A. and Hoyos, S.P. (2008) Occupational exposure to extremely low frequency electric and magnetic fields and Alzheimer disease: a meta-analysis, *International Journal of Epidemiology*, 37, 2, 329–40.

Goldbourt, U., Schnaider-Beeri, M. and Davidson, M. (2007) Socioeconomic status in relationship to death of vascular disease and late-life dementia, *Journal of the Neurological Sciences*, 257, 1–2, 177–81.

Hayden, K., Norton, M., Darcey, D., Ostbye, T., *et al.* (2010) Occupational exposure to pesticides increases the risk of incident A.D. The Cache County Study, *Neurology*, 74, 19, 1524–30.

Helmer, C., Letenneur, L., Rouch, I., Richard-Harston, S., *et al.* (2001) Occupation during life and risk of dementia in French elderly community residents, *Journal of Neurology Neurosurgery and Psychiatry*, 71, 3, 303–9.

Hogervorst, E. and Clifford, A. (2013) What is the relationship between higher levels of education delaying age at onset of dementia?, *Journal of Alzheimers Disease and Parkinsonism*, 3, e128. doi:10.4172/2161-0460.1000e128.

Hollingshead, A.B. and Redlich, F.C. (1958) *Social Class and Mental Illness: A Community Study*. New York: John Wiley.

Hulko, W. (2009) From 'not a big deal' to 'hellish': experiences of older people with dementia, *Journal of Aging Studies*, 23, 3, 131–44.

Innes, A. (2009) *Dementia Studies: A Social Science Perspective*. London: Sage.

Innes, A., Archibald, C. and Murphy, C. (eds) (2004) *Dementia and Social Inclusion: Marginalised Groups and Marginalised Areas of Dementia Research, Care and Practice*. London: Jessica Kingsley.

Johnston, D., Samus, Q., Morrison, A., Leoutsakos, J., *et al.* (2011) Identification of community-residing individuals with dementia and their unmet needs for care, *International Journal of Geriatric Psychiatry*, 26, 3, 292–8.

Jones, I.R. and Higgs, P. (2013) Class and health inequalities in later life. In Formosa, M. and Higgs, P. (eds) *Social Class in Later Life, Power, Identity and Lifestyle*. Bristol: Policy Press.

Karlamangla, A., Miller-Martinez, D., Aneshensel, C., Seeman, T., *et al.* (2009) Trajectories of cognitive function in late life in the United States: demographic and socioeconomic predictors, *American Journal of Epidemiology*, 170, 3, 331–42.

Karp, A., Kareholt, I., Qiu, C.X., Bellander, T., *et al.* (2004) Relation of education and occupation-based socioeconomic status to incident Alzheimer's disease, *American Journal of Epidemiology*, 159, 2, 175–83.

Kim, M., Park, J., Lee, C., Kang, N., *et al.* (2012) Prevalence of dementia and its correlates among participants in the National Early Dementia Detection Program during 2006–2009, *Psychiatry Investigation*, 9, 2, 134–42.

Kitwood, T. (1997) *Dementia Reconsidered: the Person Comes First*. Buckingham: Open University Press.

Kitwood, T. and Benson, S. (eds) (1995) *The New Culture of Dementia Care*. London: Hawker.

Klein, R., Day, P. and Redmayne, S. (1996) *Managing Scarcity: Priority Setting and Rationing in the National Health Service*. Buckingham: Open University Press.

Koehn, S., Badger, M., Cohen, C., McCleary, L., *et al.* (2014) Negotiating access to a diagnosis of dementia: implications for policies in health and social care. *Dementia*, 1471301214563551.

Koeman, T., Schouten, L., van den Brandt, P., Slottje, P., *et al.* (2015) Occupational exposures and risk of dementia-related mortality in the prospective Netherlands Cohort Study, *American Journal of Industrial Medicine*, 58, 6, 625–35.

Kontos, P. (2012) Rethinking sociability in long-term care: an embodied dimension of selfhood, *Dementia*, 11, 3, 329–46.

Kontos, P. and Martin, W. (2013) Embodiment and dementia: exploring critical narratives of selfhood, surveillance, and dementia care, *Dementia*, 12, 3, 288–302.

Kontos, P., Miller, K., Mitchell, G. and Cott, C. (2011) Dementia care at the intersection of regulation and reflexivity: a critical realist perspective, *Journals of Gerontology Series B*, 66, 1, 119–28.

Kovandzic, M., Chew-Graham, C., Reeve, J., Edwards, S., *et al.* (2011) Access to primary mental health care for hard-to-reach groups: from 'silent suffering' to 'making it work', *Social Science & Medicine*, 72, 5, 763–72.

Krekula, C. (2007) The intersection of age and gender – reworking gender theory and social gerontology, *Current Sociology*, 55, 2, 155–71.

Kroger, E., Andel, R., Lindsay, J., Benounissa, Z., *et al.* (2008) Is complexity of work associated with risk of dementia?, *American Journal of Epidemiology*, 167, 7, 820–30.

Kuiper, J., Zuidersma, M., Voshaar, R., Zuidema, S., *et al.* (2015) Social relationships and risk of dementia: a systematic review and meta-analysis of longitudinal cohort studies, *Ageing Research Reviews*, 22, 39–57.

Levy, J. (1988) Intersections of gender and aging, *Sociological Quarterly*, 29, 4, 479–86.

Lloyd, B. and Stirling, C. (2011) Ambiguous gain: uncertain benefits of service use for dementia carers, *Sociology of Health & Illness*, 33, 6, 899–913.

Lorion, R.P. (1974) Patient and therapist variables in treatment of low-income patients, *Psychological Bulletin*, 81, 6, 344–54.

Lynch, J., Smith, G., Harper, S. and Hillemeier, M. (2004) Is income inequality a determinant of population health? Part 2 US national and regional trends in income inequality and age- and cause-specific mortality, *Milbank Quarterly*, 82, 2, 355–400.

McCall, L. (2005) The complexity of intersectionality, *Signs*, 30, 3, 1771–800.

McEwen, B. and Gianaros, P.J. (2010) Central role of the brain in stress and adaptation: links to socioeconomic status, health, and disease, *Annals of the New York Academy of Science*, 1186, 190–222.

MacRae, H. (2008) 'Making the best you can of it': living with early-stage Alzheimer's disease, *Sociology of Health & Illness*, 30, 3, 396–412.

MacRae, H. (2011) Self and other: the importance of social interaction and social relationships in shaping the experience of early-stage Alzheimer's disease, *Journal of Aging Studies*, 25, 4, 445–56.

Marengoni, A., Fratiglioni, L., Bandinelli, S. and Ferrucci, L. (2011) Socioeconomic status during lifetime and cognitive impairment no-dementia in late life: the population-based aging in the Chianti area (InCHIANTI) study, *Journal of Alzheimers Disease*, 24, 3, 559–68.

Massey, D., McCall, L., Tomaskovic-Devey, D., Avent-Holt, D., *et al.* (2014) Understanding inequality through the lens of cultural processes: on Lamont, Beljean and Clair 'What is Missing? Cultural Processes and Causal Pathways to Inequality', *Socio-Economic Review*, 12, 3, 609–36.

Matthews, F.E., Arthur, A., Barnes, L.E., Bond, J., *et al.* (2013) A two-decade comparison of prevalence of dementia in individuals aged 65 years and older from three geographical areas of England: results of the Cognitive Function and Ageing Study I and II, *The Lancet*, 382, 9902, 1405–12.

Matthews, F.E., McKeith, I., Bond, J., Brayne, C., *et al.* (2007) Reaching the population with dementia drugs: what are the challenges?, *International Journal of Geriatric Psychiatry*, 22, 7, 627–31.

Meng, X. and D'Arcy, C. (2012) Education and dementia in the context of the cognitive reserve hypothesis: a systematic review with meta-analyses and qualitative analyses, *Plos One*, 7, 6, e38268.

Mukadam, N., Cooper, C., Basit, B. and Livingston, G. (2011a) Why do ethnic elders present later to UK dementia services? A qualitative study, *International Psychogeriatrics*, 23, 7, 1070–7.

Mukadam, N., Cooper, C. and Livingston, G. (2011b) A systematic review of ethnicity and pathways to care in dementia, *International Journal of Geriatric Psychiatry*, 26, 1, 12–20.

Muniz-Terrera, G., Matthews, F., Dening, T., Huppert, F.A., *et al.* (2009) Education and trajectories of cognitive decline over 9 years in very old people: methods and risk analysis, *Age and Ageing*, 38, 3, 277–82.

Norton, M., Smith, K., Ostbye, T., Tschanz, J., *et al.* (2011) Early parental death and remarriage of widowed parents as risk factors for Alzheimer disease: The Cache County Study, *American Journal of Geriatric Psychiatry*, 19, 9, 814–24.

O'Connor, D., Pollitt, P. and Treasure, F. (1991) The influence of education and social class on the diagnosis of dementia in a community population, *Psychological Medicine*, 21, 1, 219–24.

Page, S. and Fletcher, T. (2006) Auguste D: one hundred years on: 'the person'not 'the case', *Dementia*, 5, 4, 571–83.

Peel, E. (2014) 'The living death of Alzheimer's' versus 'take a walk to keep dementia at bay': representations of dementia in print media and carer discourse, *Sociology of Health & Illness*, 36, 6, 885–901.

Peel, E. and Harding, R. (2014) 'It's a huge maze, the system, it's a terrible maze': dementia carers' constructions of navigating health and social care services, *Dementia*, 13, 5, 642–61.

Peet, J. (2014) The influence of social location on the experience of early dementia. Unpublished PhD thesis. University of Kent.

Pietila, I. and Ojala, H. (2011) Acting age in the context of health: middle-aged working-class men talking about bodies and aging, *Journal of Aging Studies*, 25, 4, 380–89.

Qiu, C., Karp, A., von Strauss, E., Winblad, B., *et al.* (2003) Lifetime principal occupation and risk of Alzheimer's disease in the Kungsholmen Project, *American Journal of Industrial Medicine*, 43, 2, 204–11.

Qiu, C., Fratiglioni, L., Karp, A., Winblad, B., *et al.* (2004) Occupational exposure to electromagnetic fields and risk of Alzheimer's disease, *Epidemiology*, 15, 6, 687–94.

Ribeiro, P., Lopes, C. and Lourenco, R. (2013) Complexity of lifetime occupation and cognitive performance in old age, *Occupational Medicine*, 63, 8, 556–62.

Robinson, L., Tang, E. and Taylor, J.-P. (2015) Dementia: timely diagnosis and early intervention, *BMJ*, 350, doi:10.1136/bmj.h3029.

Rovio, S., Kareholt, I., Viitanen, M., Winblad, B., *et al.* (2007) Work-related physical activity and the risk of dementia and Alzheimer's disease, *International Journal of Geriatric Psychiatry*, 22, 9, 874–82.

Russ, T.C., Stamatakis, E., Hamer, M., Starr, J.M., *et al.* (2013) Socioeconomic status as a risk factor for dementia death: individual participant meta-analysis of 86 508 men and women from the UK, *British Journal of Psychiatry*, 203, 1, 10–7.

Sabat, S., Fath, H., Moghaddam, F. and Harre, R. (1999) The maintenance of self-esteem: lessons from the culture of Alzheimer's sufferers, *Culture and Psychology*, 5, 1, 5–31.

Santibanez, M., Bolumar, F. and Garcia, A. (2007) Occupational risk factors in Alzheimer's disease: a review assessing the quality of published epidemiological studies, *Occupational and Environmental Medicine*, 64, 11, 723–32.

Sayer, A. (2002) What are you worth? Why class is an embarrassing subject, *Sociological Research Online*, 7, 3.

Sayer, A. (2005) *The Moral Significance of Class*. Cambridge: Cambridge University Press.

Seidler, A., Nienhaus, A., Bernhardt, T., Kauppinen, T., *et al.* (2004) Psychosocial work factors and dementia, *Occupational and Environmental Medicine*, 61, 12, 962–71.

Sharp, E. and Gatz, M. (2011) Relationship between education and dementia an updated systematic review, *Alzheimer Disease and Associated Disorders*, 25, 4, 289–304.

Skeggs, B. (2011) Imagining personhood differently: person value and autonomist working-class value practices, *Sociological Review*, 59, 3, 496–513.

Skeggs, B. and Loveday, V. (2012) Struggles for value: value practices, injustice, judgment, affect and the idea of class, *British Journal of Sociology*, 63, 3, 472–90.

Staff, R.T., Chapko, D., Hogan, M. and Whalley, L.J. (2016) Life course socioeconomic status and the decline in information processing speed in late life, *Social Science and Medicine*, 151, 130–8.

Stern, Y. (2002) What is cognitive reserve? Theory and research application of the reserve concept, *Journal of the International Neuropsychological Society*, 8, 3, 448–60.

Stern, Y. (2012) Cognitive reserve in ageing and Alzheimer's disease, *Lancet Neurology*, 11, 11, 1006–12.

Stimson, G. and Webb, B. (1975) *Going to See the Doctor*. London: Routledge.

Strand, B.H., Skirbekk, V., Rosness, T.A., Engedal, K., *et al.* (2015) Income in midlife and dementia related mortality over three decades: a Norwegian prospective study, *eNeurologicalSci*. 1, 2, 24–9.

Sue, D.W. and Sue, D. (2003) *Counseling the Culturally Diverse*, 4th edn. New York: John Wiley.

Sweeting, H. and Gilhooly, M. (1997) Dementia and the phenomenon of social death, *Sociology of Health & Illness*, 19, 1, 93–117.

Tschanz, J., Norton, M., Zandi, P. and Lyketsos, C. (2013) The Cache County Study on memory in aging: factors affecting risk of Alzheimer's disease and its progression after onset, *International Review of Psychiatry*, 25, 6, 673–85.

Tucker, A. and Stern, Y. (2011) Cognitive reserve in aging, *Current Alzheimer Research*, 8, 4, 354–60.

Twigg, J. and Buse, C. (2013) Dress, dementia and the embodiment of identity, *Dementia*, 12, 3, 326–36.

Vergara, X., Kheifets, L., Greenland, S., Oksuzyan, S., *et al.* (2013) Occupational exposure to extremely low-frequency magnetic fields and neurodegenerative disease a meta-analysis, *Journal of Occupational and Environmental Medicine*, 55, 2, 135–46.

Vygotsky, L.S. (1978) *Mind in Society: the Development of Higher Psychological Processes*. Cambridge: Harvard University Press.

Wang, H., Wahlberg, M., Karp, A., Winblad, B., *et al.* (2012) Psychosocial stress at work is associated with increased dementia risk in late life, *Alzheimers and Dementia*, 8, 2, 114–20.

Werner, P., Goldstein, D., Karpas, D., Chan, L., *et al.* (2014) Help-seeking for dementia a systematic review of the literature, *Alzheimer Disease and Associated Disorders*, 28, 4, 299–310.

Wilson, R.S., Scherr, P.A., Hoganson, G., Bienias, J., *et al.* (2005) Early life socioeconomic status and late life risk of Alzheimer's disease, *Neuroepidemiology*, 25, 1, 8–14.

Yaffe, K., Falvey, C., Harris, T., Newman, A., *et al.* (2013) Effect of socioeconomic disparities on incidence of dementia among biracial older adults: prospective study, *BMJ*, 347, f7051.

Yip, A., Brayne, C. and Matthews, F. (2006) Risk factors for incident dementia in England and Wales: the medical research council cognitive function and ageing study, A population-based nested case-control study, *Age and Ageing*, 35, 2, 154–60.

Young, J.T. (2004) Illness behaviour: a selective review and synthesis, *Sociology of Health & Illness*, 26, 1, 1–31.

Zhong, G., Wang, Y., Zhang, Y., Guo, J.J., *et al.* (2015) Smoking is associated with an increased risk of dementia: a meta-analysis of prospective cohort studies with investigation of potential effect modifiers, *Plos One*, 10, 3, e0118333.

11

Precarity in late life: rethinking dementia as a 'frailed' old age

Amanda Grenier, Liz Lloyd and Chris Phillipson

Introduction

Ideas and assumptions about cognitive impairment, combined with approaches to ageing organised around 'success' and 'activity', have contributed to views of dementia as a 'failed' or 'frailed' old age. Alongside this, institutional and organisational practices associated with physical and mental frailties are increasingly used to mark the boundaries of health and illness in late life. For example, policies and frameworks targeted at later life tend to focus on either healthy populations (those viewed as the 'active ageing'), or those in need of care (i.e. 'the frail' and/or 'demented'), thereby sustaining distinctions between the third age as a successful lifestyle, and a 'fourth age' as a social position marked by decline (Gilleard and Higgs 2013, Grenier 2012, 2015, Katz and Calasanti 2015, Lloyd 2012, Lloyd *et al.* 2014). Socio-cultural interpretations of late life frailties have themselves emphasised age and stage-based distinctions, these identifying the fourth age as an 'unagentic' social and cultural space (Gilleard and Higgs 2010). Our concern is that such approaches can further marginalise persons who occupy locations linked with dementia and disablement.

Interpretations of dementia as a 'frailed' and 'failed' late life have become highly influential in the context of health and social care practices. The construction of 'frail' subjects, itself takes place amidst a larger 'decline narrative' (Gullette 1997, 2004), one supported by the biomedicalisation of impairment and dementia. Moreover, concerns have been raised about the dominance of biomedical approaches to memory loss, and threats to 'selfhood' and the 'civilised body' (Gilleard and Higgs 2000, Katz and Peters 2008, Kontos 2005). At the same time, the medicalisation of dementia has itself raised the status and public attention afforded the condition, and sustained its position as a distinct disease (Whitehouse and George 2008).

Ideas about dementia as impairment have been reinforced in the context of the dominance of 'the successful ageing paradigm' (Rowe and Kahn 1997), with dementia and frailty relegated to the 'fourth age'. Although unintended, the emphasis on successful ageing, combined with historical and medicalised trajectories of impairment, have crystallised the 'frailties' of physical and cognitive impairment into an 'unsuccessful' or 'failed' late life. Dementia is considered by many to represent a dreaded disease and a 'horrific' end to late life (Gilleard and Higgs 2010, Katz and Peters 2008). This sentiment operates in the public eye, through fund raising campaigns and policy frameworks, often meeting up with discourses about cost and the urgency of response. For example, the foreword to an official report on dementia care in

Ageing, Dementia and the Social Mind, First Edition. Edited by Paul Higgs and Chris Gilleard.
Chapters © 2017 The Authors. Book Compilation © 2017 Foundation for the Sociology of
Health & Illness/Blackwell Publishing Ltd.

England states that: 'We are facing one of the biggest health challenges ever, a challenge as big as the fights against cancer, heart disease and HIV. Dementia steals lives. It also imposes a huge emotional and financial cost. It is time to fight back' (Department of Health 2013: 2). One response to this has been the establishment of a 'World Dementia Council' together with the setting of a 'global dementia challenge' charged with the goal of finding 'a cure or disease modifying therapy by 2025'.[1]

Such responses to dementia are reinforced in conditions of economic austerity whereby longevity and the increased likelihood of a life with dementia, collide with the loss of rights and citizen entitlements to social welfare (Phillipson 2015). The resulting tension, as this article argues, is between ideals of independence and the emergence of new forms of vulnerability, or what we shall term as 'precariousness'. The concern of this article is that current ideas and practices organised around the 'fourth' age – including taken for granted discourses, practices and the 'imagined' – risk reinforcing unequal power relations in late life, with the potential of further marginalising persons with dementia. We suggest, therefore, that the concept of precarity be used to reconsider the socio-cultural ideas and practices that operate with regards to dementia, and shift the debates into considerations of shared processes and experiences of vulnerability that occur over time. Within this frame, use of the concept of precarity can help to draw attention to a deeper problem whereby notions of dementia as a 'frailed' old age risk being read and interpreted as a ' failed' old age.

Frailty and dementia: Discourse, practice and the 'imaginary' of the fourth age

Frailty and dementia have both emerged as conditions which are presented as 'opposites' to a 'healthy' and 'active' later life. Where medical and practice perspectives consider frailty and dementia as different states or conditions, there is also a significant overlap where discourse, practices, and the 'social imaginary' are concerned. Impairment – whether physical or cognitive – is considered to mark disease, establish practice directives, and inform socio-cultural interpretations about debility and decline. While frailty and dementia are undoubtedly different, it is the construct of the 'fourth age' that links them together. This connection results in part from the emergence of the 'fourth age' as a function – or troublesome outcome – of the dominance of success-based discourses and the third age lifestyle characterised by health, personal growth and active engagement (see Lloyd 2015). This article combines frailty and dementia to illustrate how understandings of physical or cognitive impairments – the 'frailties of the body and mind' – can be reconsidered through contemporary writing on precarity.

In biomedical and health domains, frailty has become a major site of research efforts to define the 'condition', determine practice indicators, and target health and social care practices to those at 'risk' (Lacas and Rockwood 2012, Morley *et al.* 2013, Searle *et al.* 2008). This is equally the case for dementia, where the diagnosis provides access to specialised services and community-based programs (Brooker 2007). Where health research tends to focus on dementia as a disease or 'frailty' as an indicator of risk, the 'fourth age' refers to a construct that encapsulates ideas about the 'frailties' and impairments of late life – whether physical or cognitive in nature (Lloyd 2015, Pickard 2014). The 'fourth age' is increasingly described as a complex cultural construct, a 'social imaginary' that is unknowable and, once entered, from which there is no return (Gilleard and Higgs 2010). As such, the 'fourth age' refers both to an age or staged-based period, and a cultural construct – or 'imaginary' – that espouses impairment, decline and dependency in late life (see Gilleard and Higgs 2000, Laslett 1991). Whether in practice, or the socio-cultural sphere, the 'fourth age' becomes an important discursive and symbolic marker of the boundaries between health and impairment, the proximity to death, and by extension, the expectations of late life as a period of disablement and decline (Grenier 2012). It is viewed as a liminal space and an event horizon – a location that holds the negative or less than ideal experiences of ageing (Gilleard and Higgs 2010, Grenier 2012). Falling into the 'fourth age' space, frailty and dementia occupy sites laden with associations of physical and cognitive deficits, dependence and burden, pity or weakness (see Grenier 2007, 2012, Pickard 2014).

The marginalisation of those with physical and/or cognitive deficits is reinforced by the lack of agency ascribed to persons deemed to occupy the 'fourth' age. Gilleard and Higgs (2010: 123) argue in their paper '*Ageing without agency*' that: 'The fourth age … represents not so much a particular cohort or stage of life but […] a kind of terminal destination – a location stripped of the social and cultural capital that is most valued and which allows for the articulation of choice, autonomy, self-expression and pleasure in later life'. However, an alternative perspective has been put forward by Grenier and Phillipson (2013) who suggest that conditions within the 'fourth age' can be said to challenge conventional approaches to the idea of agency. In the case of conditions such as dementia, it is possible to see how agency rather than being 'compromised' may simply differ from current interpretations, or be communicated or enacted differently. This suggestion makes the case for a critical approach to understanding the location of dementia within the life course. Such a perspective is supported by Jaworska (1999: 124, 126), who argues that 'the ability to value is independent of the ability to understand the narrative of one's whole life [and] the capacity for autonomy is first and foremost the capacity to espouse values and convictions, whose translation into action may not always be fully within the agent's mastery'. Thus, in the context of care services, the task is to value the lives, experiences and convictions of persons with dementia, even in circumstances where what is expressed seems foreign or 'unknowable'.

Although the discourses, practices, and imaginary of the 'fourth age' have yet to be fully considered in relation to dementia, approaches organised around selfhood and cultural change represent parallel concerns about dementia as an 'unagentic' and 'failed' late life. Researchers in dementia studies have stressed the importance of person-centred care and the need to challenge dominant approaches to thinking about the condition (O'Dwyer 2013). George and Whitehouse (2010: 351), among others, have argued: 'for the need to challenge the tyranny of the scientifically uncertain and socially stigmatising AD [Alzheimer Dementia] story to make both cultural understandings and social institutions more responsive, and so that persons with memory challenges and their families may tell their own stories about brain ageing rather than succumbing to the generality of a vague, imprecise, and stigmatising disease label that emphasises only decline'. Similarly, Kontos (2004) has questioned the idea that cognitive deficiencies lead to the loss of selfhood and advocated for arts-based approaches that bridge differences in communication (Kontos and Naglie 2007). Yet, the contemporary discourses and practices, including the 'social imaginary' can run counter to these ideas, and reinforce the view that people with dementia have 'less' or are without agency, with the implication that their lives are both marginal to society and less valued.

To explore this issue, the next section of this article analyses the extent to which frailty and dementia are better understood in the context of new forms of insecurity that affect the life course, as expressed through ideas associated with the concepts of precariousness and risk.

Precarity as a means to reconsider experiences of dementia

The concept of precarity has been used in a number of contexts in order to draw attention to rising insecurities in the context of global economic and social change. In articulating a perspective from critical geography, Waite (2009: 426) refers to precarity as 'life worlds characterized by uncertainty and insecurity', and a concept that implies 'both a condition and a possible rallying point for resistance'. Although precarity has been widely used in other fields, in particular with regards to changes in the labour market (Standing 2010), its application to ageing and late life is relatively new. To date the concept has been applied in discussions around ageing and employment (Bohle *et al.* 2010), financial insecurity and/or exclusion of older people (Craciun and Flick 2014), disability and citizenship (Knight 2014), and trends towards inequality in the G20 countries (Biggs 2014). In all cases, the use of precarity in gerontology and allied disciplines echo the broad application to issues of exploitation and insecurity in the labour market. The dominance of discourses of success and declining social protection, however, point to the need to consider older people outside the labour force, including those considered 'frail' by means of their cognitive and/or physical impairments.

Drawing on the concept of precarity to understand the structured and existential vulnerabilities experienced across the life-course and into late life may help reconfigure ideas and practices about physical and cognitive impairment. The insights of researchers such as Standing (2010, 2012) and Butler (2006, 2009, Butler and Athanasiou 2013) are particularly helpful in advancing our reconsideration of dementia as a 'frailed' and 'failed' late life. Although representing different theoretical standpoints, both draw attention to the vulnerabilities in which people are placed. Likewise, they ground their analysis in dependency and the need for change through a response based on a shared interdependence. Where Standing focuses on a dependency structured by the labour market, Butler emphasises shared cultural frameworks about the conditions of life, or more specifically, 'what counts as a valued life'. This section provides a brief overview of their work, emphasising aspects that are most relevant to our consideration of physical and mental frailties and the 'fourth age'.

Uncertainty, insecurity and vulnerability may be viewed as produced by shifting global, economic, social and cultural relations, as well as the choices and decisions made in such contexts. Standing's (2010, 2012) analysis draws attention to the insecurity, unwanted risks, and costly hazards of contemporary life that have resulted from globalisation, neo-liberalisation, and declining social protection. He focuses primarily on the implications of flexible labour relations and the rollback of public pensions in creating new uncertainties in late life. Drawing older people into precarious work raises issues for social care as well as labour relations. According to Standing (2010), older people can get caught in a 'precarity trap', forced to remain or re-enter the workforce in flexible and lower-income status positions. Older people with limited financial resources may themselves rely upon precarious workers as carers, and family networks may be reduced or drained by means of their own precarity.

Standing's (2010) approach draws attention to the way in which structural inequalities are reinforced through differential 'options' and 'choices' about work and care in later life. While his argument has primarily been applied to the operation of the labour market, the thrust of his critique can be extended to later life more generally. Taking a long view of the life course, it is precisely the 'cumulative effects' of precarity that shape late life, in particular where social and economic inequalities are concerned. Further, the contemporary economic conditions and austerity measures that are central to Standing's critique do not cease at retirement or in later life. This is particularly the case for groups of older people who are poorly served by traditional programmes such as pension schemes (i.e., immigrants, casual employees, women, people with disabilities, etc.) as well as carers, who may themselves be precarious by means of migration, low wages and labour market conditions. In fact, the precariousness that Standing outlines may become exemplified in late life in a context whereby reduced public support intersects with an ever-expanding for-profit market of homecare. Vulnerabilities may thus be considered to shift from labour, income and status, to 'dependence', the need for care, and the struggle to have these needs met by residual public services and private care schemes. As such, Standing's notion of the 'precarity trap' may in effect continue to snare older people as they move into late life, and most notably at the very moment that they require care.

Butler's (2009) argument is that we all experience 'precariousness' at different points in our lives, that 'interdependence' is a feature of the human condition, and that this precariousness is political. Butler's work on precariousness is chiefly concerned with the construction of subjects and the ontological questions of what it means to have a life. According to Butler (2009: 25): 'Precarity' is a 'politically induced condition in which certain populations suffer from failing social and economic networks of support and become differentially exposed to injury, violence, and death'. Her analysis draws attention to the importance of the differential construction of subjects, and how mutually held frameworks create and sustain particular responses, especially with regards to independence and dependence. Butler's interpretations of precarity shed light on the politics of ageing, whereby older people can suffer from 'unequal access to material goods, and diminished social networks, resulting in a potential vulnerability to neglect, abuse and violence'. Her approach raises questions about both life and care, and points to concerns about how the construction of a devalued 'fourth age', in the context of declining social protection, may place older people at risk of abandonment or ill-treatment.

The processes of de-subjectivation and 'othering' that lead into 'precarity' highlight the potential problems of a devalued 'fourth age'. For Standing (2010), a precarious life characterised by a chronic state of uncertainty and instability can lead to a 'truncated status' where many become 'denizens' as oppose to citizens, defined as lacking at least one group of basic rights (civil, political, economic, social and cultural). Similarly, Butler outlines a shared experience of vulnerability, and a collective de-humanisation that is used to justify the devaluation of particular lives. Butler highlights that life, and the decisions made about life, are not selfevident, but constituted by structures of recognition, and discursive power. That is, they are contingent upon mutually-held epistemological and normative frameworks that depict collectives as 'having or not having a life', and enacted through decisions and social practices. Such perceptions play a central role in accessing networks of protection and care, and are thus directly relevant to the construction and response to the 'fourth age'. She illustrates her point through the need for intensive forms of care: 'when decisions are made about providing life extending machine support to patients, or extended nursing care to the elderly, they are made, at some level, by considering the quality and conditions of life. To say that life is precarious is to say that the possibility of it being sustained relies fundamentally on social and political conditions, and not only on a postulated internal drive to live' (Butler 2009: 21). A shared schema of 'fourth age dependence' as a social and cultural burden can thus play a central role in configuring responses and sustaining power organised around a devalued notion of decline.

At the same time, a critical reading of precarity draws our attention beyond the immediate horizon of decisions about care, to recognise and confront the risks of life. Precarity underlines the fact that life is essentially 'risky'. Unlike previous social divisions organised around class, gender, geography, or 'racial' lines, precarity represents a universal form of insecurity, vulnerability, and potential suffering. Standing (2010) argues that contemporary conditions have created a '*class-in-the-making*' (italics in original) – a membership that is open to virtually every member of society whose social, economic and political relationships are destabilised by neoliberal commodification. Butler's (2009) thinking here is that our lives are, and always have been, defined as a state of precarity, based on an interdependent web of social support and obligations. She argues that: 'precariousness implies living socially, that is, the fact that one's life is always in some sense in the hands of the other' (Butler 2009: 14). This is reinforced by Turner's (1993) point that individuals may be viewed as ontologically frail rather than autonomous human beings, this arising partly through the effects of ageing and decay, but also because life itself is inherently risky.

All of these authors draw attention to an inherently shared, but unequally experienced, 'precariousness'. So, while risks or insecurities are part of the human experience, certain locations or lives are more susceptible to the hazards than others, and even more so in a context characterised by precarious work and declining social benefits. Older people increasingly find themselves as linked with precarious work, ever-shrinking social protections and safety nets, and in need of care in later life. Such conditions are then carried into late life, affecting experiences that occur in 'frailty' or dementia. Conditions of care also shape precarity and underline human inter-relatedness, as can be seen in the accounts of families and carers of people with dementia, who describe a sense of abandonment. Similarly, precarity is evident in the conditions of workers in health and social services where low pay and poor conditions of employment match precisely Standing's description of the precarious worker (Cangiano *et al.* 2009). Realities of ageing and decline combined with contemporary age and care-relations, create a greater risk of precarity, as both structured and experienced – risks that are carried across the life course and into late life.

Finally, the experience of precarity underscores the need for change. Whether drawing on the works of Butler or Standing, the concept of precarity can be employed to stress the need for a response based on interdependence as part of the human condition. Although Standing ignores the way in which labour force insecurities may be carried into late life, he calls for a progressive vision that contains the potential to influence new perspectives on late life. Standing (2010: 157) argues: 'The precariat's foremost need is economic security, to give some control over life's prospects and a sense that shocks and hazards can be managed. This can be achieved only if income security is assured. However, vulnerable groups also need 'agency', the collective and individual capacity to represent their interests'. Butler's emphasis on change is rooted in a response that is intricately tied to the relational nature of our existence – our interdependence. Highly relevant to the question of dementia and impairment in late life, she states 'the question is not whether a given being is living or not, nor whether the being in question has the status of a "person"; it is, rather, whether the social conditions of persistence and flourishing are or are not possible' (Butler 2009: 20). Here, Butler's (2009, Butler and Athanasiou 2013) thinking presents a serious challenge to existing approaches to the 'fourth age', outlining both that our response to late life should develop from an acknowledgement of fragility and limitation, and not a denial or distinction from it, and that such conditions will not naturally emerge, but must be fostered.

Shifting the discussion from the 'fourth age' as debility and decline: Unhinging age and stage-based assumptions

Precarity draws attention to the risks and inequalities across the life course and into late life, underscoring the importance of unburdening ourselves from the age and stage-based fixations that are implicit in notions of the 'fourth age'. Considering late life frailties as precarious deepens our understanding of the ideological power inherent within constructs, practices and the 'social imaginary of the fourth age'. Using precarity to understand late life illuminates the 'fourth age' as a location distinguished from youth and adulthood, and one where the devaluation of life is based on impairment and the associated costs of dependency. This assists our understanding of the multiple layers that structure deep old age as disadvantage, whereby older people with physical or cognitive frailties become 'othered' by means of the contradiction between autonomy and dependence. As such, it highlights how these ideological notions are culturally mediated and sustained through institutions and practices. Despite attempts to distinguish ageing from a negative period of the life course, the mutually reinforcing constructs of the 'third' and 'fourth age' draw us back to deeply held notions of age as impairment, dependence and decline. Arguably, the 'fourth age' is becoming constructed as old age per se. As such, there is a growing realisation that the concept of successful ageing may operate to the disadvantage of older persons with physical and cognitive impairments. Looking back, it may be the case that the pendulum has swung back to the notions Rowe and Kahn (1997), and Laslett (1991), were challenging – the view of ageing as a largely negative experience. It might also be argued that over time, understandings and approaches to late life have shifted in line with patterns of mortality, with the burdens of the 'fourth age' unequally distributed to those without resources or care networks, and where declining social protection fail to compensate for their needs.

Drawing on interpretations of precarity to understand the 'fourth age' accentuates the need for agency and the provision of care as a shared responsibility. Butler's (2009) work on precarity can be employed to underscore how the 'fourth age' is created and reinforced as devalued, through cultural priorities and practices, social structures, and care systems. Thinking about precarity with regards to late life, therefore, helps shift the focus to the conditions within which people live. Chronological age – or any proxy such as the 'third' or 'fourth age' – and the ways in which we 'imagine' or respond to these categories, can create and sustain inequalities, many of which are a result of contemporary decisions and priorities about care. The suggestion is therefore, that altering the constitution of subjects, and the responses that take place through social structures and care practices, can create change. Admittedly, 20th century patterns of extended longevity have redistributed death from a more equal distribution across the life course to one in which it is overwhelmingly associated with old age. A long life has become so commonly expected – assumed to be a right – that a 'premature' death has to be explained. While the cultural impacts of associations between age and death, and similarly dementia and old age, cannot be overlooked, the same may not be true of our understandings and responses to late life. Precarity calls attention to the construction and conditions of vulnerability, including how even the right to a long life is unequally distributed, through for example, differential mortality rates of privileged and disadvantaged groups (Marmot 2015).

Recognising vulnerability: Fostering the conditions for a sustainable life

Drawing attention to precarity emphasises the importance of responding to vulnerability and fostering the conditions for a sustainable life. An analysis of precarity can offer new insights, first, into existing critiques in the field of dementia studies; second, into how ideas about care and the accompanying care relations can naturalise and sustain inequality and disadvantage (Holstein 2015, Tronto 1993). In the context of increased longevity, late life is often accompanied by what is termed 'co-morbidity' and extended periods of 'chronic impairment', creating a new dimension to discussions about ageing and the need for care. What precarity brings to light is how the need for care, combined with potential of impairment in late life, can conflict with declining support from the welfare state. Our concern is that the relegation of people with dementia to a devalued category of the 'fourth age' can become a further rationale for poorly resourced services and threaten standards of care for older people in late life.

Recognising precarity and the inherent risks of late life could form the basis for reconfiguring understandings and care practices towards frailty and dementia (see, also, Gawande 2015). Standing and Butler argue for the need to foster conditions that make life sustainable in situations of vulnerability and insecurity. Where Standing's suggestions would mitigate the inequalities that accumulate across the life course, Butler recognises the roots of suffering as the foundation for an ethical and just response. According to Butler (2010), the response to precarity should develop from an acknowledgement of fragility and limitation. She articulates that a response capable of improving lives will not naturally occur, but must be created, arguing: 'Simply put, life requires support and enabling conditions in order to be a livable life' (Butler 2009: 21). And later, 'To sustain life as sustainable requires putting those conditions in place and militating for their renewal and strengthening. Where a life stands no chance of flourishing … one must attend to ameliorating the negative conditions of life' (Butler 2009: 23). Here, Butler's point may resonate in some ways with approaches (Barnes 2012, Sevenhuijsen 1998, Tronto 1993) which view the need for care as a political issue, and is not confined to 'abnormal' situations, nor grounded in moral and ethical duty.[2] However, where Butler, and Tronto (1993) both focus on vulnerability as a universal human characteristic, their positions are different. Where the ethics of care tends to remain grounded in a 'moral imperative to care' and a 'knoweable other', Butler focuses on relationality, the social and political conditions which give rise to precarity and precariousness, and the 'processes that render 'them' [the other] unintelligible' (see Chambers and Carver 2008: 107).[3]

In the context of this article, the social and political conditions which shape a devaluing of subjects by means of their physical or cognitive impairments, can serve to reinforce precarity, and deflect attention from the disadvantages that accumulate and affect late life, the experiences of living with dementia, and the practices of providing and receiving care. As such, the associations embedded in the constructs, practices, and 'imaginary' of the 'fourth age' may lend strength to decisions and programmes that provide only minimal public care as a form of compensation for a lack of personal or family resources, rather than universal vulnerability and the need to foster care. With few available care 'choices', and in particular accessible and affordable options, notions of the 'fourth age' which are formed, and become activated over time in line with the conditions of a life, and in the current political context, can serve to limit agency, as well as reinforce notions that agency is limited in situations of physical and/or mental frailties. The trajectories into care and the foundations for effective communication with people with dementia are thus ignored, and the potential for people living with dementia to shape the conditions within which they live go unrecognised.

Discussion: Citizenship and vulnerability in late life

The argument of this article has been that concepts such as 'precarity' can contribute to better understandings of frailty and dementia, especially when placed in the context of new forms of insecurity influencing the life course. This approach also helps shift 'fourth age' debates away from age or stage-based thinking that risk reinforcing unequal power relations and marginalising older people with physical or cognitive impairments. It does so by rendering visible how current approaches to the 'fourth age' as a 'failed' late life mask universal suffering, structures of inequality, and processes of precarity. Rooted in the idea of instability and enhanced vulnerability, precarity provides a foundation from which to more closely consider care priorities and the experiences of living with impairment. A key issue concerns how best to protect people subject to the vulnerabilities associated with late life. Whilst these conditions may be shared across a large section of the population, they are experienced by individuals – often living alone and with limited community support. The key issue which arises is how to incorporate the recognition of the vulnerabilities associated with ageing and dementia into frameworks which translate into an acceptable response that gives scope for agency (or some variant thereof) and the maintenance of human dignity.

One response is to link the analysis of precarity with an inclusive form of citizenship that challenges the responses to older people with physical and cognitive impairments. This may be illustrated through what Delanty (2000) refers to as 'cosmopolitan citizenship'. Challenging a 'deep moral contradiction at the heart of the modern state', Linklater (1998: 24) argues that cosmopolitan citizenship is used to 'remind citizens of the unfinished moral business of the sovereign state and to draw their attention to the higher ethical aspirations which have yet to be embedded in political life'. In this sense, cosmopolitan citizenship can provide a crucial bridge from our analysis of precarity in late life into pathways for enacting change. A framework that is capable of responding to precarity in late life requires attention to both shared vulnerabilities, and the unequal experiences of such conditions. Linklater (1998) cites Beitz's view that political communities should widen their ethical horizons until the point is reached where no individual or group interest is systematically excluded from moral consideration. Such an approach challenges the construction of old age as a form of 'otherness' – a central feature of approaches to dementia and 'frailty'.[4] Insisting on the political component of cosmopolitan citizenship, Linklater (1998: 28) states: 'The argument is that, if it is to have real meaning, cosmopolitan citizenship must involve rather more than moral commitments not to exploit the weaknesses of others – more than the ethical resolution to treat all other human beings with care and compassion. It requires political action to build communication communities in which outsiders, and especially the most vulnerable among them, have the power to 'refuse and renegotiate offers' and to contest unjust social structures' (Linklater 1998: 28). As such, cosmopolitan citizenship represents an important framework when considering how to move beyond a 'precarious' old age.

This model of citizenship underscores the importance of inclusion, agency and negotiation that is fostered in part through communication, in this case, even in circumstances where agency is considered to be reduced. A critical analysis drawing on precarity, when combined with an inclusive notion of citizenship, holds the potential to recognise and respond to the needs of older people with dementia. Precarity highlights the severity of the problems that exist for a large number of older people. This leads us to argue that it is 'precarity' rather than 'activity' and 'success' that may be a more realistic model for understanding late life, and especially the lives of older people with physical and cognitive impairments. A careful consideration of the 'fourth age' as a form of symbolic exclusion can create the space to reconsider the foundations of constructs and care practices, and 'what it means to live in a "frail" state'.

In some ways, insights from dementia studies have pioneered a reconsideration of late life care. Discussions framed around 'personhood', 'selfhood' and 'othering' have drawn attention to the need to change medical and social practices, particularly the interactions between professionals and people living with dementia, and the reconfiguration of care spaces (see George and Whitehouse 2010, Kontos 2004). Models such as The Eden Alternative (2012) or other dementia-friendly spaces (Mitchell *et al.* 2004) reflect alternative notions of what care 'should look like'. Such responses have played an important role in reconfiguring dementia, but we also need perspectives that address the socio-cultural and political challenges to interpretations of dementia as a 'frailed' and 'failed' late life. Dementia is by its nature one of the most challenging areas in which to argue against age and stage-based thinking given that it is a chronic, physiologically based condition, leading to death, mostly occurring in old age. Yet, it is a site where constructs, practices, and the 'social imaginary' of the 'fourth age' reinforce negative valuations of dependence as a problem, and sustain notions of living with dementia – or other end of life stage conditions – as void of agency and potential. Dementia and other 'frailties' that fall within the 'fourth age' signify that mastery over the body cannot be won, that death is inevitable, and simply a question of time (see Lloyd 2000). Such devaluations are, of course, worsened in a context where political notions of dependence interpreted as costly burden can result in non-existent or poor levels of care for older people.

Shifting the focus from constructs that reinforce the negative valuations of age, to a recognised shared vulnerability, acceptance of the limitations of life and death, and shared political responsibility can help to unhinge dementia and impairment from a 'frailed' and 'failed' late life into a foundation from which to develop new types of care relationships. To do so however, relies on a critical analysis of the constructs, practices, relations, and contexts within which care for people with dementia takes place. Relocating dementia to a more 'normalised' life course space however, must not become another rationale for neoliberal care models to relegate care onto families, individuals, or the lowest cost service provider. Change must also be accompanied by a social and cultural ethos of care, the prevention of inequalities, the alleviation of suffering, and the opportunity to flourish throughout the life course and into late life. Understandings and practices for older people with physical and/or cognitive impairments must, therefore, be repositioned in a space where it is possible to recognise and address vulnerability, inequalities, suffering, as well as the moments of pleasure and joy that can exist in deep old age. We must create structures and programs where 'care', and the alleviation of suffering, is both important and possible, and begin to more closely consider and respond to the relationship between cultural, social and biological life, and death.

Conclusion

In conclusion, the contemporary response to dementia in the context of longevity and austerity creates a need to examine the inequalities of late life, the failures of the system with regards to care, and to develop new cultural narratives of deep old age (Phillipson 2015). This will involve a willingness to normalise late life and frailties that occur over time, and recognition that communication and agency may look different in later life, and be as much socio-cultural as biological. Turning to an analysis of precarity throughout the life course and in late life outlines the differences that exist, including how late life contains the vulnerabilities of the human condition, the accumulation of structured inequalities, and the socio-cultural assumptions and notions of 'failure' that are associated with impairment. Precarity makes two contributions to the discussion: first, it moves thinking away from the dominance of individualised age or stage-based frameworks that are rooted in success, and by consequence, position dementia as a 'frailed old age'. Second, it renders visible a shared vulnerability, as well as the desire for control, and the inability, or the lack of political will, to address dependency, interdependence and human suffering. Our suggestion is, therefore, to pair the analysis of precarity with a response that balances an inclusive form of citizenship, recognition, and shared responsibility to vulnerability. Only from this point, can we alter current understandings of late life, structures and relations of care, and attempt to alleviate rather than sustain the suffering that may exist in late life. Such approaches would create responses to older people with dementia not because they are pitied or sick, but because they are valued, and because a clearer understanding of their experiences prevails.

Acknowledgements

The authors wish to thank the Social Sciences and Humanities Research Council for funding on Precarity and Aging (435-2016-0933), and Brian Budd and Rachel Weldrick for their assistance with the review of literature.

Notes

1   http://www.dementiadaily.org.au/dr-dennis-gillings-world-dementia-envoy-a-cure-for-dementia-by-2025/
2   In the feminist ethics of care, care is a political issue that should be brought out of the private and into the public, and debated, not only in terms of cost and organization, but the potential to respond to need and support human flourishing (see Barnes 2012, Sevenhuijsen 1998, Tronto, 1993). Tronto (2013), for example, argues that 'all humans are extremely vulnerable at some points in their lives' (p. 164), and it is this vulnerability that underscores both the political nature of care ethics and the need for care. However, in Tronto's work, the primary focus is on the moral imperative to provide care.
3   The differences between these positions are the subject of philosophical debate and in particular, that of ontology. Chambers and Carver (2008: 107) state the following: 'even in the case of Joan Tronto's deft articulation of an ethic of care, her understanding of 'relationality' bears little or no resemblance to Butler's. In Tronto's understanding of caring, the 'other' is always a concrete, knowable and intelligible other. She writes: 'that 'others' matter is the most difficult moral quality to establish in practice' (Tronto 1993: 130). Butler, however, does not focus her attention on intelligible others (those who would then be cared for, be granted rights, be recognised), but on the very processes that render 'them' unintelligible … Tronto's account concerns itself solely with actual 'beings' and not with the Being of those beings. Butler's 'relationality' not only precedes but also undoes any so-called 'ethic of care'. Thus, in describing Butler's political ontology by way of highlighting the 'primacy of relationality', we are at the same time, and in no uncertain terms, rejecting any variant of individualised ontology'.
4   It also links with arguments from the ethics of care. The political dimension of the ethic of care can, for example, be linked to the concept of citizenship and the possibility of changing conventional responses to people with physical and cognitive impairments. Sevenhuijsen (1998) for example, articulates a view of citizenship that is grounded in an ethics of care, and inclusive of a range of voices. She argues that: 'citizenship is not conceptualized exclusively in terms of a liberal rights model but first and foremost as an activity and a normative approach which can lead to a search for the best course of action in public contexts' (Sevenhuijsen 1998: 148). In models of citizenship based on the ethics of care, conflicts of interests are recognised and discussed through processes that ensure that weaker voices are included.

References

Barnes, M. (2012) *Care in Everyday Life: An ethic of care in practice*. Bristol: The Policy Press.
Biggs, S. (2014) Precarious ageing versus the policy of indifference: International trends and the G20, *Australian Journal on Ageing*, 33, 4, 226–8.
Bohle, P., Pitts, C. and Quinlan, M. (2010) Time to call it quits? The safety and health of older workers, *International Journal of Health Services*, 40, 1, 23–41.

Brooker, D. (2007) *Person-centred Dementia Care: Making Services Better*. London: Jessica Kingsley Publishers.

Butler, J. (2006) *Precarious Life: The Powers of Mourning and Violence*. London: Verso.

Butler, J. (2009) *Frames of War: When is Life Grievable?* London: Verso.

Butler, J. and Athanasiou, A. (2013) *Disposession: The Performative in the Political*. Cambridge: Polity Press.

Cangiano, A., Shutes, I., Spencer, S., Leeson, G., *et al.* (2009) *Migrant Care Workers in Ageing Societies. Research Findings in the United Kingdom*. Oxford: COMPAS.

Chambers, S.A. and Carver, T. (2008) *Judith Butler and Political Theory: Troubling Politics*. London: Routledge.

Craciun, C. and Flick, U. (2014) 'I will never be the granny with rosy cheeks': Perceptions of aging in precarious and financially secure middle-aged Germans, *Journal of Aging Studies*, 29, 1, 78–87.

Delanty, G. (2000) *Citizenship in a Global Age: Society, Culture, Politics*. Maidenhead: Open University Press.

Department of Health (2013) *Dementia: A State of the Nation Report on Dementia Care and Support in England*. London. Available at https://www.gov.uk/government/uploads/system/uploads/attachment_data/file/262139/Dementia.pdf (Last accessed 20 May 2015).

Gawande, A. (2015) *Being Mortal: Illness, medicine and what matters in the end*. London: Profile Books and Wellcome Collection.

George, D. and Whitehouse, P. (2010) Dementia and mild cognitive impairment in social and cultural contexts. In Dannefer, D. and Phillipson, C. (eds) *The Sage Handbook of Social Gerontology*. London: Sage Publications.

Gilleard, C. and Higgs, P. (2000) Aging, Alzheimer's, and the uncivilized body. In Malacrida, C. and Low, J. (eds) *Sociology of the Body: A Reader*. Don Mills: Oxford University Press.

Gilleard, C. and Higgs, P. (2010) Aging without agency: Theorizing the fourth age, *Aging and Mental Health*, 14, 2, 121–8.

Gilleard, C. and Higgs, P. (2013) The fourth age and the concept of a 'social imaginary': A theoretical excursus, *Journal of Aging Studies*, 27, 4, 368–76.

Grenier, A. (2007) Crossing age and generational boundaries: exploring intergenerational research encounters, *Journal of Social Issues*, 63, 4, 713–27.

Grenier, A. (2012) *Transitions and the Lifecourse: Challenging the Constructions of 'Growing Old'*. Bristol: Policy Press.

Grenier, A. (2015) Transitions and time. In Twigg, J. and Martin, W. (eds) *Handbook of Cultural Gerontology*. London: Routledge.

Grenier, A. and Phillipson, C. (2013) Re-thinking agency in later life. In Baars, J., Dhomen, J., Grenier, A. and Phillipson, C. (eds) *Age, Meaning and Social Structure*. Bristol: Policy Press.

Gullette, M.M. (1997) *Declining to Decline: Cultural Combat and the Politics of the Midlife*. Virginia: University of Virginia Press.

Gullette, M.M. (2004) *Aged by Culture*. Chicago: University of Chicago Press.

Holstein, M. (2015) *Women in Later Life: Critical Perspectives on Gender and Age*. London: Rowman and Littlefield.

Jaworska, A. (1999) Respecting the margins of agency: Alzheimer's patients and the capacity to value, *Philosophy and Public Affairs*, 28, 2, 105–38.

Katz, S. and Calasanti, T. (2015) Critical perspectives on successful aging: does it 'appeal more than it illuminates'? *The Gerontologist*, 55, 1, 26–33.

Katz, S. and Peters, K.R. (2008) Enhancing the mind? Memory medicine, dementia, and the aging brain, *Journal of Aging Studies*, 22, 4, 348–55.

Knight, A. (2014) Disability as vulnerability: Redistributing precariousness in democratic ways, *The Journal of Politics*, 76, 1, 15–26.

Kontos, P. (2004) Ethnographic reflections on selfhood, embodiment and Alzheimer's disease, *Ageing and Society*, 24, 6, 829–49.

Kontos, P. (2005) Embodied selfhood in Alzheimer's disease: Rethinking person-centred care, *Dementia*, 4, 4, 533–70.

Kontos, P. and Naglie, G. (2007) Tacit knowledge of caring and embodied selfhood, *Sociology of Health & Illness*, 31, 5, 688–704.

Lacas, A. and Rockwood, K. (2012) Frailty in primary care: A review of its conceptualization and implications for practice, *BMC Med*, 10, 4.

Laslett, P. (1991) *A Fresh Map of Life: The Emergence of the Third Age*. Cambridge: Harvard University Press.

Linklater, A. (1998) Cosmopolitan citizenship, *Citizenship Studies*, 2, 1, 23–41.

Lloyd, L. (2000) Dying in old age: Promoting wellbeing at the end of life, *Mortality*, 5, 2, 171–88.

Lloyd, L. (2012) *Health and Care in Ageing Societies*. Bristol: Policy Press.

Lloyd, L. (2015) The fourth age. In Twigg, J. and Martin, W. (eds) *Handbook of Cultural Gerontology*. London: Routledge.

Lloyd, L., Calnan, M., Cameron, A., Seymour, J., *et al.* (2014) Identity in the fourth age: perseverance, adaptation and maintaining dignity, *Ageing and Society*, 34, 1, 1–19.

Marmot, M. (2015) *The Health Gap: The Challenge of an Unequal World*. London: Bloomsbury Press.

Mitchell, L., Burton, E. and Raman, S. (2004) Dementia-friendly cities: designing intelligible neighbourhoods for life, *Journal of Urban Design*, 9, 1, 89–101.

Morley, J.E., Vellas, B., van Kan, G., Anker, S.D., *et al.* (2013) Frailty consensus: a call to action, *Journal of the American Medical Directors Association*, 14, 6, 392–97.

O'Dwyer, C. (2013) Official conceptualizations of person-centred care: Which person counts? *Journal of Aging Studies*, 27, 3, 233–42.

Pickard, S. (2014) Frail bodies: Geriatric medicine and the constitution of the fourth age, *Sociology of Health and Illness*, 36, 4, 549–63.

Phillipson, C. (2015) The political economy of longevity: Developing new forms of solidarity for later life, *The Sociological Quarterly*, 56, 1, 80–100.

Rowe, J. and Kahn, R. (1997) Successful aging, *The Gerontologist*, 37, 4, 433–40.

Searle, S., Mitnitski, A., Gahbauer, E., Gill, T.M., *et al.* (2008) A standard procedure for creating a frailty index, *BMC Geriatrics*, 8, 24, 1–10.

Sevenhuijsen, S. (1998) *Citizenship and the ethics of care: Feminist consideration on justice, morality, and politics*. New York: Routledge.

Standing, G. (2010) *The Precariat: The New Dangerous Class*. London: Bloomsbury Press.

Standing, G. (2012) The precariat: From denizens to citizens? *Polity*, 44, 4, 588–608.

The Eden Alternative (2012) The Eden Alternative domains of well-being: Revolutionizing the experience of home by bringing well-being to life. New York. Available at http://www.edenalt.org/wordpress/wp-content/uploads/2014/02/EdenAltWellBeingWhitePaperv5.pdf (Last accessed 20 May 2015).

Tronto, J. (1993) *Moral Boundaries: A Political Argument for an Ethic of Care*. New York: Routledge.

Turner, B. (1993) Outline of a theory of human rights, *Sociology*, 27, 2, 489–512.

Waite, L. (2009) A place and space for a critical geography of precarity? *Geography Compass*, 3, 1, 412–33.

Whitehouse, P. (with George, D). (2008) *The Myth of Alzheimer's: What You Aren't Being Told about Today's Most Dreaded Diagnosis*. New York: St. Martin's Griffin.

Index

Ageing, Dementia and the Social Mind, First Edition. Edited by Paul Higgs and Chris Gilleard.
Chapters © 2017 The Authors. Book Compilation © 2017 Foundation for the Sociology of
Health & Illness/Blackwell Publishing Ltd.